HOW TO WIN IN SMALL CLAIMS COURT IN CALIFORNIA

Second Edition

Royce Orleans Hurst
Mark Warda
Attorneys at Law

SPHINX® PUBLISHING
AN IMPRINT OF SOURCEBOOKS, INC.®
NAPERVILLE, ILLINOIS
www.SphinxLegal.com

Second Edition, 2002

Published by: **Sphinx® Publishing, An Imprint of Sourcebooks, Inc.®**

<u>Naperville Office</u>
P.O. Box 4410
Naperville, Illinois 60567-4410
630-961-3900
Fax: 630-961-2168
www.sourcebooks.com
www.SphinxLegal.com

This publication is designed to provide accurate and authoritative information in regard to the subject matter covered. It is sold with the understanding that the publisher is not engaged in rendering legal, accounting, or other professional service. If legal advice or other expert assistance is required, the services of a competent professional person should be sought.

From a Declaration of Principles Jointly Adopted by a Committee of the American Bar Association and a Committee of Publishers and Associations

This product is not a substitute for legal advice.

Disclaimer required by Texas statutes.

Library of Congress Cataloging-in-Publication Data
Hurst, Royce Orleans, 1947-
    How to win in small claims court in California / Royce Orleans Hurst, Mark Warda.--
2nd ed.
        p. cm. -- (Legal survival guides)
    Includes index.
    ISBN 1-57248-194-3
    1. Small claims courts--California--Popular works. I. Title: Small claims court in
California. II. Warda, Mark. III. Title. IV. Series.

KFC976.Z9 H87 2002
347.794'04--dc21
                                                                                          2002021050

Printed and bound in the United States of America.

VHG Paperback — 10 9 8 7 6 5 4 3 2 1

To Hyman Wolfson, JD, LL.M., CPA, MBA

1920–1996

My law and mediation partner, my father, my friend

CONTENTS

USING SELF-HELP LAW BOOKS

Before using a self-help law book, you should realize the advantages and disadvantages of doing your own legal work and understand the challenges and diligence that this requires.

THE GROWING TREND

Rest assured that you won't be the first or only person handling your own legal matter. For example, in some states, more than seventy-five percent of the people in divorces and other cases represent themselves. Because of the high cost of legal services, this is a major trend and many courts are struggling to make it easier for people to represent themselves. However, some courts are not happy with people who do not use attorneys and refuse to help them in any way. For some, the attitude is, "Go to the law library and figure it out for yourself."

We write and publish self-help law books to give people an alternative to the often complicated and confusing legal books found in most law libraries. We have made the explanations of the law as simple and easy to understand as possible. Of course, unlike an attorney advising an individual client, we cannot cover every conceivable possibility.

COST/VALUE ANALYSIS

Whenever you shop for a product or service, you are faced with various levels of quality and price. In deciding what product or service to buy, you make a cost/value analysis on the basis of your willingness to pay and the quality you desire.

When buying a car, you decide whether you want transportation, comfort, status, or sex appeal. Accordingly, you decide among such choices as a Neon, a Lincoln, a Rolls Royce, or a Porsche. Before making a decision, you usually weigh the merits of each option against the cost.

When you get a headache, you can take a pain reliever (such as aspirin) or visit a medical specialist for a neurological examination. Given this choice, most people, of course, take a pain reliever, since it costs only pennies; whereas a medical examination costs hundreds of dollars and takes a lot of time. This is usually a logical choice because it is rare to need anything more than a pain reliever for a headache. But in some cases, a headache may indicate a brain tumor and failing to see a specialist right away can result in complications. Should everyone with a headache go to a specialist? Of course not, but people treating their own illnesses must realize that they are betting on the basis of their cost/value analysis of the situation. They are taking the most logical option.

The same cost/value analysis must be made when deciding to do one's own legal work. Many legal situations are very straight forward, requiring a simple form and no complicated analysis. Anyone with a little intelligence and a book of instructions can handle the matter without outside help.

But there is always the chance that complications are involved that only an attorney would notice. To simplify the law into a book like this, several legal cases often must be condensed into a single sentence or paragraph. Otherwise, the book would be several hundred pages long and too complicated for most people. However, this simplification necessarily leaves out many details and nuances that would apply to special or unusual situations. Also, there are many ways to interpret most legal questions. Your case may come before a judge who disagrees with the analysis of our authors.

Therefore, in deciding to use a self-help law book and to do your own legal work, you must realize that you are making a cost/value analysis. You have decided that the money you will save in doing it yourself outweighs the chance that your case will not turn out to your satisfaction. Most people handling their own simple legal matters never have a problem, but occasionally people find that it ended up costing them more to have an attorney straighten out the situation than it would have if they had hired an attorney in the beginning. Keep this in mind while handling your case, and be sure to consult an attorney if you feel you might need further guidance.

LOCAL RULES   The next thing to remember is that a book which covers the law for the entire nation, or even for an entire state, cannot possibly include every procedural difference of every jurisdiction. Whenever possible, we provide the exact form needed; however, in some areas, each county, or even each judge, may require unique forms and procedures. In our state books, our forms usually cover the majority of counties in the state, or provide examples of the type of form which will be required. In our national books, our forms are sometimes even more general in nature but are designed to give a good idea of the type of form that will be needed in most locations. Nonetheless, keep in mind that your state, county, or judge may have a requirement, or use a form, that is not included in this book.

You should not necessarily expect to be able to get all of the information and resources you need solely from within the pages of this book. This book will serve as your guide, giving you specific information whenever possible and helping you to find out what else you will need to know. This is just like if you decided to build your own backyard deck. You might purchase a book on how to build decks. However, such a book would not include the building codes and permit requirements of every city, town, county, and township in the nation; nor would it include the lumber, nails, saws, hammers, and other materials and tools you would need to actually build the deck. You would use the book as your guide, and then do some work and research involving such matters as whether you need a permit of some kind, what type and grade of wood are available in your area, whether to use hand tools or power tools, and how to use those tools.

Before using the forms in a book like this, you should check with your court clerk to see if there are any local rules of which you should be aware, or local forms you will need to use. Often, such forms will require the same information as the forms in the book but are merely laid out differently or use slightly different language. They will sometimes require additional information.

CHANGES IN THE LAW

Besides being subject to local rules and practices, the law is subject to change at any time. The courts and the legislatures of all fifty states are constantly revising the laws. It is possible that while you are reading this book, some aspect of the law is being changed.

In most cases, the change will be of minimal significance. A form will be redesigned, additional information will be required, or a waiting period will be extended. As a result, you might need to revise a form, file an extra form, or wait out a longer time period; these types of changes will not usually affect the outcome of your case. On the other hand, sometimes a major part of the law is changed, the entire law in a particular area is rewritten, or a case that was the basis of a central legal point is overruled. In such instances, your entire ability to pursue your case may be impaired.

Again, you should weigh the value of your case against the cost of an attorney and make a decision as to what you believe is in your best interest.

INTRODUCTION

In 1998, California voters approved Proposition 220, an amendment permitting the judges in each county to merge their Superior and Municipal Courts into a single Superior Court in each county. The purpose of the change was to improve services to the public by consolidating state resources and using them more efficiently. Early reports on Proposition 220 seem to indicate that the consolidation is improving services to the public and that small claims courts are becoming even more user friendly.

Most counties have chosen to divide the cases into general and limited jurisdiction cases, using the same criteria as the former superior and municipal courts previously used. Small Claims are now generally heard in limited jurisdiction courts and the procedural rules have largely followed the rules formerly known as municipal court rules. Nevertheless, administrative changes are still in flux in several counties and local forms are still evolving. It has always made sense to check with the court clerk to make sure the forms you are using contain the most recent revisions. With the recent overhaul of the courts, it is essential to take the time to be certain that you are using the latest forms.

The main purposes of this book is to bring together in a concise format all the information and forms you need to navigate the small claims process in California. Preparation will make the process far less intimidating. It will give you the confidence to exercise your legal rights as a consumer of products and services. It will help you decide whether the battle is worth fighting and how to make the court system work for you.

The book is divided into chapters, which provide you with both general and specific information regarding each part of the process. Chapter 1 is an overview, answering basic questions such as how much you can sue for, the kinds of cases you can bring and what kind of damages you can get. It also tell you how to start your case, how to decide if you need an attorney and where to go for additional help. Chapter 2 helps you decide whether you have a winnable case, and if you do, whether it is worth your time and energy to pursue it. In fact, sometimes merely filing and serving a small claims case will get results from people who know they owe money but needed an extra push to get around to paying it. It is also useful to keep in mind the many alternatives available to resolving civil disputes.

Increasingly popular is the process of mediation and Chapter 3 explains how it works. This procedure has many advantages over litigation, especially in situations where you want to maintain a relationship, such as your landlord, your roommate, your neighbor or your employer. You can choose to mediate at any time in the process, including the day of the hearing and after an appeal is filed. Some counties even require the parties to attempt mediation and have mediators waiting in the courtroom on the days hearing are set.

Chapter 4 goes into detail on who can sue and who can be sued, where to file, how much to ask for, and how to find and serve the defendant. Chapter 5 contains an explanation of the most common kinds of cases.

Chapter 6, while largely devoted to the needs of the defendant, is invaluable reading for the plaintiff as well. Knowing what the other side is going to do is just as important and having your own strategy worked out.

Chapter 7 explains the basic rules of evidence and Chapter 8 explains how to present your case to the judge. Following the guidelines in these two chapters may very well make the difference as to whether you win or lose.

Before filing your case it is advisable to read the entire book. Sometimes information relating to the last steps of the process are important in preparing the initial steps, or a decision made in the beginning may effect the procedure at the end. For example, Chapter 9 tells you how to collect your judgment if you win. But going through the whole process and winning a judgment may be useless if a person or company has no money and there is nothing to collect.

Chapter 10 tells you who can appeal and how to file the appeal. Attorneys can represent the parties at an appeal, requiring a cost-benefit analysis.

Following Chapter 10 is a glossary explaining the legal terms used in the book. Appendix A contains a listing of the county court websites and the names and addresses of the small claims advisor in each county. Appendix B contains a list of mediation programs by county. Appendices C, D and E contain the applicable statutes and rules. Appendix F contains a list of questions to ask the judgment debtor to find out the amount and location of his assets.

Appendix G contains handy checklists to follow to make sure you have covered all the bases. Appendix H contains sample demand letters to use when requesting payment or reimbursement prior to filing suit. Last but not least, Appendix I provides the California Small Claims Judicial Forms, ready for you to use. Make copies first and save the originals for your final draft. There is also a list of local forms for the counties that use them in Appendix J.

While the small claims court was designed to make it possible to take court action without the expense of an attorney, legal advice can be very valuable in determining whether or not to sue, or if you are the defendant, what claims or defenses to present. If you need legal advice, there are many attorneys who offer free or low cost consultations in the hope that you will hire them, now or in the futrue. Most county bar associations can refer you to an attorney who will give you an initial consultation for a reasonable price.

SMALL CLAIMS COURT, GENERALLY

1

Small claims court is a forum where people with "small" disputes can have a judge, a commissioner, or an attorney acting as a temporary judge decide their legal rights. It is usually located in a courtroom set aside in the county courthouse. The parties cannot be represented by an attorney in California although attorneys can represent themselves if they are bringing or defending a claim. The rules of procedure are simplified so that cases can be heard within forty days of filing, or seventy days, if the defendant lives out of the county where you are filing the initial paperwork. It is important to note that some counties have local rules and procedures that must be followed in addition to the more general state rules.

How Much You Can Sue For

The small claims court has *jurisdiction* of up to $5,000, meaning that $5,000 is the upper limit of a judgment that the small claims court can award. This amount includes interest and does not include costs and fees. Even if the judge deciding your case thinks you should recover $10,000, the law limits the amount you can recover to $5,000. Very few states have a higher limit.

There is an exception to the $5,000 limit–if you file more than two small claims actions in one year. The limit for the third and every other case you file for the rest of the year will be $2,500(unless the claim is filed by *public entities*, such as school districts and cities). There is no limit on the number of claims where you can ask for $2,500 or less. There have been efforts in the state legislature to raise the amount you can sue for in auto accident cases to $10,000. So far, these efforts have failed, probably because of the strong consumer attorney lobby.

TYPES OF CASES
The most common kind of case involves a request for money, such as when someone damages your property and refuses to pay for it, or your landlord refuses to return your security deposit. Small claims actions for unlawful *consumer practices* are filed against almost every kind of company including collection agencies for harassment, automobile dealerships for representing that used vehicles are new, banks for excessive fees, property management firms for discrimination, and auto repair franchises for misrepresenting the cost of fixing your vehicle. Suits against governmental entities, such as transportation and water district counties, and the State of California have increased since they rarely pay legitimate claims made against them.

NOTE: *A suit against the government (e.g. a city vehicle crashed into your motorcycle) requires special claims procedures within specific time periods.*

Local merchants sue customers for wrongful *stop payment* orders where the damages include the amount of the check and up to $1,500 in penalties under California's bad check statute.

Some other cases are personal injury suits involving:

- auto accidents;

- injury as a result of a product that did not operate the way it was supposed to (such as a chair that did not hold a normal person's weight); or,

- injury resulting when someone pulls a chair out from under you as a prank.

If a person did not mean to injure you, this is an example of *negligence*, which is another kind of case. Examples of negligence include:

- a store owner failing to clean up spilled liquids within a reasonable time;

- your neighbor failing to restrain his or her dog that bites a member of your family. (Even if a dog never bit anyone before, you can sue the owner in small claims court under the theory of *strict liability*. There is no such thing as a free bite.);

- a property owner's lax security resulting in unnecessary exposure to criminal activity; or,

- the failure of restaurant employees to wash their hands after using the lavatory resulting in food poisoning.

The possibilities of negligent behavior are endless.

You can sue when the terms of a contract are breached and you suffer losses as a result.

Example: The blinds you ordered for your windows were measured incorrectly and are six inches too short.

You can bring an action when an intentional act of someone caused you harm, such as when your neighbor punched you in the face causing a broken tooth or ordered his or her dog to attack you.

There are very few lawyers who will take on a personal injury lawsuit where the damages are under $5,000 because it simply is not cost-effective for them. On the other hand, injured people with $3,000 or $4,000 in damages rarely want to pay a percentage of the fee (often amounting to over $1,000). As a result, many of the above mentioned personal injury suits are heard in small claims court.

REMEDIES OTHER THAN MONEY

The small claims court also hears *equitable actions*. These are special kinds of cases where the plaintiff requests that the judge order someone to do something other than pay money. Some examples of equitable actions follow.

SPECIFIC
PERFORMANCE

In some cases money is not an adequate remedy. For example, suppose you purchased an oil painting to be delivered on Saturday. If the seller refuses to deliver the painting, you could sue him for *specific performance* which means you ask the judge to force him to deliver the painting to you.

RESCISSION

If a deal was made under a *mistaken* assumption or under extreme pressure known as *duress*, you could sue for rescission of the contract. Rescission is discussed in Chapter 6.

RESTITUTION

If you were the seller of an oil painting, and the buyer obtained possession without paying for it, you could ask for *restitution*, meaning it would be returned to you. Getting an item back is often better than getting a money judgment that may never be paid.

REFORMATION

Where a written agreement does not express the true understanding of the parties, a court can *reform* the contract to express their intent.

Example: If you sign a receipt to sell a 1988 auto to your neighbor and accidentally write 1998, you probably will not have to deliver a 1998 car to him. If he sued for that you could ask the judge to *reform* the contract to reflect the correct date.

NUISANCE

Another special kind of case is a *nuisance* action. Loud music from the apartment upstairs is a private nuisance if it only bothers you. Another example is your neighbor's cat that uses your daughter's sandbox as a litter box. But if several people in a particular neighborhood are subject to the same nuisance, such as noxious fumes from a factory or a house where drugs are sold, it is a *public nuisance*. (This is an example of the type of situation where consulting a lawyer for advice makes financial sense since the cost can be spread among several people.) Each person can sue for money damages and request that the court order the person responsible for the nuisance to prevent it from happening.

PROCEDURE

When you file a claim, you are the *plaintiff* and the person or company you are suing is the *defendant*. Filling out the claim is fairly easy. (See form 2, p.183.) You then hand over the claim to the court clerk who checks it for accuracy and directs you to the cashier to pay.

The clerk will then assign a time and date for the hearing. Be sure to find out whether the court has night or Saturday sessions if you prefer them. If some days are better for you than others, be sure to let the clerk know. You can also file your claim by mail. However, very few people take the chance since a careless mistake will result in the claim being sent back to you unfiled and you will have to start over.

After the case is filed, it is up to you to make sure the lawsuit is delivered to the other party properly under the rules of service and that your witnesses show up promptly on the date of the hearing. It is up to you to prepare your case and present it to the judge. If you fail to appear for your own case, the judge can decide it against you. Therefore, if you are inclined to forget to show up at important engagements, make sure you have asked your family members to keep reminding you of the date and have at least one of them plan to go with you.

After your case has been heard, the court will usually make its decision within three weeks of the hearing. You will receive the judgment in the mail, which starts the time period running for an appeal. After the 30–day appeal period is over, formal collection procedures can begin.

NEEDING AN ATTORNEY

Small claims court in California was designed for people who do not plan to use an attorney. In fact, attorneys are normally not permitted in small claims court in California. However, if the amount of money in dispute is substantial, or the law is confusing to you, you may wish to obtain a consultation with an attorney just to make sure you are on the right track.

Cases with a value of more than $5,000 are often filed in small claims court despite only being able to get a $5,000 judgment. In situations where the attorneys' fees would cost more than the amount above $5,000 that the case is worth, it may make sense to take advantage of the benefits of small claims court.

Example: If the contractor you hired to build your swimming pool refused to finish the job, and you paid another contractor $7,200 to do the work, the $5,000 you could win in small claims court still leaves you $2,200 short. If an attorney tells you that he would charge you only $1,500 to represent you in court, it seems that you would still come out ahead by $750 by using the attorney.

However, it costs $86 to $97 to file a case in limited jurisdiction courts (formerly municipal courts) if the request is for less than $10,000—$66 to $77 more than you would pay in small claims court. So, now you are only ahead by approximately $675. If the lawyer plans to take depositions, subpoena records, or hire an expert, that $675 may not be enough to cover the costs of this litigation.

A thorough financial analysis weighing the benefits against the costs would be very helpful. Another important issue to consider is whether the type of lawsuit allows the winner to collect money spent to hire a lawyer. Even simple one-page contracts sometimes have an attorney's fee paragraph hidden in the small print. Since no attorneys are permitted to represent you in small claims court, neither party will be required to pay the other's lawyer.

There is no way of guaranteeing a result. If you file the claim in small claims court and lose, you will probably wonder if you would have won if you had hired an attorney to pursue the case. On the other hand, if the attorney loses in court, you may be responsible for your opponents' attorney fees as well as your own. In that situation, you will surely regret not having filed the case in small claims court. In fact, even though lawyers are allowed to represent parties during the appeal of a small claims case, the hiring of an attorney is usually not cost-effective and few do so.

OTHER PLACES TO GET HELP

COURT CLERKS

It is important to remember that the court clerks are not attorneys and are prohibited from giving legal advice. Nevertheless, they are often excellent sources of information regarding the preparation of forms and the procedures adopted by the local courts. You should always listen carefully to the advice of the clerk. They have the "inside track" on the preferences and nuances of their particular court. Some clerks have worked at the courthouse for so many years that they are more knowledgeable than many attorneys, commissioners, and judges on small claims matters. Be polite and do not argue with them.

Astute attorneys know that a court clerk can be your best friend or your worst enemy. They can put your case on the top of the pile or on the bottom. They can direct your case to the judge who takes all day to hear two cases or to the judge who will get you in and out of the court in less than an hour. Even if you are only going to the courthouse to pick up a form, do not let the clerk see you looking unkempt. They may take it as a sign of disrespect for the court and they will remember you.

SMALL CLAIMS
ADVISOR

Under California Code of Civil Procedure, Section 116.940 all counties are required to provide advice on small claims court. The person providing this advice is called the *small claims advisor* and may be available in person or by telephone. Smaller counties may share an advisor with other counties. Appendix A contains the name, address and telephone number (where available) of the advisor for each county. In addition, Appendix A contains the Web address for each county court. There is also a form called INFORMATION FOR THE SMALL CLAIMS PLAINTIFF, which is an information sheet setting forth the basic small claims rules. (see form 1, p.181.)

LOSSES YOU CAN RECOVER

As a general rule, you can only recover actual out-of-pocket losses directly relating to the subject matter of the case.

Example: If you are suing a dry cleaner for ruining a dress, you can sue for the replacement value of the dress (depending on whether it was brand new).

If you are suing an auto mechanic for improperly repairing your car, you can sue for the cost of repairs if they do not exceed the value of the car.

If you loaned money that has not been repaid, you may be entitled to interest as well as the principal of the loan.

In a personal injury case, you are entitled to a whole range of damages including the intangible loss of enjoyment of life known as *pain and suffering*, economic loss and future medical treatment.

You generally cannot recover for the fact that you missed a day of work because you did not have the dress or car. Nor can you recover lost wages for time you spend in court or your travel costs to court, even if you had to fly in from out-of-state or drive a long distance.

In some situations, under specific statutes you may be entitled to recover additional damages based on "punishing" or making an example of the defendant, sometimes called *penalties* or *punitive damages*. If you are the prevailing party, meaning you won on a significant issue in the case, you probably will be awarded your costs of the suit. These include your filing fee, sheriff's fee and witness fees. It is up to you to decide if it is worth spending $100 in costs to win a $50 case since you would be entitled to $150 if you win.

As discussed in the next chapter, you should ask for as much as possible within the small claims court in order to improve your negotiating position (even if you know you will not be granted everything in court), but as a practical matter, you usually will not get much more than the out-of-pocket losses.

TERMINOLOGY

While the court system strives to make small claims court as simple as possible, there are still legal terms that are used to describe many forms and procedures. These are defined in the glossary following Chapter 10 of this book.

BEFORE YOU SUE 2

Everyone, including attorneys, feels anxiety before presenting a case in court. Before you file a case, you should first decide whether you want to deal with the anxiety and whether it is worth your time and effort to go through the whole process. Even though a trial in small claims court is much quicker and easier than a case in limited jurisdiction or superior court, you will have to spend a lot of time preparing your case, filing the correct forms and collecting the judgment.

Maybe you want to file a case because you feel you have been ripped off, but a trial itself can be an emotionally draining experience, even if you win. It will be even more upsetting if you lose, especially if you end up paying damages to the other side. Most cases settle out of court because you can never predict what result you will get in court. No matter how right you are, or how strong your case is, the court can rule the other way for any number of reasons.

You should almost always attempt to resolve the dispute before filing the case. In fact, the law governing small claims procedures requires you to ask the other side to pay the amount owed before you file the lawsuit. The reason for this rule is that many people come to court and say they have not paid the amount owed simply because they were never asked. It is a good practice to make the request in writing and keep a copy of it to present to the court as evidence that you have tried to resolve the matter. Use a mail service that requires a signature to prove that your opponent received it. Even though few first class letters are lost by the post office each year, it is amazing that so many small claims litigants claim not to have received items placed in the mail.

DECIDING WHETHER YOU HAVE A CASE

In order to win a lawsuit against someone, you must be able to prove they are liable under some acceptable legal theory. In many instances, a person who has clearly suffered a loss may not be able to win his or her case because the law does not allow liability. Before filing your case you must find a legal theory that will allow you to win. Some cases are easy. If a person did something intentionally (like hitting you in the jaw) or failed to do something that was legally required (like pay back a loan) then you have a clear case.

Sometimes you must use a more complicated theory, such as *negligence* or *implied warranty*. In cases like these you will only win if the facts of your case fit into the legal definitions. If you are struck by lightning while walking at an amusement park, the owners will probably not be liable because the courts consider lightning an "act of God" and not the legal responsibility of the landowner. (A person once tried to sue God for an act of God. He served the papers on a local church as an "agent of God." But the court said that the church was not legally able to accept service of process for God so the court "did not have jurisdiction over the defendant.")

Another instance for deciding whether you have a case is where you have leased a house from a landlord. When you signed the lease, you agreed to take care of minor maintenance and the landlord agreed to charge you less rent. Now suppose you fixed a board on the steps and later it broke, causing you to fall and break your leg. Even though the landlord owns the property and has insurance against liability, the landlord (or the landlord's insurance company) will probably not be liable because you had a duty to maintain the premises and you are the one who improperly fixed the step that broke. On the other hand, if the landlord supplied you with defective materials to fix the step, the landlord, the supplier, and the manufacturer may all be liable for your injury and your own improper maintenance would be considered merely an insignificant factor in determining fault.

If you signed a contract or received any documents or papers from the other party relating to the transaction, you should read them very carefully before filing a claim. Sometimes the contract will limit your legal rights or your right to bring suit. If a sales person made oral promises about a product but the contract said that the product was sold "as is" and that "oral representations cannot be relied upon," you may be out of luck. Or if your contract with your stock broker says that you agree to have your case decided outside of court by a private individual, known as *arbitration*, you may have given up your right to sue in court.

In some cases, the papers used by the party may not have any legal effect. Parking lot machines often hand out "tickets" that say they are not liable for any loss or damage to your vehicle on the premises. However, in some instances, California law says otherwise and this over-rules the wording on the parking ticket. Receipts you receive for bringing clothing to a tailor for alterations, a car in for repairs, or a computer in for required maintenance may say that the shop is not liable for damages. Sometimes California law allows you to recover anyway.

GETTING INFORMATION

If you have any doubts about your rights, you should either check with an attorney, do some research yourself, or both. Many types of claims are explained in this book, but you may want to do some extra legal research to find more information, other causes of action, or other grounds for your suit. You can do legal research at the law library found in most county courthouses or at the law library in some law schools.

Law schools often restrict use of their law libraries to their own students and attorneys, so check first. Some college libraries have substantial law sections, especially if they offer paralegal or other law related degrees.

The Internet contains excellent sources of information, many of them easily searchable. For example, the entire California Code is available and can be searched by code section, keyword or subject. The web site is:

http://www.leginfo.ca.gov/index.html

The California court cases available on the Internet at no charge is limited at this time, but will be expanded over the years. The web site is:

http://www.courtinfo.ca.gov

You can also find services on the Internet that will do your research for you (for a fee, of course) and there are some databases available for a fee. There are several books on the market explaining how to do legal research.

PROVING YOUR CASE

Even if you have a good case, you will not win if you do not have enough proof to convince the judge or commissioner that you are right. If all you have is a verbal agreement, it will be your word against the other party and the judge will have to decide who is more believable. If you do not have any evidence and the other side has evidence that supports their position, it is unlikely that you will win.

Be sure to read the rules of evidence in Chapter 7. Also, ask a friend (the one that always tell you the truth) what he or she believes are the best points of the other side's case. As a participant in the situation you will not be able to effectively judge the merits of the arguments on either side as objectively as your friends. He or she may be able to point out the weaknesses of your case, a legal rule, or other reason that you could lose the case.

YOUR TIME AND EFFORT

Even if you have a valid legal claim, not all claims are worth bringing to court. Sometimes it may cost you more to take off work than the claim is worth. If there is a chance that the other party can also sue you, then you are risking more than just your time and effort.

In many cases the principle seems more important than money to the wronged person. If you enjoy the process of righting the wrong, especially if someone took advantage of you, be sure to consider what the case will involve before you start it.

On the other hand, there is always the possibility that it might not be worth the time and effort for the other side to fight your case. If the amount involved is small (in their perspective) and they will have to take off work or hire any attorney, they may just pay you without a trial. So merely filing the case may get results.

COLLECTING IF YOU WIN

If the person you want to sue has no money, it may be a waste of time to get a judgment. You cannot garnish the wages of the self-employed, unemployed, and those receiving most types of government income (unemployment, social security benefits, etc. are exempt). The most difficult parties to collect from are small corporations with no assets or unemployed people who have no assets.

For example, equity in the amount of at least fifty thousand dollars in a primary residence is exempt from collection, as is a certain amount of equity in a car or household furnishings. Sometimes a company or person with a lot of real estate or other assets may be worth pursuing. The judgment can be filed in court as a right to proceeds of some of the property when it is sold. You will be paid at that time, which may be several years in the future.

The old saying "you can't get blood out of a turnip" applies here. Consider carefully whether the judgment you spent time and court costs to obtain will end up being a worthless piece of paper. (Of course, you can hope that the defendant may some day win the lottery and be able to pay you, but you are better off hoping that you will win the lottery instead and no longer care about the defendant's finances.)

If you are not sure if the party is worth suing, you might want to first read Chapter 9 in this book before filing your claim. It explains how to find out the extent of assets owned by a company or person.

DEMANDING PAYMENT AND SETTLING

California law requires that you "demand" payment from the other person before you file your claim in small claims court. While there is no requirement that the demand be written, it makes sense not to rely on your memory as to the date you requested payment and what you asked for. Some judges interpret the requirement to mean that a written request was made, so you should do so, by return-receipt mail, so you can prove that the other party got your letter. Even though the letter is often called a *demand letter*, it is much more effective to be polite and business-like in your letter. (A sample demand letter is provided in Appendix H.)

Before filing your suit, either before or after you have written the required letter, you should attempt to work out a settlement with the other person. In some circumstances you can try to negotiate directly with the other person, or you can have another person act as the go-between if you do not want to do it yourself. You can ask a lawyer, a friend, a spouse, or someone both you and the other person know and respect. (This person can also be a witness to prove that you tried to settle the case.)

The next chapter explains how you can use mediation to resolve your dispute. (You do not have to like each other to use mediation.) Appendix B contains a list of county sponsored and private mediation services available in each county.

DEADLINE FOR FILING SUIT

Whenever you are negotiating to settle a case, you should be careful not to miss the time limit for filing your case. This time limit is a deadline, and the laws that set the deadlines are called the *Statutes of Limitations*. If you have not done so already, you should immediately turn to Appendix E, which contains a list of the various time periods for filing your case. You should then calculate the very last day you can file your lawsuit and write it in a calendar or a place where you absolutely cannot miss it. You should also write reminders in your calendar for six months before the deadline and one month before the deadline.

Example: A California lawyer who was so caught up in negotiating a several million dollar settlement for her client forgot about her case's deadline. A few minutes after the court closed on the day of the deadline, the insurance company representative "changed his mind" and decided not to settle. Luckily, it was a case where the federal courts had jurisdiction and she was able to call a lawyer in Hawaii where the courts were still open and get the case filed in time.

Even though the story above is fictional, missing the deadline has happened to many people, including lawyers. If the deadline is near and the person you are negotiating with seems to be delaying, you may have to file your suit to avoid missing the deadline. Even though insurance companies are required to inform you of how long you have to sue, you may not have paid attention to the information if it was written in a letter which contained a lot of other information. Or, you may be negotiating with someone who does not have insurance. Remember, once the deadline has passed, you can never file the claim.

> ***Warning:*** If you are planning to sue a government agency, you *must* file a governmental claim first and you need to be aware of the time limits for filing the various types of claims. A list of the time periods for governmental claims is provided after the Statutes of Limitation in Appendix E, and a sample Notice of Claim Against Governmental Agency is provided in Appendix H.

> ***Warning:*** You should not sue anyone unless you have a valid claim. If you file a suit and the judge decides there is no legal or factual merit to it, he or she may decide the judgment against you and award costs to the other party.

USING MEDIATION TO RESOLVE YOUR CASE 3

Alternative Dispute Resolution (ADR) is the term used to describe the processes for resolving disputes without going through a crowded court system. *Mediation* is, by far, the most popular dispute resolution method and it is now being used to resolve all kinds of disputes including:

- divorce;
- employment;
- probate;
- civil cases;
- misdemeanors; and,
- juvenile cases.

Because the small claims process is based on providing an inexpensive, uncomplicated and convenient forum for cases that do not warrant the expense of formal litigation, it is especially well-suited for small claims disputes such as:

- landlord/tenant;
- consumer/merchant;
- professional/client;

- auto accident property damage;

- neighborhood nuisance;

- business and contracts; and,

- personal loan disputes.

TYPES OF MEDIATION

Many small businesses and individuals are now turning to mediation either before they file their claim or very early in the process after it is filed. There are two basic kinds of small claims mediation. The first process begins when one of the parties decides that he or she would like to attempt mediation and contacts a private mediator or a non profit organization which provides mediation services to the community. The contact with the other party is done by the mediator. If both side agree, a mediation session is set up.

Because setting up the mediation session requires coordination, cooper-ation and knowledge of the facts and law early in the process, it just does not take place as often as same-day mediation (discussed next). As public awareness of the benefits of mediation increases, and as more mediation programs become available, the number of participants in this *pre-hearing* type of mediation is increasing.

The second type of small claims mediation is commonly called *same-day* mediation. These mediation sessions take place on the date of the hearing at the courthouse, in a jury room, a court office, or the cafeteria. When there is a severe space crunch, mediations may take place in the hallway. Due to the time constraints, the mediation session will usually be restricted to less than an hour. Added to these disadvantages is the pressure of being "ordered" or strong-armed into mediation by the expectations of the court that you will attempt mediation before your case will be heard. The so-called voluntary nature of the process is somewhat compromised and this is reflected in the lower resolution rates for same day mediation as compared to pre-hearing mediation. Nevertheless, the only requirement the court can realistically impose is that the parties show up at the mediation. They cannot make you settle.

In contrast to this scenario, a pre-hearing mediation takes place away from the courthouse. Another advantage is that you and the other party can determine when to schedule the mediation. This is an especially important consideration if the county in which you must file the lawsuit does not hold night sessions and you do not want to lose a day of work.

ADVANTAGES TO MEDIATION

There are many advantages to mediation. Some people like the informality of mediation and not having to "dress up" for court. There are no forms to file when you mediate a case. The only paperwork necessary will be the agreement if you resolve the case.

Mediation allows you and the other party the opportunity to try to work out a settlement rather than taking your chances on the ruling of judge or commissioner who may not be familiar with the type of business or with the laws which apply to the situation.

Many people feel that the most important advantage is that people who mediate agreements are much more likely to abide by the terms of the agreement because they feel connected with the process of reaching the outcome. Furthermore, when cases are mediated, the the range of potential solutions is much greater and more creative than a judge would be allowed to fashion from the bench.

Example: In a case where money is owed, the parties can:

- decide to trade their services or merchandise instead of repayment in cash;

- make an agreement where goods or services are given to a person who is not part of the dispute;

- work out a payment schedule based on irregular incomes.; or,

- apologize and renew their business or personal relationship.

The parties are limited only by their imaginations, their willingness to cooperate, and their desire for a reasonable and fair result. It is one of the few situations in life where you really have nothing to lose by trying it.

Finding Services

Many counties, bar associations, non-profit, consumer and private organizations have mediation services where the parties meet together with one or two trained *neutrals* who help you resolve your case. (A list of these services is included in Appendix B.) The small claims advisor in your county usually has a list of local attorneys, psychologists, accountants and other professional mediators who charge a fee. But check first with the non-profit agencies because many of the professional mediators do volunteer mediation with non-profit agencies as a public service. Several of these non-profits have very reasonable fees for mediation.

Procedure

Whenever the mediation takes place, the procedure is somewhat standard. The parties meet privately with one or two mediators and engage in a process of *facilitated negotiation*, which means the mediators' role is to guide you through the process and to facilitate the meeting. They help you and the other party set an agenda and focus on the issues. The mediator often commends the parties for choosing mediation and asks for their commitment to the process.

In conjunction with making an opening statement where the mediation procedure is explained, the mediator also tries to establish a sense of equality and rapport between the participants. The mediator ascertains whether the participants in the room (or hallway) have full authority to settle the case or have the means to contact the ultimate decision-maker during the mediation. (It is a good idea to anticipate the opportunity to mediate and obtain settlement authority in advance if you are appearing on behalf of someone else.) The parties then each have an opportunity to make an opening statement where they point out the strengths of their position and voice their individual concerns. The mediator may probe and ask clarifying questions during the opening statements.

The parties then communicate directly with each other while the mediator guides the discussion. Every mediation is different, but most parties exchange information, talk about their point of view and try to understand the other parties' position. They discuss ways to manage conflict that can be applied to future situations. The mediator guides them to break down misunderstandings by helping them open the lines of communication and then identify and focus on common goals.

CAUCUS At some point during the discussion, the mediator may suggest a *caucus*, which is a private meeting with each party. The mediator may review the strengths and weaknesses of the case and try to channel the party in a more constructive direction, give feedback on the person's style of negotiation or suggest reasons why the other party may not be accepting their proposals. During the caucus, the parties have an opportunity to tell the mediator information that they do not necessarily want to disclose to the other party. The mediator will keep this information confidential if the party so desires. The parties will then go back into joint session, and the mediator will attempt to help the parties integrate their interests into a workable solution and write a mutually acceptable agreement.

CONFIDENTIALITY The agreement can later be used as evidence of the failure to perform the contract in a later small claims action, but everything that was said during the mediation is private. Any information obtained in the mediation session, and the dialogue within a session is, by law, confidential. No one can obtain that information through any court or lawful process, even through a subpoena requiring the mediator to appear in court.

MEDIATED
AGREEMENT

Although there are mediated agreements that are not fulfilled, they have a much better chance of being followed than a court judgment. To encourage people to mediate, some courts in California use a mediated agreement form that allows for the case to be taken off calendar pending fulfillment of the agreement. If the defendant defaults, the plaintiff can petition to have the agreement converted to a judgment. Defendants benefit from the fact that a mediated settlement, unlike a judgment, results in no damage to credit records.

If the parties do not reach an agreement, they still have the right to appear before the judge and argue their case. At its best, the parties address each other's interests, rather than their positions, and attempt a win-win solution rather than a decision where one party wins and the other loses. It does not preclude attorney participation at any stage of the procedure if the parties choose to include them. Mediation can take place at any time during the dispute including the day of trial, or even after the decision from the judge.

FILING AND SERVING YOUR CASE 4

This chapter explains who can file a case, how to name the person being sued, where to file the case and the various fees and charges attached to each procedure. This chapter also tells you how to serve the defendant.

THOSE WHO CAN SUE AND BE SUED

Before you file your lawsuit you must be sure that you are suing the proper legal entity and that your own legal status is designated properly. If this is not done you may lose your case, or your judgment may be worthless.

MINORS   In California, *minors* are people under eighteen years of age who have not been *emancipated* under the law. They cannot sue or be sued except through their parent or legal guardian. If you are a minor who wants to sue someone, you must use the APPLICATION AND ORDER FOR APPOINTMENT OF GUARDIAN AD LITEM—CIVIL. (see form 3, p.189.)

If you wish to sue a minor it makes sense to sue his or her parent or legal guardian. However, you should be aware that under most circumstances a parent is not liable for the acts of his or her child except for auto accidents where the child was authorized to drive, and for acts that are "malicious and willful." Such acts include things like driving at an extremely high speed through a school zone while children are crossing the street.

INCOMPETENT PEOPLE	*Incompetent* is a legal word meaning that, due to some physical or mental condition, a person is unable to bring or defend a suit on their own behalf. If you wish to file a suit on behalf of an incompetent person you must use the APPLICATION AND ORDER FOR APPOINTMENT OF GUARDIAN AD LITEM—CIVIL to have yourself or another person appointed. (see form 3, p.189.)

If you are suing an incompetent person you should name their guardian ad litem as defendant if they have one. Otherwise the court will need to appoint one. The incompetent would be named in the lawsuit as: *Lorraine B. Little, by and through her Guardian ad Litem, Silvia T. Little.*

SPOUSES

A husband or wife who sues or who is sued with his or her spouse, may appear and participate on behalf of the spouse if the claim is a joint claim. However, the spouse must give his or her permission and the court must agree that the interests of justice would be served. The lawsuit would name them as Florence Flighty and Filbert Flighty, or Filbert Flighty and Mrs. Filbert Flighty, or Florence Flighty and Mr. Flighty.

SOLE PROPRIETORS

The appearance in court must be made by the business owner of a sole proprietorship unless the suit is only for collection of an unpaid bill. Under those circumstances the sole proprietor can send an employee who prepares or keeps the business records, subject to Evidence Code 1271, and is knowledgeable about the facts and circumstances of the unpaid bill.

If you are suing a sole proprietorship, check the *fictitious name* listings at the county clerk's office to find out the correct name of the person who owns the business. Sometimes businesses are owned by many more people than the one person who may have identified himself to you as the owner. Name both the owner individually and the company name in your lawsuit. The format would be as follows: *Ura Skunk, an individual and Ura Skunk d.b.a. (doing business as) Silly Smells.*

PARTNERSHIPS AND OTHER UNINCORPORATED ASSOCIATIONS

A partnership and other unincorporated associations, even though made up of individuals, can sue in the name by which it is known, the name it has assumed, or in the name of all the individuals. Any partner may make the appearance in court for the entire partnership.

When bringing suit against a partnership or unincorporated association, the safest route is to name each individual as well as the partnership.

CORPORATIONS

The suit should be brought in the name of the corporation and the claim should be signed by an officer or director or a regular employee appointed by the corporation's board of directors. The key point is that this person must have been hired to perform other duties in addition to making appearances in small claims court.

When you are suing a corporation, you will probably need to check with the Secretary of State's office to obtain the names and addresses of the officers and of the person or corporation designated to receive lawsuits against the corporation. In a suit against a corporation, the defendant should be named by its corporate name, or its corporate name and its *subsidiary*.

You can find out the exact name of a corporation and the agent for service of process online at **http://www.kepler.ss.ca.gov/list.html**, by visiting an office of the Secretary of State, or by sending a fee to their Sacramento office. The fee is currently $10 unless you are only requesting a computer printout. To find out whether it has changed, call 916-653-7315. The address is:

Secretary of State
1500 11th Street, 3rd floor
Sacramento, CA 95814
Attn: The IRC Unit.

The branch offices are located in Fresno, Los Angeles, and San Diego.

A corporation with assets is a good target, but a *shell* corporation with no assets is not. This means it can be dissolved, making your claim worthless. An individual may have no assets or may file bankruptcy, but it is not as likely or as easy as dissolving a shell corporation. A new corporation can always be started, but an individual is stuck with his or her credit record for years.

In such a case, it is better if you can sue some of the individuals in the corporation. This can be done if:

- the individuals signed documents without their corporate titles;

- the company name was used without the words "Inc.," "Corp.," or "Co." after it;

- the individuals committed some sort of fraud; or,

- a corporation does not have enough funds to pay a judgment.

Ignoring a corporate entity and suing the individuals behind it is called *piercing the corporate veil* and much has been written about it in legal books and periodicals. If you think you will need to pierce a corporate veil to win your case, you should research the subject further in your nearest law library. To find out who the officers of a corporation are you can obtain a *Statement of Officers* from the Secretary of State for $5 from the address above.

ATTORNEYS Attorneys can only appear as *real* parties in small claims court; not as representatives of anyone else. If an attorney and someone else are injured in an automobile, the attorney can represent himself but not the other person who was in the car. When an attorney is a member of a partnership of lawyers, (many law firms are set up that way) the attorney can represent the partnership. If all of the officers and directors of a corporation are attorneys, any one of them may prosecute an action on behalf of the corporation.

ASSIGNEES A person who has received an assignment of rights, known as an *assignee*, generally cannot appear in small claims court. The exceptions are trustees in bankruptcy, and holders of security agreements, retail installment contracts, or lien contracts.

OWNER OF RENTAL REAL PROPERTY In a suit involving rental property, the appearance can be made by either the owner of the property or the property manager if the manager has other duties and was not hired for the specific purpose of appearing in small claims court. The claim must relate to the rental property.

When *serving* the landlord (see p.36.), it is permissible to serve the manager of the building if the manager will not provide the owner's address and if the manager rented the apartment to you.

NON-RESIDENT
OWNER OF
REAL PROPERTY

A non-resident owner (owner who lives elsewhere) may defend the small claims case by submitting *declarations* (a written document under penalty of perjury stating his or her case), or by asking another person to appear who does not receive compensation for making the appearance, or both. This provision is only for the defense of the action and does not include a counter-claim.

DEPARTMENT OF
CORRECTIONS
AND YOUTH
AUTHORITY

If either the Department of Corrections or the Youth Authority is a plaintiff, they can appear by a regular employee but when named as a defendant, they are permitted to appear by declaration to challenge the pleading defects.

MEMBERS OF
THE ARMED
SERVICES AND
INCARCERATED
INDIVIDUALS

If a member of the Armed Services is stationed outside the state of California on an assignment that is scheduled to last more than six months, the member may file the claim by mail for a claim that arose before the out-of-state assignment was made. The member can choose whether to submit declarations testifying to the facts under penalty of perjury or have someone else appear instead. This someone else must:

- not be a lawyer;

- not be compensated; and,

- have appeared in small claims court on behalf of others less than four times during the past twelve months.

A person who is incarcerated in a county jail, a Department of Corrections facility or a Youth Authority facility is allowed the same choices as someone in the armed services.

GOVERNMENT
ENTITIES

Except for the federal government, you can sue any government agency in small claims court. You can also sue an employee of the government, if the employee caused you injury while "in the course and scope" of employment. It is very easy to confuse one government entity for another and sue the wrong one. For example, even though a street may run through a city or town, it may be under the jurisdiction of the state rather than the city. Some hospitals may appear to be private hospitals but they come under the umbrella of the government.

In order to sue a government entity, you are required to file a claim against the proper agency within six months of the *accrual date*, which is usually the date the incident occurred. A sample Notice of Claim Against a Governmental Agency is included in Appendix H. The claim must be rejected before you file your small claim action. If you do not get an acceptance or a rejection within forty-five days, the claim is deemed rejected by law and you can file in small claims court. A copy of the rejection form—if you received one—should be attached to your small claims action when you file it. You only have six months from the date of rejection to file your lawsuit.

If you missed the claim filing deadline, do not give up. There are many exceptions for late claims and there are a few specific situations where a claim is not required at all. You will either need to do some research or consult with an attorney to find out how to file an application for a late claim.

The claim against the government entity must contain:

- your name and address;

- the address where notices should be sent;

- the date, place, and circumstances giving rise to the claim;

- the name of any government employee responsible (if you know);

- a description of the injury; and,

- the specific dollar amount of damages being claimed.

Some government entities have their own claim form but most will accept any format that contains the required information.

A claim against the state must be delivered to an office of the Board of Control and a claim against local agencies must be delivered or mailed to the clerk, secretary, or governing body. If you are unsure of the name or address of the government you are suing, the county clerk in each county should keep a roster of public agencies for you to review. Most government agencies will give you the name and address of the person and the place to send a claim over the phone. Be cautious, however, since not every public entity is easily recognized by its name.

OTHERS The judge in a small claims action has been given the discretion by the legislature to allow another person to help someone who cannot effectively present or defend their case. This issue most often arises when a non-English speaking person is either the plaintiff or the defendant. The small claims court usually has a list of interpreters who can help non-English speaking plaintiffs. Some charge for their services, some do not.

If there is no available interpreter on the day of the hearing, the court will usually postpone the hearing to allow the party to find one. If there is no available interpreter on the new date, the judge may use his or her discretion to either postpone the matter again or to allow a family member or friend to interpret.

Other situations where this issue arises occur when judges relax the rules to permit a representative to appear for a non-resident motorist.

WHERE TO FILE YOUR SUIT

You must file your small claims suit in the right county. The official legal term is *venue*. The general rule is that proper venue is the county where the defendant lives. Venue, however, has lots of rules which expand this definition, and the plaintiff may choose among any of the counties where venue is proper, even if the location is inconvenient for the defendant. Some of the other places where venue would be proper are:

- where a business or branch office is located;

- where a corporation does business;

- where an injury occurred;

- where a buyer signed a contract (automobile or retail installment contract);

- where buyer resided when contract was signed (automobile or retail installment contract); or,

- where buyer presently resides (retail installment contract only).

The defendant can write a letter to the court explaining the inconvenience and hope that the court will transfer the case. However, if moving the case is going to cause hardship for the plaintiff, there is much less likelihood of transferring it out of the county where the plaintiff filed.

If the defendant is a business, venue is proper in the county where the business or branch office is located. A case against a corporation is properly filed where the corporation has its principal place of business, where the contract was breached, or where the obligation or liability arose. A tort action such as an automobile accident case is venued in the county where the injury occurred. If a tort action is being brought against a corporation, the liability arose where the injury occurred.

If you are seeking recovery for a bad check, or suing your landlord for return of your security deposit, then you should file your claim in the county where the check was issued or where the rental property is located. A case based on contract can be filed in the county in which the contract was signed or where it was to be performed.

A case based on a retail installment account, a sales contract or motor vehicle finance sale can be brought where the buyer lives, where the buyer lived when the contract was signed, where the buyer signed the contract or where the goods or vehicle are permanently kept.

An objection to the proposed venue can be made in a written letter to the court or by an appearance on the day of the hearing. If the defendant does not appear, the court will investigate the facts and make a determination as to whether venue is correct. If it is not, the case will be dismissed with the right to refile the case. If venue is correct and the defendant is not present, the case will be continued for at least fifteen days. If all the parties are present and agree to proceed, the case will be heard.

FEES

The fee to file your claim is $20. If you have filed more than twelve cases during the previous twelve month period, the filing fee is $35 for subsequent filings.

There is an additional fee of $6 to have the court clerk serve the defendant by certified mail, or you can pay $25 to the marshal or sheriff for personal or substituted service. (see p.35.) Marshals usually require thirty days lead time. The marshal can also serve subpoenas. The court will waive the fees if you cannot afford to pay them. This is not a decision you get to make. There is a form in Appendix I that contains the conditions you have to meet for a waiver of fees. (see form 5, p.193.)

There is a fee of $10 to file a REQUEST FOR POSTPONEMENT of the court date. (see form 10, p.203.) There is also a $14 fee for a judgment creditor examination and a $14 fee to file a motion to vacate the judgment.

If you cannot afford to pay court fees, you can apply for a waiver. You will need to fill out an APPLICATION FOR WAIVER OF COURT FEES AND COSTS. (see form 6, p.195.) To see if you qualify for the waiver, you will need to review the requirements on the Information sheet on waiver of court fees and costs, also included in Appendix I.

HOW MUCH TO SUE FOR

When filing a suit you should always ask for the highest amount allowed for the claim.

Example: If someone hit your car and you got estimates of $100, $150, and $175 to fix it, you may be happy if that person paid you $100. If they offer to settle the case, you should seriously consider accepting it. But if you have to sue for damages, sue for $175, plus any other amounts you can reasonably add to the bill such as car rental, lost time at work, taxi fares, etc. You might not get the full amount, but asking for it will provide the judge with room for compromise.

BEGINNING YOUR CASE

To begin your case, you must file a PLAINTIFF'S CLAIM AND ORDER TO DEFENDANT. (see form 2, p.183.) The instructions to complete the form can be found at the end of form 2. The claim form is the same whether your case is based on breach of contract or negligence. In only one circumstance is there an *attachment* and that is for a dispute between you and an attorney over fees after a non-binding arbitration has taken place.

You are not required to go into a lot of detail on the claim form. However, you will need to know all of the elements required for each type of case when you prepare it and when you present your case during trial. The next chapter explains the various types of lawsuits and the necessary elements.

FORMS

The approved Judicial Council forms are in this book in Appendix I. However, some counties have devised their own forms for some situations. Appendix J lists the counties that have devised their own forms, but check with the court clerk in your own county to see if there are any new county forms. You can also download forms from the internet. See Appendix I for more information.

There are forms for most actions you may wish to take in your case, such as listing additional plaintiffs or defendants (form 9), requesting a postponement (form 10), dismissing your case (form 15). Check the list in Appendix I for the form you need.

STATUTES

The statutes governing small claims court are contained in Appendix C of this book. They are very useful to have with you when you are presenting your case in court. The temporary judge hearing your case may be unfamiliar with the law and quoting from the source will make you appear knowledgeable.

SERVING THE PAPERS ON THE DEFENDANT

One requirement in successfully suing someone in any court is that they be properly *served* with the papers. The purpose for this delivery of the court papers rule is to be sure the defendant knows about the suit and has the right to respond to it. As explained below the papers may be served by certified mail, but if the defendant refuses to sign for them you will have to use personal or substitute service. For this you will need the home or business address of the defendant. If you do not know the defendant's physical address, read the section beginning on page 38.

CERTIFIED MAIL

Service of a lawsuit is less formal in small claims court than superior court actions. Service of the claim may be made by the clerk of the court mailing the claim to the defendant by *restricted certified mail*, which means that only the defendant can sign for it. Service is complete when the defendant signs the return receipt, which must be at least ten days before the hearing if the defendant lives in the same county and fifteen days before the hearing if the defendant lives in a county different from the one where the action is filed. This kind of service is the cheapest and the easiest but least reliable because the defendant can refuse delivery and write "return to sender." If someone else signs by mistake, the service is not valid. The service by certified mail can only be accomplished by the court clerk and you have to rely on the court and the post office directing the return receipt to the right file.

PERSONAL SERVICE

Another way to serve is *personal service*. This is accomplished when the defendant identifies himself to the server (unless the defendant is known to the server) and "handed" the lawsuit. If the defendant refuses to accept the lawsuit, it can be dropped at his or her feet. This service may be done by any person:

- over eighteen who is not a party to the lawsuit;

- a registered process server;

- the sheriff; or,

- the marshal.

Commercial process servers advertise in the yellow pages, legal news papers and on the Internet. It is best not to have witnesses to your lawsuit do the service. Law firms almost always use process servers and you can ask any legal secretary to recommend one to you.

SUBSTITUTE
SERVICE

A defendant can also be served by *substitute service*. This means that the claim can be left at the defendant's office with the person in charge or at the place of residence with a person who is an adult. After the claim is substitute served, it must be mailed within ten days to the defendant at the address where it was substitute served. In addition, the mailing must be at least twenty days before the hearing, or twenty-five days before the hearing if the defendant lives out of the county. Substituted service can be done by anyone over eighteen.

OUT-OF-STATE
OWNER
OF RENTAL
REAL PROPERTY

If the owner of your rental property is not a resident of California and has no agent for service in California, the owner can be served by the court through certified mail ($6-8) or by another person over age 18 leaving a copy with the defendant directly. The process server can also serve the defendant by leaving a copy of the lawsuit papers with an adult member of the defendant's household or an adult in charge of receiving legal papers or mail at the defendant's primary place of work. The process server must then mail a second copy to the defendant addressed to where the first copy was left.

When serving the landlord, it is permissible to serve the manager of the building if the manager will not provide the owner's address and the manager rented the apartment to you.

The appearance can be made by either the owner of the property or the property manager if the manager has other management duties and was not hired for the specific purpose of appearing in small claims court. The claim must relate to the rental property, the manager must not receive extra pay for appearing in small claims court and has appeared no more than four times during the calendar year to represent others in small claims court.

OUT-OF-STATE
DRIVERS AND
OWNERS

Another exception to the general rule is that the small claims complaint cannot be served on a defendant outside the state of California. If the defendant is an out-of-state driver who was involved in automobile accident in the state of California or an out of state owner of an automobile involved in an accident in California, the claim must first be served on the California Department of Motor Vehicles (DMV) before serving the out-of-state driver.

In most cases, the court clerk is the only person permitted to serve by certified mail. But out-of-state drivers and vehicle owners are exceptions to that rule. The plaintiff will be responsible for service on the Director of the DMV or by certified mail. Mail the claim to:

DMV
Attention Legal Office
E_128, 2415 First Avenue
Sacramento, CA 95818.

Make out a check or money order to the Director of the DMV in the amount of $2.00. (If you are reading this book in 2003 or later, contact the DMV at 916-657-6421 to make sure the fee is still $2.00.) Service on the Department of Motor Vehicles is effective on the day the return receipt is received back from the DMV.

The out-of-state driver and owner can also be served by the the court clerk through certified mail ($6-8), by the plaintiff by registered mail, or by a process server leaving a copy with the defendant directly. The process server can also serve the defendant by leaving a copy of the lawsuit papers with an adult member of the defendant's household or an adult in charge of receiving legal papers or mail at the defendant's primary place of work.

There is an additional step to take. Contact the sheriff's department in the county where the driver lives and have them serve another copy of the claim on the driver and/or the owner. This service must also take place at least 15 days before the hearing. Request a certificate of service from the sheriff, make copies of it and the two return receipts , and then file them with the small claims clerk at least three days prior to the hearing.

NOTE: *The rules for service for out of state owner of rental real property or out of state drivers and owners are very confusing. Do not hesitate to call the court clerk and ask for assistance in these two instances.*

PROOF OF
SERVICE

You should make sure that the proper **PROOF OF SERVICE** has been filed in the court file prior to your hearing. (see form 8, p.199.) Usually, this is a paper signed by the sheriff or process server stating that the papers were properly delivered to the defendant. Most process servers will file the **PROOF OF SERVICE** done by their agency, but if a friend or family member served the defendant, you will have to file the proof of service yourself. If the court served the defendant by certified mail, make sure the receipt is in the court file.

WHEN YOU CANNOT FIND THE DEFENDANT

It is not unusual to discover that the individuals and businesses you want to sue are not easy to locate. They may either have unlisted phone numbers, post office boxes, fictitious names, or they have gone out of business. You can always hire a private investigator to do a search for you. A thorough search will reveal property, bank accounts, tax liens and prior lawsuits against the company or individual. This information can be very helpful in determining whether your lawsuit is worth pursuing and how to go about collecting on your judgment (more about this later.) (see Chapter 9.)

LAST KNOWN
ADDRESS AND
PUBLIC RECORDS

If you want to start or do the search yourself, there are several things you can do. If you are familiar with the last known address, you can mail a letter to the old address requesting an "address correction only" from the post office or you can send a certified letter and see who signs for it. Sometimes the post office does not have the old address on file, either because a forwarding address was not given to the post office or the forwarding order expired.

If the only address you have for a business is a post office box, you are permitted to obtain the name and address of the holder of the box if you can show that the box is used for business purposes. Libraries also contain "reverse directories" that provide the address that goes with the phone number (they are also available on the Internet). The tax assessor has records linking property addresses to their owners, as well as death, birth and marriage records, all available to the public to review. Much of this information is now online.

DMV   There is a commonly held belief in California that personal information can no longer be obtained from the Department of Motor Vehicles. While it is true that the DMV has made it more difficult to obtain information, it is certainly not impossible. The DMV does not consider a post office box to be confidential information and will make that information available after you fill out a form. If you want the street address you will have to provide justification (such as the need to serve the lawsuit) and some information you already have about the defendant. The key is following the DMV's instructions to the letter because the applications for information are scrutinized very carefully.

INTERNET   The Internet is very helpful in locating both individuals and businesses. There is an excellent selection of directories providing all kinds of information. One links area codes and prefixes with locations. Another links phone numbers with business and residence addresses.

The social security death index will provide information as to where a person was born or died. You can find information revealing the financial status of most major and some not so major companies. There are also services on the web which will perform fairly sophisticated searches for less than $20. If you are not computer-savvy, you can probably find one or two people among your family and friends who can help you in your quest for information.

TYPES OF CASES 5

This chapter contains a brief explanation of the most common types of cases that can be brought in small claims court. If your case falls into more than one category, list all of them on your claim. For example, if you are suing an auto repair facility for negligent repair of your auto, you may also have a case for breach of contract, and breach of warranty.

If your claim does not fall into any of these categories, it does not mean that you do not have a case. There are many legal theories and more are evolving every year. If you feel you have a case you should either do some legal research yourself or consult with an attorney.

Even if you can prove all the elements of a particular claim, you should try to anticipate any defenses the defendant will have. Before filing your case, be sure to read Chapter 6 to find out if any of the defenses mentioned apply to your case and could negate your claim.

For example, if you are in business using a fictitious name and have not filed a fictitious name statement, make sure you do so before you file suit. Another common defense is that the suit is beyond the period allowed by the statute of limitations. Before you file, be sure to check the list in Appendix E.

BAD CHECKS AND "STOP PAYMENT" CHECKS

A person who writes a check that is dishonored by the bank for lack of funds is civilly liable for the face value of the check and may have to pay penalties of up to three times the face value of the check (with a minimum of $100.00 and a maximum of $1500.00. If the person who receives the bad check writes a demand letter and sends it by certified mail, the person who wrote the bad check has thirty days from the date a demand letter was mailed by certified mail to pay the amount of the check, the service charge and the costs of mailing. If the customer fails to pay within thirty days, then he is liable for the amount of the check (subtracting any partial payments made within the thirty-day period) and a penalty equal to three times the amount of the check. However, the check writer is no longer liable for any service charges or the costs of mailing the demand letter.

If someone has stopped payment on a check written to your business or to you personally, you may also be able to take advantage of the penalty provisions of this statute. You must send a demand letter to the maker of the check by certified mail, in which you tell them that you plan to seek these extra damages. Be sure to save the receipt for certified mail because you will need to prove to the court that you sent this letter.

If your case is based on a bad check, the notice from the bank containing the information about the check coupled with a receipt showing the services you provided or the merchandise purchased should be sufficient to prove that the defendant owed the money to you.

If your case is based on a stop payment, you will have to prove that the stop payment order was not based on a *good faith* dispute with you. Grounds for a good faith dispute include:

- services not rendered;

- goods not delivered;

- goods or services that were faulty, not as promised, or otherwise unsatisfactory; or,

- where the customer claims an overcharge.

This may be difficult to prove if the person who stopped payment called you immediately after he or she stopped payment to explain why he or she stopped payment, and either returned the merchandise or wrote you a letter stating the facts of the dispute (the car engine burned up on the way home from the repair shop).

You will also need to show that you made a reasonable attempt to resolve the issues (mediating the dispute is considered a reasonable attempt) and wait 30 days from the date you mailed the notice before you file your case.

BREACH OF CONTRACT

Breach of contract is an action to recover money damages for failure of one party to abide by the terms of an oral or written contract. To win a suit for breach of contract you must prove that:

- there was an agreement;

- the defendant either did not perform or performed improperly; and,

- that you either performed or were ready to perform your part of the agreement.

If the breach was failure to pay a sum of money or to deliver some item, the proof and the evidence will be easy. But if the breach involved the quality of an item or service, the proof required will be more complicated.

Example: Mike agreed to pay John $2,000 to purchase his 1957 Chevy "if it runs." The car had been sitting in John's garage for years and would not start. John got it started the next week, Mike drove it around the block. He then paid John $1,500 cash and $500 by check and drove home. On the way home the car broke down and the service station that towed it said the engine was beyond repair and would have to be replaced at a cost of $1,000. Mike stopped payment on the check and sued John for the $1,000 it would cost for a new engine. John countersued Mike for $500 for the stopped payment on the check.

To Mike it is a simple case. He was supposed to get a car that runs for $2,000. To John it is also a simple case. The car did run and he was supposed to get $2,000. To a judge looking at the case, it is much more complicated. Some of the questions the judge will have are: What exactly was said between the parties? Did John make any representations about the car? Did John tell Mike that the car hadn't been driven in years? Is either party an expert on cars? What exactly was wrong with the engine? Did Mike get other estimates on the engine?

Actually, Mike and John should probably go to mediation to come to a settlement with which they are both happy. But if they insist on fighting it out in court, they should do their homework and have evidence that will answer all the questions the judge will have. This may mean written estimates and witnesses who heard their negotiations or saw the car before and after it broke down.

CONTRACT RESCISSION

A contract can be cancelled if a party to the contract was induced to enter into the contract through *fraud* or *misrepresentation*, or if the bargain fails through no fault of the party. A contract can also be rescinded if the contract was unlawful, unconscionable, or against public policy, such as contracts selling English language encyclopedias to single adults for personal use who speak only German.

For example, a car dealer may enter into a contract to sell a new car. If the car dealer knew that the car he was selling had been returned to the dealership as the result of defects, the contract can be cancelled.

Another example is a homeowner selling a house without disclosing the fact that the roof has to be replaced. On the other hand, it is not fraud if the seller did not know about a defect in his house when he sold it. A contract to rent a stadium may fail without fault because the stadium burned down before the event was to be held.

Example: A contract to cut down a tree can be rescinded if a storm uproots the tree before the contract could be performed.

The point of *rescission* (cancellation) is to restore the parties to the position they were in prior to entering into the contract. Therefore, a party requesting rescission must return everything of value he received under the contract if it is possible to do so. There is also a requirement of giving notice to the other party. If a small claims case for rescission is filed, it is deemed to be both notice and an offer to restore the benefits.

Rescission can be used as the basis of a claim for damages, as a defense, or as a counterclaim.

NOTE: *Parties who have entered contracts through misrepresentation or fraud may be entitled to punitive damages which are not available in small claims court. If rescission is based on a consumer contract, damages in the form of penalties may be available to the claimant.*

WARRANTY

A claim for a breach of warranty is one of the most useful. There are two types of warranties, *express* and *implied*, and there are three kinds of implied warranties of title, merchantability, and fitness for a particular purpose.

EXPRESS
WARRANTY

An action for breach of *express warranty* exists when a product or service does not live up to oral or written statements describing how well the product will perform. To win such a case, a person must prove four things:

1. the product had a warranty;

2. the product did not perform as represented;

3. that the person relied on the warranty to purchase the product; and,

4. that damages were suffered as a result.

IMPLIED
WARRANTY

The theory of *implied warranty* is used when a product does not live up to its basic purpose. Most new products, and some used ones, come with implied warranties, but the warranties rarely cover everything that can go wrong.

Warranty of Title. If you were sold an item that the seller did not own and that you had to return to the rightful owner (such as stolen property), you could sue the seller for breach of the implied warranty that he had *title* (right to own) to the property he sold you. To do so, you must prove that:

1. you paid for the item; and

2. you did not obtain title to it.

Warranty of Merchantability. When goods are sold by a dealer in such merchandise, unless they are sold "as is," there is an implied warranty that they are fit for the ordinary purpose for which they are made. If a washing machine does not wash, it is not *merchantable*. If bread is moldy, it is not merchantable.

To win a claim for breach of the warranty of merchantability, you must prove that the goods were not merchantable when received. If, for example, a car broke down two weeks after it was purchased, you could not collect for breach of such a warranty unless you could prove that at the time of the sale the car was in such a condition as to make it unmerchantable. If a part was ready to break, you would probably win. If it broke because you hit a bad bump in the road, you would probably lose.

Warranty of Fitness for a Particular Purpose. When a seller represents himself as being knowledgeable about a product and sells it to a person for a known particular purpose, there is an implied warranty of *fitness* for that known purpose. For example, if a body building gym sells a piece of pipe for use as a weight lifting bar and the bar bends when weights are attached, there would be a breach of a warranty even if it was a perfectly good pipe for other purposes.

To win a suit for an implied warranty, you need to prove that the seller was knowledgeable about the product and that you relied on this knowledge when you purchased the item.

LEMON LAW CASES

California's lemon law is applicable to vehicles used by small businesses as well as individual consumers. The purpose of the lemon law is to give the buyer of a defective vehicle still under the original warranty the *presumption* that they are entitled to replacement or refund. The presumption is based on the manufacturer making at least two attempts (previously four attempts) to fix the problem or in the alternative, the fact that the vehicle has been out of service for 30 days. There are of course, many hoops to go through before you find out that the manufacturer is not going to give you a replacement vehicle. These include the written notice to the manufacturer and submission of the dispute to manufacturer's arbitration program.

If you have a new car, the value of your vehicle will be well in excess of the small claims limit, and you will probably want to file your case in superior court. But this is not true of every potential lemon law case, especially where the law applies to used vehicles. If the value of your vehicle comes within the small claims limit, or you are willing to forgo the amount of your claim in excess of the limit, you can bring the case in small claims court, whether or not you go through the lemon law procedure.

However, failure to go through the arbitration procedure with a manufacturer who uses a certified arbitration program will prevent you from taking advantage of the presumption. It is very important to carefully read the statute and the rules governing the arbitration program before filing your case.

If you have a car that is out of warranty, and is defective, you can sue the car manufacturer for breach of merchantability if you have been trying to get them to fix the problem since the time the vehicle was still under warranty. First write a demand letter asking the manufacturer to stand by their warranty and give them a specific amount of time to honor it. Then file your case. You will need to be very careful in naming the car manufacturer by their legal name. Choose the court which is most convenient for you since venue is everywhere they do business.

You should also check with the National Highway Traffic Safety Administration (NHTSA) and request the federal government's file on your vehicle to see if there are enough reports about the defect to have put the manufacturer on notice of the problem. (United States Code, Title 15, Section 1402.) If you can prove that a problem with the car was concealed from you there is a possibility you can get the car contract rescinded. If so, you will want to file your case in municipal or superior court so you can get punitive damages.

If you bought your vehicle "as is" , you should analyze the entire situation. Was the "as is" sign conspicuous? Were you being rushed? Did the salesperson tell you that the "as is" sign did not matter—they would fix or replace the vehicle anyway? Is your case against the manufacturer? ("as is" only protects the seller.) Was the sign confusing? Did they already void the "as is" by performing some repairs? Was there a failure to disclose defects, thereby constituting a deceptive sales practice?

CONSUMER CONTRACTS

In response to consumer complaints, the state of California has amassed an enormous number of statutes governing consumer contracts. Appendix D contains a list of the California and Federal consumer laws most often encountered in small claims actions. There is also a list of the cancellation periods, known as *cooling off* periods. The consumer laws contain these cancellation periods because the legislature was aware that many people have difficulty saying "no" to high pressure salespeople. For example, home repair contracts made after a disaster such as an earthquake can be canceled for up to seven days after the contract is signed, but only for up to three days under normal conditions.

If a contractor failed to permit you to cancel the contract during the cooling off period, and assuming you have proof that you attempted to cancel, you will substantially increase your chances of recovering your money in small claims court. Even if you do not have written proof, be sure to include the information on your claim and let the judge or commissioner know during your presentation that you attempted to cancel the contract. There is always the chance that the contractor will admit his refusal to allow you to cancel.

All of the statutes are available in law libraries, on the Internet, and through the Department of Consumer Affairs, a state agency which oversees compliance with these statutes. If you think your small claims suit may be based on a consumer protection statute on the list, be sure to research the statute thoroughly prior to filing a lawsuit because many of them contain special procedures. You should also consider the fact that most of the violations of the consumer statutes provide for attorney's fees, thereby making it reasonable to obtain legal representation and file your case in a court where the limits are higher.

Following are several types of consumer contracts that are covered by statutes.

HOME
IMPROVEMENT
CONTRACTS

Contracts made under the Home Improvement Act and The Swimming Pool Act are overseen by the Contractors State License Board, an arm of the Department of Consumer Affairs. The Board licenses contractors to provide services to improve real property, including remodeling, room additions, repairs of mobile homes, electrical work, and many other improvements only after the contractor meets certain requirements such as posting a bond for $7,500 ($10,000 for swimming pool contractors).

The bond is provided by companies called *bonding* companies. (The name of a contractor's bonding company can be obtained by calling the Board at 800-321-2752.) You may have a better chance of collecting damages from a bonding company than a fly-by-night contractor so be sure to name and serve the bonding company in your lawsuit. The one catch is that the bonding company can only be sued for up to $4,000.

To be successful in a suit against a home contractor, the work must be defective. You cannot sue the contractor merely because the contractor was not licensed.

If you win your lawsuit against the contractor, be sure to notify the Board because it will not renew a contractor's license if there is an unpaid judgment on the contractor's record. Also, if you are being sued by a contractor, be sure to find out if the contractor was licensed at the time the work was done because under most situations, the contractor cannot sue on home improvement contracts unless the requirements of licensing were substantially met. If the contractor had been previously licensed but unknowingly failed to renew, the court may consider that the contractor *substantially* complied.

UNLAWFUL
COLLECTION OF
PERSONAL
INFORMATION

When a consumer pays with a credit card or check, the law restricts the amount and type of information a merchant can collect. (California Civil Code (Cal.Civ.Code), Sec.1747.8.) Merchants cannot request or require that the consumer write any personal information, including address and telephone number, on any form associated with the credit card transaction when the credit card is used to pay for goods or services.

The merchant cannot ask the consumer to provide personal information that the merchant records and they cannot use credit card forms with pre-printed spaces for personal information. The merchants can require that you produce a picture i.d. but they cannot record any information from the i.d.

There are, of course, several exceptions to these restrictions. For example, if you use a credit card to obtain a cash advance the law does not apply. The law also does not apply when you put down a deposit using a credit card, when the information is needed for shipping purposes, or if some federal law or regulation requires obtaining the information. One other exception are credit cards issued by gasoline stations where a merchant is required by contract to collect the personal information.

You can, of course refuse to show merchants your identification. If they refuse to make the transaction, you can tell the merchant that you plan to complain to the credit card issuer since this practice is not permitted by most credit card issuers. The credit card issuer can revoke the merchant's right to accept credit cards. Most merchants will relent rather than attempt to justify their actions to the credit card issuer.

Merchants who accept a check for retail goods or services cannot require a consumer to provide a credit card or record the credit card number in connection with any part of the transaction. They cannot require the consumer to sign a statement agreeing to allow the consumer's credit card to be charged to cover the amount of the check in case the check bounces and they cannot contact the credit card issuer to find out if the amount of credit available to the consumer will cover the amount of the check. If the check is used for a deposit, a cash advance or to pay a credit card bill, the merchant can require that you produce the credit card number.

If the merchant violates these rules, they can be sued in small claims court for the unlawful collection of personal information. Because it is very difficult to place a value on personal information, you may want to consider suing for the highest amount possible. (If this is your first or second small claims action in one year, the amount is $5,000; otherwise you are limited to suing for $2500.) The amount you recover may depend on whether the judge feels that the request was a mere slip-up of a new employee or a deliberate policy set by the store. (If the merchant has a practice of violating the credit card laws, there may even be a basis for a "class action".) Some judges feel that privacy rights are very important while others feel that the gathering of this information is not a substantial intrusion in the modern world.

TELEMARKETING CALLS

Who has not run out of the shower to get the phone, only to find out that it was an unsolicited phone call? You can use the small claims court to stop them.

Under the Telephone Consumer Protection Act, telemarketers are required to put you on a list of phone numbers not to call upon request. So next time they call, ask to be put on the do-not-call list. Better yet, ask them for a copy of their "written policy" which they are required to supply upon request. The telemarketer is permitted one mistake during the next year. After that, you can sue for $500 for each unwanted call, treble damages for wilful or knowing violations. The law also applies to unsolicited faxes, and automated calls, and calls received before 8 A.M. or after 9 P.M. It does not apply to non-profit agencies, political organizations , polling companies or to businesses with which you have an established relationship. You may want to consider purchasing one of the gadgets that are available to deliver recorded "do not call" message when a telemarketer calls.

Although the federal statute does not apply to unsolicited messages sent by e-mail, California's statute does, but in a limited way. In order to sue under the state's anti-spam legislation make sure the defendant meets the requirements of doing business in California and using equipment located in the state to send unsolicited advertising. (California Business and Professions Code, Sec. 17538.4 and 17538.45.) The law, passed in 1998 and held up on appeal in January of 2002, requires advertisers to enable recipients to remove their names from future e-mail transmissions, by means of either a toll-free telephone number or a return e-mail address. It also requires senders to identify advertisements by including "ADV:" at the beginning of the subject line of each message. If the ad pertains to adult material, the subject line must say "ADV:ADLT".

Unfortunately, some of these unwanted interruptions come from out of state or entities that do not have an agent for service of process in the state. In fact, many unsolicited communications come from out of the country. California' s small claims statutes requires that a defendant either reside in the state, or have an agent for service of process in the state (except for certain auto and real estate cases) so be careful to ascertain where the solicitations are coming from.

CASES AGAINST CREDIT REPAIR AGENCIES

The stated purpose of Credit Services Organizations (CSOs) is not to provide credit, but to obtain loans and extensions of credit for consumers who have credit problems. They also offer to help consumers repair or correct their credit history. While there are legitimate credit repair organizations, some of them operate unscrupulously, selling services that consumers can obtain themselves for no charge, or selling incorrect and inaccurate advice.

The law now requires these organizations to register with the state, obtain a bond, provide notices to the consumer telling them what they can and cannot do, and how and when they can charge for their services. A full listing of the requirements can be found in the California Civil Code, Section 1789.

A suit can be brought in small claims court for any damages caused as a result of a violation of the statute. Before filing in small claims court, you should be aware that it is possible to obtain both punitive damages and attorney fees under the statute, perhaps justifying a case in municipal or superior court, rather than small claims.

PROMOTIONAL GIVEAWAYS

Have you ever wondered whether people actually get a free television or diamond bracelet just for attending a sales presentation? The answer is that failure to disclose the odds of receiving the incentive, as well as other specific information about the promotion is not only a misdemeanor under the California Business & Professions Code, Section 17534, but private parties can sue for *treble* (triple) damages and attorney's fees if the promised gift is not received.

PRODUCTS LIABILITY CASES

A *products liability case* exists when a person is injured or suffers financial loss as the result of a defective product. This kind of case may be brought against the manufacturer, assembler, component supplier, advertising agency, distributor, retail establishment, repairer, and anyone else in the chain of commerce. There are several theories under which you can bring your lawsuit. The easiest one to prove is *strict liability*, which makes the defendant liable even if there is no *negligence* or wrongdoing. To win a case under strict liability, it is only necessary to show that a particular product, when used as intended, caused the injury. A products liability case may also be brought under the theory of warranty discussed on pages 45 to 47.

You can also bring a products liability case based on negligence. You do this by showing that the defendant owed a duty to guard against injuries resulting from foreseeable misuse to the consumer who was injured, that the manufacturer breached this duty, and that injury was caused as a result of this breach of duty. One example of a negligence situation is where the plaintiff misuses a chair by standing on it. If the chair breaks, injuring the plaintiff, a product liability case based on a reasonable misuse may result.

If you do not know whether the defect in your product is a manufacturing defect or whether it occurred later, it may be reasonable to name and serve all of the parties in the "stream of commerce" and let them fight it out among themselves. You can sue the company that produced the food, the one that shipped it, and the place that prepared it.

In some cases, each defendant will make a better case against another defendant than you could because of a greater familiarity with the product. In cases where it is obvious where the defect arose, you are likely to raise the ire of the judge or commissioner if you parade ten defendants into court. But do not let the inexpensive price of an item scare you off if the damages it caused are substantial. (A faulty washing machine hose can result in an expensive flood.)

Before bringing suit, you should find out if any of the California consumer statutes cover the product and whether there are any special requirements you need to follow. At the very least, you should give notice to all the defendants before you sue them, giving them a sufficient opportunity to resolve the problem without going to court.

AUTO ACCIDENTS AND OTHER NEGLIGENCE CASES

You can bring an action to recover money for damages sustained in an automobile collision as a result of negligence of either individuals, government entities, companies, and the owner of the vehicle (including rental car agencies). It is especially important to remember to sue both the owner and the driver.

In California, a suit for personal injury must be filed within a year of the date of the accident with very few exceptions to extend the filing period. (Children have until their nineteenth birthday to file a lawsuit for personal injuries, even if the injury occurred when the child was only five years old.) If the negligent person or entity is the government, you only have six months to file a claim against the government.

When you compute your damages, be sure to include your actual medical expenses, even if they were paid by your medical insurance company. If you belong to an HMO, finding out the value of your medical treatment is a little more complicated, but there are books that list approved billing rates for all medical procedures. Check with the bookstore or library of a medical or nursing school near your home.

You can also sue for out-of-pocket expenses and lost wages including:

- the value of any sick or vacation days used up;

- time taken off for doctor's appointments;

- the cost of repairing or replacing your vehicle or other damaged items;

- the cost of a rental vehicle;

- mileage for medical care; and,

- a reasonable amount for pain and suffering.

These damages can quickly add up, so make sure your case is small enough to file in small claims court. A general rule of thumb is that to be cost-effective enough to hire an attorney, the case needs to be worth more than $7,000; otherwise, you would gain nothing since the the lawyer's fees would be approximately $1500-$2,000.

The value of your case is rarely the figure first offered to you by the claims adjustor. It is the claims adjustor's job to pay you as little as they can. Generous claims adjustors do not keep their jobs very long.

Most attorneys will give you a free consultation on a personal injury case since they do not charge fees until the case is concluded. Gather a few opinions on the value of your case. If any attorney tells you that he can get you a lot more money than you can get for yourself, try offering one third of your settlement for every dollar above the $5,000 you can get for yourself in small claims court. If the attorney is still interested, your case is probably worth more than $7,000.

CLASS ACTIONS

A *class action* is a court procedure where a matter involving a number of individuals may be litigated by a few without the need or expense of joining every member into the suit. Class actions keep the courts from being overwhelmed by individual lawsuits. The class action puts together several small claims that otherwise might not warrant individual litigation. The class action procedure encourages the filing of one case on behalf of all people harmed or potentially harmed by the defendants.

One of the main benefits of class action lawsuits is the ability to spread the costs of litigation among many people. For example, it may be prohibitively expensive for one individual to hire an attorney to give advice or an expert to testify. When many individuals are involved the cost becomes more manageable.

There is no official class action designation in small claims court but it is a good forum for neighbors or tenant groups to bring individual nuisance actions against the same defendant. Several cases against the same defendant on the same theory are informally considered *class actions* in small claims court. In some circumstances, it makes sense to let the court personnel clerk know how many individuals will be filing small claims actions so that the cases can be coordinated and scheduled for the same day.

If all of the cases are heard on the same day, the cooperation of the police department, local elected representatives and other city agencies and non-profit organizations may be easier to obtain. On the other hand, another strategy the group may use might be to schedule their individual cases to take place over a substantial period of time, forcing the defendant to appear in court numerous times.

The small claims court has been the chosen forum for a suit involving 170 neighbors claiming that they suffered damages caused by airport noise. Other claims brought on the nuisance theory include suits against property owners for failing to stop illegal drug activity on rental property and against a property owner for incessantly barking dogs.

HOMEOWNER ASSOCIATION CASES

Small Claims Court is often the fastest and most cost-effective method for homeowner and condominium Associations to collect delinquent assessments, fines, and penalties. It is only when the dollar amount has accumulated above the jurisdictional limit that there is a need for the association to file a superior court action.

In addition to the financial disputes the associations have with the individual property owners, the associations have made use of the equitable powers of the small claims court to enforce architectural requirements, pet issues and disallowed use of private residences.

LANDLORD PROBLEMS

Whether it is called last month's rent, pet deposit, security deposit, new tenant fee, or cleaning fee, if it is for the purpose of protecting the landlord from damage or default, it is fully refundable if the tenant fulfills his or her obligations under the rental agreement.

DEPOSITS
As a tenant, you can sue in small claims court if the landlord refuses to return the deposit (or permit access to meet the conditions for return of the money), or if the amount collected is in excess of two month's rent on an unfurnished rental and three months rent on a furnished rental. You can also sue if the landlord uses more than a reasonable amount of the deposit for any purpose other than unpaid rent, cleaning, and replacement or repair of the apartment caused by the tenant or his guests. The landlord may not use the deposit for normal "wear and tear," and this issue is where there are the greatest number of disputes. Good evidence of normal "wear and tear" includes rental agreements that contain a description of the premises, photos taken just before you move in to compare with photos taken just before you move out, and a letter written to the landlord describing the premises as soon as you become aware of them after moving in.

The landlord is required to either return the deposit within three weeks after you move out or to send you an accounting of how the deposit was spent. After first writing a letter to the landlord requesting the return of your deposit (see Appendix H for an example), return receipt requested of course, you can sue for the return of the deposit and up to $600 in penalties if the refusal to return the deposit was unreasonable. In those counties where the landlord must pay interest on the deposit, you can sue for the accumulated interest as well.

RETURN OF PROPERTY

If you left something on the premises by mistake, or under some other reasonable circumstances, (your piano mover did not show up on moving day) the landlord is required to return it as long as you follow specific steps set forth in the law including writing a letter requesting the return of the property within 18 days of moving out. If the landlord refuses to return the property within a reasonable time after you have followed those steps, the landlord will be liable for damages for the value of your property and up to $250 in penalties.

The steps you must take include writing a letter, paying the landlord's reasonable costs of removal and storage, and removing the item from the landlord's premises within three days. After the landlord receives your letter, he or she must write a return letter within five days individually listing all the items and the cost of removal and storage for each.

UNINHABITABLE RENTAL UNIT

A tenant can sue a landlord in small claims court if a landlord does not make needed repairs to a rental unit in a timely fashion. In order to win such a lawsuit, the tenant must prove that the unit is *uninhabitable*, that a housing inspector notified the landlord in writing to repair the condition, and that the condition lasted at least sixty days after receiving written notice from the housing inspector. An uninhabitable rental unit is one that is considered unfit for humans to live in. These include but are not limited to functioning plumbing, doors that lock, buildings free from infestation, and well-lighted staircases.

If the landlord is liable, a tenant can collect up to $1000 for damages you can itemize incurred as a result of the condition. For example, if you had a leaky roof during a rainstorm, you can collect the expense of staying in a hotel as special damages.

In order to determine if the unit is legally unliveable or uninhabitable, the landlord must comply with housing and building codes in addition to maintaining the integrity of the structure, plumbing, utilities, ventilation, cleanliness etc. On the other hand, the tenant has the responsibility to keep from damaging the unit, common areas, equipment, or fixtures. Basically, if the tenant caused the conditions that made the unit uninhabitable, the tenant will not be successful in a suit against the landlord.

TENANT PROBLEMS

Eviction actions are not handled in small claims court, but a landlord may have reason to sue a tenant in small claims court after a tenancy has ended. This section discusses such claims briefly.

DAMAGE TO
RENTAL
UNITS

If a tenant has done damage to the unit greater than the amount of damage or security deposit, the landlord may want to take the tenant to court. Of course, he must take into consideration all the factors discussed in Chapter 1, such as whether it is worth the time and whether a judgment against the tenant would be collectable.

To win such a case you must have good evidence that the damage was done to the unit during the tenant's occupation. This would require testimony or photos of the unit before and after the tenant rented the unit. Normal "wear and tear" would not usually be chargeable against a tenant. If a unit had not been painted in five years, the cost of painting could not be charged to a tenant who only rented it for the fifth year unless unusual damage was done to the walls.

UNPAID RENT

If a tenant leaves a unit owing back rent, a landlord can sue the tenant in small claims court. This would usually be a simple case to prove unless there was some sort of complicated agreement between the parties for payment of rent in other than cash. For example, if the tenant was to do some work to the unit in lieu of rent, then the exact terms of the agreement as well as photos and an expert opinion of the quality of the work would be helpful to the judge.

CIVIL RIGHTS COMPLAINTS

The Unruh Civil Rights Act prohibits discrimination against a person by a business establishment based disability. (California Civil Code, beginning with Sec. 51.) It also prohibits denial or interference with a disabled person's access to specified public accommodations. At the same time, it does not require any construction, alteration, repair or modification of new or existing structure. It also declares that a violation of the rights of any individual under the Americans with Disabilities Act (ADA) of 1990 shall also constitute a violation of The Unruh Civil Rights Act.

In 1998, a bill was passed by the California legislature and signed into law providing that claims brought under the Unruh Civil Rights Act may be brought in small claims court if the amount of the damages sought in the action does not exceed the current jurisdictional limit of small claims court of $5,000. The bill further clarifies that nothing in the Unruh Civil Rights Act may be construed to relieve building owners of their obligations under existing law to make their buildings accessible to people with disabilities.

This is a great advantage for individuals who had previously been forced into municipal court for ADA discrimination complaints, even if they were only claiming minimal damages. Before the passage of this legislation, many small claims courts did not routinely accept discrimination cases because of confusion over whether the small claims court had jurisdiction. The new section of California Civil Code Section, 52.2 under The Unruh Civil Rights Act specifies that the Small Claims Courts has jurisdiction to hear these cases.

ATTORNEY-CLIENT PROBLEMS

If you lost money or property because of negligence or other wrongdoing on the part of your attorney, you can sue the lawyer in small claims court to recover the money or the value of the property. If you have a dispute with an attorney concerning fees, you can request a trial de novo in small claims court after first going through a non-binding arbitration. See the ATTORNEY-CLIENT FEE DISPUTE (ATTACHMENT TO PLAINTIFF'S CLAIM) for this purpose, and to vacate, correct, or confirm either a binding or non-binding arbitration award. (see form 35, p.255.) Confirmation is required before collection procedures are initiated. You will have thirty days to file after the date the arbitration award was mailed.

DEFENDING YOURSELF 6

Typically, you will first become aware that you are being sued when you are served with (receive a copy of) the PLAINTIFF'S CLAIM AND ORDER TO DEFENDANT. (see form 2, p.183.) Be sure that you read all of the documents you receive carefully. They will tell you why you are being sued, when your response must be filed, and where the hearing is taking place.

IGNORING THE SUMMONS

Some people consider themselves *judgment proof* and make the big mistake of ignoring a small claims case. If the party does not show up on the day of trial, the judge does not have to decide between two estimates of damages and the judgment could end up being much more than the case was worth. Defendants who plan to file for bankruptcy, and as a result, ignore a small claims case, may be very surprised to find out that not every judgment will be wiped out. Even though judgments are only good for ten years, they can easily be renewed for another ten years. What a surprise it will be for the "no-show" defendant to find a lien on their house when it is finally sold fifteen years in the future.

Many defendants merely show up in court and give their side of the story without any preparation. This is certainly better than not showing up at all. The problem with this type of defense is that it increases the likelihood of having insufficient proof to substantiate the defendant's position. These defendants appear unorganized, confused about the law and rules that apply to their case, and mixed up about the chronology of events that make up their defense.

Anyone who plans to offer this kind of defense will benefit from spending a few hours sitting in small claims court and watching some cases. It will be easy to pick out the parties who are prepared and those who are not. Any defendant who has opened this book to this chapter first, hoping to avoid reading the information that relates to plaintiffs should go back to the beginning and read the entire book. All the information is helpful to defendants too.

If you have a counterclaim against the plaintiff, you become a plaintiff on your case as well as a defendant. You will need to fill out the DEFENDANT'S CLAIM AND ORDER TO THE PLAINTIFF in Appendix I. (see form 11, p.205.) Keep in mind the fact that you have both roles. You will have to prepare the counterclaim in the same way a plaintiff prepares the claim. You will need to know the rules of evidence, and the ins and outs of preparing and presenting your case.

THE NEXT STEP

Before you spend a lot of time and money on the defense of the lawsuit, you need to know whether the case is worth defending. If you know the claim is true, you should contact the other party and try to settle the matter. You should not waste the court's time and incur additional expenses if you know you owe, at least some of the money you are being sued for. If you do not have the cash on hand, you could offer to sign a promissory note to make regular payments or you could sign a stipulation in the court case to make payments.

Whether or not to defend a case is a personal decision. For example, if you are unemployed, and have lots of free time on your hands, you may be more inclined to delve into the lawsuit than someone who is employed. Some people feel that the amount of money that is at stake is the main issue. They will need to make a calculation of the amount of damages in dispute and decide if the money is worth their time. Or if they have no money to pay and they know they owe it, they may be able to work out a payment plan with the plaintiff. One way of handling the situation is to write a letter to the plaintiff and make an offer to settle the case. You may get a counter-offer, or your offer may even be accepted.

Another possibility is to contact a mediation service (listed in Appendix B) and tell them you want to mediate your dispute. They will contact the plaintiff for you. Some people feel that in certain situations, it is not the money, but the principle that they want to defend. This type of case lends itself to the type of mediation where the interests and positions of the party are explored in reaching resolution as opposed to merely settling the case.

There are several defenses based on improper procedures followed by the plaintiff. You will need to determine which ones apply and whether they were followed in your case. For example, were you named and served correctly? Is the plaintiff named correctly? Was the case filed in a court that has venue? Has the plaintiff fulfilled all the prerequisites to filing a small claims suit? Is the contractor licensed? Did the plaintiff write the required demand letter? Any one of the above can be fatal to the plaintiff's case (or counterclaim). These defenses are discussed later in this chapter.

Decide if you have defenses based on principles of law. For example, if the plaintiff fell in the parking lot in front of your store, are you responsible for the plaintiff's injuries? Who owns the parking lot? Are you responsible for the upkeep? You may have to do some investigation into the facts of the situation.

ATTORNEYS Should you contact an attorney? There are several reasons you may want to seek legal advice. Perhaps the principles of law are complicated. If there is more than one plaintiff asking for the $5,000 limit, you may have a situation where legal advice is essential. You may have a potential case against the plaintiff where you are unsure whether it should be heard in small claims court. Maybe you just need reassurance that you can handle the defense yourself, or that you are on the right track.

INSURANCE

One other important factor that is often overlooked is the possibility that your homeowner's, auto, or business insurance policy covers you on the plaintiff's claim. Send a copy of the plaintiff's claim to your agent and your insurance company (certified mail) and ask them to provide a defense and pay the claim if necessary. Sometimes, if the insurance company is unsure about whether the policy covers you, they will pay anyway to avoid future litigation over the issue. In many situations, they will do the investigation of the facts and save you a lot of time even if it ends up that you are on your own.

TRANSFERRING THE CASE

If the value of the claim is more than $5,000, you will need to file a motion if you want to transfer the case to a court that has jurisdiction to award more than $5,000. A form for the motion is in Appendix I. (see form 12, p.207.)

YOUR DEFENSES

Before you decide to settle the case you should review your defenses in the matter and see if the claim is legally enforceable. There are many possible defenses to a claim that you (and the plaintiff) may not know about. Not all of them are listed below.

Read the following possible defenses and see if any of them apply to your case. If you think any may apply, be sure to mention them to the judge if your case does go to court. Some of the defenses may just delay the case, and if you are in a hurry to get it over with, you might not want to use them even if they do apply. Many of them are defenses that could win the case for you.

IMPROPER SERVICE OF PROCESS

If the claim is not served on you or your company properly then the court does not have jurisdiction and the judgment is void. However, if you appear in court and do not object to the service then you waive the right to contest it, making the judgment valid.

You can appear only for the purpose of contesting the service. If you ignore it, you may have more aggravation later in having a judgment set aside or in trying to stop seizure of your property. If you appear to contest the service, you may be able to have the service set aside so that the plaintiff has to start over. But then, you may just aggravate the judge who will eventually hear your case.

VENUE

Are you being sued in the right court? See page 31, "Where to File Your Suit," to find out if you are being sued in the right court. If not, you might be able to have the case moved (or you might prefer not to). This may just delay the case, but perhaps the plaintiff will drop the case if he has to travel to another county. You can write a letter to the court explaining why venue is improper and hope that the judge agrees with you. Another possibility is to show up and bring it up at that time. If you choose to write a letter, make sure you receive notice from the court indicating whether the case has been continued or dismissed.

CORPORATE REGISTRATION

If the plaintiff is a corporation, it must be current in its registration to maintain a suit. You can call the Secretary of State in Sacramento at 916-653-7315 to check on a corporation's status or look on the Internet. If it is not current, you can order a certificate of proof of non-active status (current fee $10) from the following address:

Secretary of State
1500 11th Street
Sacramento, CA 95814

This may only delay the case, but if the corporation is a few years behind in filing, it may be too much trouble and expense to file and then start up the suit again. The fees are hundreds of dollars to reinstate a corporation.

FICTITIOUS NAMES

If the plaintiff is using a fictitious name that is not registered, then he or she may not bring a suit. If you defend the suit on this basis, you will usually delay the case a couple of months while the plaintiff is complying with the registration requirements. The plaintiff may then feel it is too much trouble and not go through with the case.

Under Sections 17900-17930 of the California Business & Professional Code, every business doing business under a name which is not its legal name must file a FICTITIOUS BUSINESS NAME DECLARATION in the counties where the business operates. (see form 4, p.191.) The registration expires after five years or forty days after a change in ownership. Check with the clerk to see if the plaintiff has properly registered. If not, bring it up to the judge.

LACK OF
CONSIDERATION

Promises to make gifts are not enforceable. Therefore, if you signed a promise to pay someone and never received anything in return, the promise would be unenforceable. This can be used in many kinds of cases.

Example 1: If you promised to give your neighbors your old car when you got a new one, they could not win a suit for the car if you changed your mind, since they didn't do anything for the car. However, if you told them you would give them your old car if they mowed your lawn every week, and they did mow your lawn, then they could sue you and win.

Example 2: If you agreed to pay $1000 for a diamond ring and signed a promissory note to the seller, then discovered the stone to be glass, you could probably avoid paying the note because you got nothing for it. (You could probably also use the fraud or the mutual mistake defenses.) However, if you borrowed the money from a third party such as a bank, you could probably not avoid repaying the bank for the loan because the bank is not responsible for the condition of the item you bought.

Also, if you bought something and signed a promissory note and then the dealer sold the note to a bank or other lender, you could probably not avoid paying the note. The bank would be considered an innocent buyer of the note and the law encourages the easy sale of notes. Many businesses that sell questionable products quickly sell the loan papers so that the buyers cannot stop payment.

STATUTE OF FRAUDS
Certain agreements are not enforceable if they are not in writing (California Civil Code, Sec. 1621). Even if the facts are true and money is owed, the *Statute of Frauds* provides that these agreements just will not be enforced by the court if they are not written. The writing need not be a formal contract. Cancelled checks and short memoranda signed by the promisor have, in some cases, been held to be sufficient. The following are circumstances when the agreement must be in writing:

- sales of any interest in real estate;

- most leases of real estate for more than one year;

- promises to pay the debts of another person;

- agreements that take longer than one year from the making of the agreement to perform;

- agreements that cannot be performed within the lifetime of the promisor; and,

- authorization for an agent to buy or sell real estate.

SPANISH LANGUAGE
There are some circumstances where businesses are required to provide a Spanish version of the contract at the time the contract is signed. These include leases for residential units for a period of more than a month, unsecured loans, and certain legal contracts. Furthermore, if a defendant can show that the material terms of the Spanish contract were different than the English language one that was signed, the judge may very well rescind the contract.

MINORS
An agreement entered into by a minor, unless *emancipated*, is generally not enforceable in court. In California, the exceptions to this are if the minor continues to fulfill the agreement after reaching age of majority (over 18) or if the agreement was for things necessary for the minor's support, such as certain food and clothing items. Thus, if a minor signed an agreement to buy a car, it would probably not be enforceable, but if he signed a check to pay for milk, bread or cereal it probably would be. (California Civil Code, Sec. 1556 and 1557.)

PAYMENT

Obviously, if you have already paid the money claimed to be owed, this would be a defense to the claim. Perhaps the money was credited to a wrong account or not credited at all. To prevail with this defense you should have some evidence that you have made payment, such as a cancelled check or a receipt.

ACCORD AND SATISFACTION

If a debt is in dispute and the parties agree to a settlement, such as acceptance of fifty percent of the debt, this should finally settle the matter. If one party later claims the whole amount in a suit, the settlement agreement would be a defense. This agreement of *accord and satisfaction* should of course be in writing, but even if it is not, it may be enforceable.

STATUTE OF LIMITATIONS

The laws of every state give time limits on how long claims can be brought. After a certain time, claims will not be allowed by the court, no matter how valid they are. Thus, if a person waits too long to file a suit, his or her claim may not be enforceable. The time limits for the different types of claims are set out in Appendix E.

FRAUD OR MISREPRESENTATION

If you were defrauded in a transaction, or if important facts were misrepresented to you, you may have a valid defense.

Example: If you bought a car and later found out the odometer was set back, you can use that as a defense if you are sued for the price of the car. Usually though, such claims should be used for a counterclaim. (See Chapter 6.)

MISTAKE OR ERROR

If both parties were mistaken about an agreement they entered into, it can usually be voided. For example, if both parties believed a gem to be a diamond, but it turned out to be a fake, then a sale of it could be rescinded. If only the seller knew it was a fake, this defense would not work, but the fraud defense might.

BREACH OF CONTRACT

If the plaintiff did not fulfill his side of an agreement, he may not be able to sue you to collect on it. Thus, if improper goods or services were provided, the seller should not be able to collect. For example if you hired someone to paint your house and they did a sloppy job, or if you contracted for a catering service for a wedding and they showed up four hours late, they would have breached the contract. In the painting example, you can also argue that they breached an implied warranty to do the job in a workmanlike manner (see the next subsection). Explain to the judge that the plaintiff failed to fulfill his side of the agreement.

IMPLIED
WARRANTIES

Even if a provider of goods and services does not provide a written warranty, the law implies three types of warranties in most business transactions. These are:

1. that the seller of goods actually owns them and can legally sell them;

2. that the the goods or services are *merchantable* (they perform the function they are supposed to); and,

3. if the seller is knowledgeable about them and sells them for a particular purpose, that they will fulfill that purpose.

For more details on warranties see page 45.

USURY

Usury is defined as charging excessive interest. Usury laws are complicated, consisting of a combination of federal and California law. In general, the law permits parties to contract for interest on the unpaid balance on a *personal loan* at a rate less than ten percent per year. Furthermore, there are many exceptions to the general rules. For example, a loan to be used primarily for home improvement or home purchase is not regarded as a personal loan and therefore, the allowable rate is five percent over the amount charged by the Federal Reserve Bank of San Francisco. The penalties for violating usury laws are severe, and people who believe that they have been charged excessive interest rates should research the laws or check with an attorney.

ARBITRATION

To avoid litigation, many parties are putting *arbitration* clauses in their contracts. These clauses provide that the parties agree that in the event of a dispute under the contract they agree not to file suit but to go to an arbitrator. There are several different versions of these clauses. Some of them require *non-binding* arbitration before suit is filed. Therefore, neither party is required to accept the arbitrator's decision. The decision is often used as a basis for later negotiation. Others say that the arbitrators decision will be final. If the contract being sued on has such a clause, the judge may be required to dismiss the case if the clause has not been followed. Of course if a party is suing about a matter which is not covered under the contract, or the arbitration clause, then the clause would not apply.

DURESS

If an agreement is made under *duress*, then it may not be enforceable. For example, if someone confronts you with a gun and says "sign a $1,000 check to me or I will shoot you," you could stop payment on the check since your agreement would have been given under duress.

Duress has to be serious, however. If a mechanic says he will not return your car unless you pay for it and you pay because you need the car even though you feel the work was done wrong, this might not be considered to be duress, because you have other options. For example, you could have sued to get your car back. But small claims court judges are flexible and it might work if you can convince the judge of the necessity of having the vehicle.

ILLEGALITY

Agreements that are illegal cannot be enforced in court. If you write a check to pay for illegal drugs, prostitution, or illegal gambling, the court will not help the person you paid collect the check.

LICENSE

In certain situations people can give up their right to sue by granting a written or an implied license to the other person. For example, if two people agree to a boxing match, one of them cannot later sue the other for battery if he is hurt. By agreeing to participate in a fight he implicitly gave the other person a license to hit him. If the fight were under the auspices of a club or organization, the parties were probably required to sign an agreement that contained a license as well as a waiver of the right to sue.

WAIVER

A *waiver* is a contract where people give up an important right, in this case, the right to sue. Restaurants, bars, social clubs, and other groups that hold any types of contests usually require all participants to sign *waivers* of their right to sue. The participants are usually too excited about entering the contest to read what they are signing, but if they try to go to court they learn that they have waived their right to sue.

School districts, sports organizations, and even police departments who use minors as informants may require that a waiver be signed. Interpretation of a waiver can involve several complicated legal issues which may require research of the case law on the validity of the waiver.

RELEASE   Similar to a waiver is a *release*. For example, suppose a landlord and a tenant get into a lawsuit, each making claims against the other. They did not want to take a chance in court, so they agree to settle. They both sign releases of the other and dismiss the case. If six months later the tenant finds a cash receipt proving that he paid more rent than he realized, he probably would not be able to sue because he already signed a release. Releases may also require analysis to ascertain whether the "injury" was contemplated by the parties when the release was signed.

SALES OF   Sales of goods are governed by a set of laws called the Uniform
GOODS   Commercial Code. If you are being sued over a transaction involving a sale of goods, there might be some rule which covers your case. For example, if you sold defective goods and the buyer did not give you proper notice that they were defective, then he may not be able to win a suit against you.

BANKRUPTCY   If a person files *liquidation bankruptcy*, most of the debts listed can be wiped out and completely discharged forever. If a person files a bankruptcy petition while a case is pending, all actions against the person and his property must stop. If you are the plaintiff, and a defendant tells you that he has filed bankruptcy, you should call the local federal bankruptcy court to confirm that it has been filed. If you take any action after you have been informed of a bankruptcy, then you may be held in contempt of federal court. If you are told that an attorney is handling the bankruptcy, all future contact must be through the attorney.

In a *reorganization bankruptcy*, the debts will not be wiped out, but the court will approve a schedule for payment for them. Still, a creditor may not take any actions against the debtor while he or she is in bankruptcy.

SETTLING THE CASE

Whether or not you have any defenses to the case, it is usually better to negotiate a settlement than to take a chance with a judge's decision. No matter how sure you are of your case, you can easily lose if your witness does not show up, the other side is more believable, or if any number of things go wrong.

It is often better to take only a partial victory than to risk complete defeat. If the plaintiff understands that he may never be able to collect his judgment, he might accept 50¢ or even 25¢ on the dollar for a cash settlement.

Even if you know you owe the full amount, you should try to avoid a judgment being issued against you. This will be damaging to your credit rating. The best arrangement for both sides is to enter into a Stipulation to Stay Entry of Judgment. This is an agreement by which the parties agree that if the defendant makes payments according to a certain schedule, no judgment will be entered. If you can come to such an agreement, check with the judge or court clerk to see if your agreement can be entered in the court file and approved by the court. It is important for the defendant to keep payment by the schedule or else the judgment will be quickly filed. If the payments are made, no judgment will ever be filed.

Some counties have dispute settlement programs where parties can talk to a mediator and avoid the trouble of court. But such mediation is not binding, and a person who does not get his way may go to court anyway.

COUNTERCLAIMS

The best defense is a good offense, so the best way to defend yourself is to find a reason to counterclaim against the plaintiff. If the only claim pending is the plaintiff's claim against you, the plaintiff will be eager to try the case because the worst that can happen is that he won't win. However, if you file a suit against the plaintiff, there is a risk of losing that was not present before. There is also a better chance of having the case against you dropped or of settling the case when neither party wants to risk losing.

In most states, if you have claims based upon the transaction the plaintiff is suing over, then you must bring up these claims in a countersuit of the same case. This is called a *compulsory counterclaim*. However, in California, the Code of Civil Procedure, Section 426.60 provides that this rule does not apply so that related claims can be the subject of a new lawsuit. Unrelated claims against the plaintiff may be raised in a counterclaim.

However, because it is cheaper and less time-consuming to handle your claims in the same suit the plaintiff has brought, you should probably do so. Only if you were not aware of a claim until after the suit was over, or if your claim is higher than the $5,000 limit of small claims court, would you want to file a new case.

If the value of the claim you have against the plaintiff is more than $5,000, the defendant can either waive his or her right to the amount in excess of $5,000 or file a motion to transfer the case to either municipal court (if less than $25,000) or superior court (if more than $25,000).

After you are served with the PLAINTIFF'S CLAIM AND ORDER TO DEFENDANT, your claim must be filed on the plaintiff at least five days before the hearing, or one day before the hearing only if you were served with the plaintiff's claim less than ten days before the hearing. (see form 2, p.183.) The time periods are very important. If you are late with your service, the judge probably will not hear your counterclaim.

CROSS-CLAIMS AND THIRD PARTY CLAIMS

If you discover or know that a third party is responsible for the plaintiff's damages, and that person is not named as a defendant in the plaintiff's case, you may need to file a separate action against that person. If the claim against the third person will be in small claims court, try to get both set for the same date and put a note on the claim form that it is related to Case Number *(insert #)* which is set for *(insert date)*. You will probably need to follow the procedure for a continuance, but it doesn't hurt to save the court some time and work in locating the plaintiff's case.

REQUESTING A CONTINUANCE

If you are the defendant, or the plaintiff on a counterclaim filed by the defendant, the failure to show up in court is likely to end up as a default judgment against you and there is no guarantee that the judge will vacate the default judgment later. Furthermore, you will have lost your right to appeal the merits of the case in superior court.

On the other hand, you can request a postponement of the small claims action if the date falls during a planned vacation, an important occasion, a busy time at work, you have a preference for an evening or Saturday hearing, or any other legitimate reason. You can obtain a continuance of fifteen days or more by making a request to the small claims clerk at least ten days before the hearing and paying a $10 fee. You can accomplish this in person or in a letter, but make sure you send a copy of the letter requesting the continuance to all the other parties to the action. As a final resort, you can show up in court and ask the court to set a new date. Most courts will do so if the request is reasonable. For example, if you were not served or served improperly, it is reasonable to obtain a continuance.

Methods of Payment

If you prefer to make payment to the court and have the court pay the plaintiff, you can file a **Request to Pay Judgment to Court** with the entire amount of the judgment. (see form 23, p.231.) This service is not free and fees vary for the service. Another option is to pay the judgment in installments. This is accomplished by filing a **Request to Pay Judgment in Installments**. (see form 24, p.233.) This procedure is not automatic. A hearing must occur where the court reviews the income of the debtor to determine how much should be paid each month.

Appeal

If you decide to appeal, the **Notice of Appeal** must be filed within thirty days of the date of the small claims decision. (see form 19, p.223.) Or if the clerk mails the **Notice of Entry of Judgment**, it must be filed within thirty days of the mailing as indicated on the form. (see form 17, p.219 and Chapter 10.)

If you won on your counterclaim, write a letter to the plaintiff asking for payment before you start collection procedures. Follow the procedures for collection that are discussed in Chapter 9. After the judgment is paid, you will be required to file an **Acknowledgment of Satisfaction of Judgment** with the small claims court. (see form 34, p.253.)

Rules of Evidence 7

The purpose of evidence is to help convince the judge that your claims are true. In small claims court the rules of evidence are much more relaxed and informal than in courts where attorneys present the cases. You will not find a lot of objections being made because it is assumed that the judge knows which evidence is most reliable and admissible without help from the parties. Nevertheless, if you know of some major problem with the other side's evidence that would not be obvious to the judge, you should speak up. For example, if the other side brings photos showing damage to their vehicle that you know was already on the vehicle before your accident, you will need to tell the judge because there is no way the judge would have this knowledge.

When your case is in municipal or superior court, there are rules of discovery which allow one side to ask the other side questions about the case and get answers under penalty of perjury. Discovery also allows the party to obtain important documents from the other side that they either know the other side has, or thinks the other side may have. None of these pre-trial discovery procedures are permitted in small claims court. The only hope a party in a small claims case has to obtain documents from the other party to prove his case is to require him to bring the relevant documents to the hearing by issuing a SMALL CLAIMS SUBPOENA FOR PERSONAL APPEARANCE AND PRODUCTION OF DOCUMENTS (SMALL CLAIMS SUBPOENA). (see form 14, p.211.)

The good news is that the *hearsay* rules do not apply in small claims court either. These are rules that require witnesses to have first-hand knowledge of matters about which they are testifying. If the information is second-hand, most other courts will not allow it into evidence, unless it falls into specific exceptions. (Hearsay is a very complicated concept.) Hearsay rules do not apply to small claims appeals either so you can prepare your case without worrying about whether you will be able to use the same evidence if the defendant loses and appeals the case.

THE FOUR TYPES OF EVIDENCE

Whether you are trying a case in superior court, municipal court, or small claims court, there are four basic types of evidence: real, demonstrative, documentary, and testimonial.

REAL EVIDENCE
Real evidence is usually a thing that was involved in some event such as a crumbled fender, the written contract, the bad check or the ruined coat. This type of evidence has several advantages. It gives the judge the opportunity to actually see what happened. It is also much more reliable evidence than just telling the judge what happened. If you can bring this type of evidence with you to court, do so. Obviously, you will not want to disturb the courtroom by wheeling a huge trash bin into the court, but you could have it in a truck in the parking lot in case you can interest the judge enough to go outside and view it. Bring photos just in case the judge does not want to take the time to leave the bench.

The problem with real evidence is that you also have to convince the judge that it has not been changed since the day of the incident. For example, if you continue wearing the jacket you claimed was damaged by the dry cleaner, it will be difficult to prove that it is in the same condition. Whenever you have real evidence, try to preserve it in a separate place.

If someone else has the evidence you need to prove your case, make sure you remember to serve a subpoena to bring the item to court.

DEMONSTRATIVE EVIDENCE

Maps, diagrams, charts (such as time lines), scale models, photos, computer animations, site plans, and videos are all *demonstrative* in nature. Several studies have shown that people are more likely to remember oral testimony when they have been shown a visual at the same time. If your case could be more easily explained, bring items to court that illustrate what happened. Sometimes, the use of demonstrative evidence can be very compelling because it is in a format that is easy to understand, especially when you are trying to explain something that is difficult to put into words. For example, if you are trying to show the judge where vehicles were in relationship to each other after a collision, a drawing would help the judge understand. The problem with this type of evidence is that you sometimes need a witness who can testify that the demonstrative evidence is accurate.

DOCUMENTARY EVIDENCE

The category of *documentary evidence* is very broad. It includes medical and inventory records, contracts, invoices, statements, public records, newspapers, magazines, and computer print-outs.

Documentary evidence runs into the same problems every time. For each piece of documentary evidence that you have, you should ask yourself the following two questions:

1. *Is there a parol evidence problem?*

Parol evidence is another term for oral evidence. This rule holds that oral evidence may not be used to contradict a written agreement. An exception to this rule is that when a written agreement is ambiguous, then parol evidence may be used to explain what the parties intended.

Example: If a lease says that the rent is $500 per month, you cannot expect to win if you tell the judge that the landlord agreed to accept $50. However, if you start taking care of the lawn and the landlord accepts $450 for the next six months while you take care of the lawn, then oral evidence could be used to explain what the parties intended.

2. *Is there a best evidence problem?*

Best evidence is pretty straightforward. If there is some other evidence that is better than the document you have, you will need to explain why you don't have the better evidence. For example, if you bring a newspaper to prove what the weather was on the day of the incident, a forecast is not as good as a newspaper story describing what the weather was on that day. A newspaper story is not as good as official records of the weather. Whenever you think that the documentary evidence is going to be an issue in your case, bring the original of the document, subpoena the originals, or get certified copies from public agencies.

TESTIMONIAL
EVIDENCE

One of the best kinds of evidence you can have is a *disinterested* witness testifying in court. Parties and members of their family can be witnesses but it is much better to have a witness who is not likely to be *biased*.

It is also very important to find out what the witness will say before bringing them to court. If there is more than one witness to an event, only bring the best witness.

To make sure a witness will appear in court with or without documents, you can subpoena him or her. Even if you are sure the witness will show up, it is sometimes better to use the subpoena process. An employer is more likely to cooperate with an employee who presents a subpoena as the reason why they will be late or absent from work. A subpoena tells the witness where to go, when to be there and what to bring. A subpoena lets the court clerk know the number of the case and where the witness should report, if the case is being heard in another courtroom.

If you want to subpoena someone, you will need to obtain a SMALL CLAIMS SUBPOENA from the clerk and fill it out. (see form 14, p.211.) It consists of three pages: Page one is entitled *Small Claims Subpoena for Personal Appearance and Production of Documents and Things at Trial or Hearing and Declaration.* Page two is the *Declaration in Support of Small Claims Subpoena for Personal Appearance and Production of Document and Things at Trial or Hearing.* Page three is the *Proof of Service.*

If you want to subpoena records but you do not know the name of the person who is in charge of the records, write "custodian of records" on the subpoena where you fill in the name and address. You will also have to fill in page 2 stating which documents you need and why you need them. A copy of the subpoena must then be delivered to the witness. Unlike service of the lawsuit, you can do this yourself. Actually, anyone over 18 can serve the subpoena, including the marshal or sheriff. The original is returned to the court with a proof of service before the trial. An excellent source of help in filling out the three page subpoena can be found at:

http://www.co.kern.ca.us/courts/BMC%20Self%20Help%20Web/WP21A.htm.

The web site is complicated, but the information is worth finding.

If the witness you subpoena is one of your friends, they may not want payment, but you must pay them if they ask at the time they receive the subpoena, so have the money ready.($35.00 and twenty cents a mile). Besides, if you win, you will be able to collect the cost of subpoenaing the witnesses if the judge feels that the testimony of the subpoenaed person or records was reasonable.

Warning: If you know that a witness will be at the trial to testify for the other side, then you do not have to subpoena them. However, if the witness does not show up, you are out of luck.

TESTIMONY BY DECLARATION

Suppose your only witness cannot come to the hearing. There is a procedure you can utilize where the witness writes a statement containing what he or she knows, declaring under oath that everything in the statement is true and correct. If you plan to proceed in this manner, make sure the declaration is in the correct format because the judge will not give any credibility to a letter that is not dated or signed. There is even a possibility that the judge will not accept the written statement at all. Plus, a live witness who shows up at the hearing is more memorable.

Testimony by Telephone

It is best to check with the court clerk to see if you will be allowed to present telephone testimony by someone who cannot come to court. Some judges allow it and some do not.

Expert Witnesses

In some cases, the testimony of an expert witness is the most convincing evidence for your case. For example, when trying to prove some repair work was done incorrectly, it is best to have a skilled technician or mechanic testify that he or she examined the work and it was done wrong. Your own testimony or the testimony of your accountant brother-in-law is not as compelling.

There are many ways to find an expert. Sometimes, a competitor of the defendant will know people who are expert in the field. The literature on a certain subject may contain the names of people who are knowledgeable in that area. The *Jury Verdict Reporter* publishes a semi-annual index of all experts who have testified during the past six months. This index is available in many law libraries.

You will probably have to pay an expert a substantial sum of money to examine the work and to come to court on your behalf. You can submit a written declaration prepared by the expert, but it will not be as effective as having the expert in court.

Oral Agreements

It is not necessary that an agreement be in writing to win in court. In most cases an oral agreement is fully enforceable. The only problem is convincing the judge that there actually was such an agreement.

Usually in a case involving an oral agreement, either one person will deny that there was an agreement or the parties will disagree over the terms of the agreement. It will be up to the judge to decide which side is telling the truth. Sometimes the judge will find inconsistencies in one side's story, and other times the judge will just have to use his or her gut feeling to decide who is telling the truth.

Occasionally there will be some evidence to support an oral agreement.

Example: If you loaned a friend some money and she paid you $100 a month by check, you could bring your check register showing a $100 deposit from her every month. Or, you could subpoena her bank records to show that she wrote you a check each month. If she denies that there was ever a loan, she will have to come up with a good story about the checks to convince the judge that she is not lying.

JUDICIAL NOTICE

There are some things that are so generally known that you may not have to bring proof to court. These include the laws of the state and federal government, the fact that the world is round, and gestation takes nine months. Under *judicial notice*, you do not have to prove the fact, so evidence is not needed. For example, you do not have to bring an original or photocopy of the Constitution with you to court to prove its existence. In general, the procedure is to ask the judge to take judicial notice of a certain fact, and the judge will either agree to do so or decline. Whenever a fact can be reasonably disputed, it is unlikely that the judge will agree to judicial notice.

PROOF

The burden of proof in a civil case is called the *preponderance of evidence.* Many people, including several lawyers, mistakenly believe that preponderance refers to the amount of evidence when it really means that the party who has the more *convincing* evidence will win. Sometimes, the most convincing evidence consists of only one sheet of paper.

Preparing and Presenting Your Case 8

The best advice I ever got as an attorney was to prepare every case as though it were going to trial. (In California, only 5% of civil cases actually do.) So I am passing this advice to you. The better prepared you are to try your case, the more confident you will feel.

Preparing for Trial

The most important thing to remember when preparing your case is to make it organized, clear, and complete. There are many different ways to go about this. Making a list of all the facts you need to prove and which witnesses or documents you will need to prove them can help you break your case into manageable activities. In some cases, reviewing each element of the law that must be proven will be most beneficial. Sometimes a chronological history of events provides the most organized evidence.

After you are familiar with what you have to prove and know which documents you will need, gather the evidence and make copies for the other parties. Make an extra copy for you to refer to while the judge looks at the originals.

Be sure you know in which courtroom your trial will be held. In counties that have more than one courthouse be sure you know which courthouse to go to. (Even lawyers have been known to show up at the wrong courtroom.)

It is a good idea to get in touch with all your witnesses to remind them of the court date and to let them know whether to expect a subpoena. Do not forget to thank them for helping you out.

NOTE: *As explained in Chapter 1, if you need advice there should be a small claims advisor available by telephone or in person in all counties in California. See Appendix A.*

SUBPOENA PROCESS

Follow the procedures for subpoenaing witnesses and documents in Chapter 7. In addition to the subpoena, it is a kindness to prepare written instructions to give to your witnesses telling them how to get to the court, what time they need to be there and what to do when they get there. Offer to pay for a babysitter if for no other reason than to prevent them from bringing children to court. (It is also kind to write down the location of the rest rooms, the cafeteria, and the price and location of the parking lot.)

DISQUALIFYING A JUDGE

It does not happen often, but in some cases you may not want a particular judge, commissioner, or attorney (acting as a *pro tem* or temporary judge) on your case. For example, if you had a similar case before the judge previously and he or she severely criticized you, you may wish to use the disqualification procedures.

To do so, you must explain to the judge before you present your case that you have an honest belief that he or she is prejudiced against your case and you wish to have another judge preside over your case as allowed by California Code of Civil Procedure, Section 170.6.

On the other hand, you are not required to sign a stipulation allowing a commissioner or attorney to hear your case if you prefer a judge. Be forewarned, requesting is frowned upon and will increase the time you spend in court while waiting for a very unhappy judge to hear your case.

PRESENTING YOUR CASE

As you get closer to the hearing date, you may find it helpful to write a concise statement of the case, one or two pages at most. You can use the statement as your opening statement to explain the case to the judge. It will also help you keep your thoughts organized.

A week or two before the hearing, present your case to a family member or friend who is unfamiliar with the facts and ask them to critique your presentation and let you know if there are any holes in your argument that you need to fill. A few days before the hearing, review and re-organize your evidence and arguments in the order you plan to present them. Make sure you do not eat or drink anything that you know will cause you to feel ill the night before the hearing.

If you have not settled the case and if the defendant has not *defaulted* (failed to show up), then a trial (also called a *hearing*) will be held. The purpose of the trial is for the judge to hear both sides of the case and decide who should win and the amount of damages. Even if the defendant does not show up, you will have to present your case.

The hearing is your only chance to present your case to the small claims court. You cannot tell the judge that you are not ready (unless it is a real emergency) or that you forgot to bring some of the evidence to court.

FOOD

If you normally eat breakfast, do not skip it on the day of trial. If the courthouse does not have a cafeteria, bring snacks. Although you cannot eat inside the courthouse except in specifically designated areas, it may be a long day and a granola bar or a piece of fruit may be a lifesaving treat.

PROMPTNESS

Make sure you arrive at the courtroom on time. Sometimes the clerks give important instructions as soon as the court session begins. If you arrive late, you will miss the instructions.

PATIENCE

Before your case is heard, you will have to sit patiently in the courtroom and wait your turn. It is a bad idea to bring children with you to court. Children get restless from sitting quietly for a long time. If they cry or behave badly, you will have to leave the courtroom. Gum chewing, eating, drinking, talking, and portable radios are also prohibited. In some courtrooms, you are not allowed to read newspapers, magazines, or books while court is in session.

SPECIAL ASSISTANCE

If you think you will need assistance, call ahead. The court has earphones to turn up the volume on the proceedings. If they know you will be in a wheelchair, they can make provisions for allowing your chair to be on the counsel side of the swinging door that separates the audience.

PROCEDURE

The procedure for presenting your case may include any or all of the following:

- opening remarks by the judge;

- plaintiff's opening statement;

- defendant's opening statement;

- plaintiff's evidence;

- defendant's evidence on plaintiff's claim;

- defendant's evidence on counter-claim;

- plaintiff's evidence on claim of defendant;

- plaintiff's closing argument;

- defendant's closing argument;

- rebuttals; and

- judge's decision.

When it is your turn to present your case, come up to the *counsel table* appearing confident, competent, and truthful. State your name and wait for the judge to tell you to proceed. Speak clearly, reviewing your written statement to make sure you do not forget any major issues. If the judge asks questions and you do not know the answer, do not make up an answer (that is called *perjury*). Do not exaggerate or make claims for which you have no evidence. If the judge asks to see documents, hand them to the bailiff or the court clerk. Do not approach the bench unless the judge clearly asks you to (this is unlikely).

Do not interrupt when it is the other side's turn to speak. Be mentally prepared to be patient and courteous throughout the entire procedure no matter what is said by the other party. Take notes instead. You will have an opportunity to dispute the evidence presented by the other side when it is your turn.

JUDGMENT

After the case has been presented the judge will probably not give you the decision even if he or she has already decided the outcome. The judge is more likely to take your case *under submission* to avoid dealing with an unhappy loser. You probably will not receive the decision for a few weeks. It will come in an envelope from the court clerk on a form called Entry of Judgment. The decision will not be final until the appeal period of over thirty days from the mailing of the judgment has taken place.

> ***Warning.*** A small claims judgment will probably make its way to the credit report of the losing party.

In order to avoid the consequences of having a major blip on your credit record, you can ask the judge to issue a *conditional judgment* with a follow-up hearing to fulfill the judge's requirements. Some courts do not issue conditional judgments. Check with the small claims advisor in the county where the case is venued before the hearing.

If the judge renders a judgment against two or more parties, he or she is required to clearly state the basis for liability and the amount of damages for each.

Costs   The prevailing party is entitled not only to the costs incurred in bringing the suit, but also to costs incurred in collecting the judgment and accrued interest. These costs include the filing fee, the costs of service and sometimes the costs of subpoenaing witness or documents. You have up to five days after the hearing to ask for your costs by using a special form called MEMORANDUM OF COSTS. (see form 20, p.225.)

VACATING A DEFAULT JUDGMENT

If you are a defendant and do not show up, your case may still be heard without you if the judge determines that service was proper after examining the proof of service filed by the plaintiff. The fact that you are not present does not absolve the plaintiff of the requirement of "proving up" the case (often called a *default prove-up*). The defendant has thirty days after receiving the NOTICE OF ENTRY OF JUDGMENT (see form 17, p.219) to file a REQUEST TO CORRECT OR VACATE JUDGMENT, and complete a declaration stating the reasons why he or she did not show up. (see form 21, p.227.) The other party will be notified by receiving a NOTICE OF MOTION TO VACATE JUDGMENT AND DECLARATION. (see form 22, p.229.) A hearing will be scheduled where the judge determines whether there was *good cause*, such as unexpected illness, for the absence. If the motion is granted, some judges will go ahead and re-hear the merits of the case immediately upon granting the motion to vacate. Other judges schedule a new date in the future. If you have not previously asked the court clerk or the small claims advisor whether this judge holds the re-hearing on the same day as the motion to vacate, be prepared to go forward with your case.

NOTE: *If you cannot afford to pay the judgment, you can make a request to the court to pay it in installments. (see form 24, p.233.)*

COLLECTING YOUR JUDGMENT 9

If the judgment is in your favor, the euphoria you feel upon winning may quickly fade if you wait until after the hearing to find out if the defendant has any property with which to satisfy the judgment. Winning the case does not necessarily mean that you will collect, at least right away. Sometimes a person or company is called *judgment proof* meaning that the judgment obtained against the person or company is worthless because they have no money to pay it.

NOTE: *Judgments can be renewed every ten years and there is always the chance that the defendant will win the lottery, or want to sell a piece of property upon which a lien is attached, making it possible for you to collect the money that is owed. If the defendant filed a Chapter 7 or 11 in bankruptcy court, you may still be able to collect the judgment.*

ASK FOR YOUR MONEY

If you won the case, write a letter to the defendant asking for payment before you start collection procedures. (You cannot start them until the 30-day appeal period is over anyway.) Sometimes, the defendant (now known as the *judgment debtor*) will pay the judgment to keep his or her employer from finding out about it through *garnishment* procedures. You may receive payment because the judgment debtor does not want to lose another day from work to appear for a judgment debtor exam, so be sure to mention this in your letter. At the end of the 30 day appeal period, the debtor will be required to submit a Statement of Assets if the judgment is not paid. That is another incentive for the debtor to pay up.

On the other hand, if you think the judgment debtor is likely to remove all of his or her money from the only bank account you know about, or is likely to quit his or her job to avoid garnishment of wages you may want to lay low until the appeal period is over, so that you can file a lien on the property before the judgment debtor can dispose of it. The steps you take prior to collection require careful analysis of all your options.

If you do not want to get involved in the collection process, you can hire a collection agency to obtain the funds for you. Most work on a percentage basis. You can hire an attorney who specializes in collection matters but negotiate a fee in advance to avoid surprise later.

COLLECTION METHODS

WAGE
GARNISHMENT

Garnishment is the most frequently used legal procedure to collect money in a small claims case. This means that the person's employer gives you part of the defendant's wages each pay day until the debt is paid. To collect your money this way, you must find out where the person is employed. You then ask the small claims court for a Writ of Execution and fill it out. It will cost you another $7.00. When the court issues this writ, the sheriff or marshal will deliver it to the debtor's employer. The employer pays the money to the court and the court pays the money owed to the winning party. The employer is the *garnishee*. The court then pays the winning party.

If the judgment debtor is your landlord or owns other rental property, you can garnish the rents paid by the current tenants. The procedure is the same as for a wage garnishment except you instruct the Sheriff to do a rent garnishment instead of a wage garnishment.

JUDGMENT DEBTOR EXAMINATION If the judgment has not been paid, you can file an **APPLICATION AND ORDER TO PRODUCE STATEMENT OF ASSETS AND TO APPEAR FOR EXAMINATION**. (see form 13, p.209.) A judgment debtor examination is a procedure where the debtor is required to return to court and answer, under penalty of perjury, the creditor's questions about the location of assets. You can also subpoena the debtors financial records by obtaining a subpoena duces tecum from the court clerk. Appendix F contains a list of suggested questions for a judgment debtor examination.

Before beginning the exam, ask the judgment debtor if you can tape record the exam. If you get permission, record the permission and the testimony. Having a recording will make it easier to listen and not be as concerned with getting the information down on paper.

RETAIL BUSINESSES A *till tap* is know as a crime when anyone other than the sheriff enters the retail establishment of a debtor and takes enough money to satisfy the judgment from the cash register. You will need to obtain a **WRIT OF EXECUTION** first. (see form 27, p.239.)

> ***Warning:*** The sheriff's fee for a till tap or keeper can turn into several hundred dollars.

Another similar procedure is where the sheriff goes to the place of business and sits by the cash register all day waiting for the money to come in. This procedure, called a *keeper levy*, is popular with collections against doctors or lawyers where customers trickle in all day. The keeper keeps the checks.

ABSTRACT OF JUDGMENT An **ABSTRACT OF JUDGMENT–CIVIL** is a document that is recorded in the county where the debtor owns property. (see form 16, p.217.) The effect of the abstract is that it places a lien on any property, or buildings on the property, that the debtor may own in the county. There is no requirement to ascertain in advance whether property is owned in the county or not. In fact, the lien operates on any purchase of property in the county by the debtor as well as any sale of property by the debtor.

If you know the debtor owns property but you do not know where, record an ABSTRACT OF JUDGMENT in several counties. You may get lucky.

WRIT OF
EXECUTION—
REAL PROPERTY

If the creditor does not want to wait until the property is sold, a WRIT OF EXECUTION can be obtained and filed with the county recorder. (see form 27, p.239.) This authorizes the sale of the property to the highest bidder at a public sale. All of the money in excess of the judgment and interest are given to the debtor. These sales do not usually fetch market value on the property, so the debtor usually ends up losing a large part of his equity in the property.

WRIT OF
EXECUTION—
PERSONAL
PROPERTY

The court can issue a WRIT OF EXECUTION against an individual judgment debtor, which is an authorization for the collection of property. (see form 27, p.239.) The judgment creditor gives the WRIT OF EXECUTION to the marshall or sheriff with written instructions describing the property. The marshall is authorized to remove the property and put it in safekeeping. It can later be sold at a public sale. If the property to be seized is in a bank or brokerage account, the marshall directs the third party to turn over the property. If someone owes you money, that person is directed to pay the money to the marshall.

The debtor has ten days after the property is seized to file a CLAIM OF EXEMPTION (WAGE GARNISHMENT) with the court. (see form 29, p.243.) For property other than wages, the debtor also has ten days to file a CLAIM OF EXEMPTION (ENFORCEMENT OF JUDGMENT) form. (see form 28, p.241.) These claims state that the property is exempt from execution or necessary for the support of the debtor or the debtor and his family. The creditor then has ten days to request a court hearing to dispute the exemption with the NOTICE OF OPPOSITION TO CLAIM OF EXEMPTION. (see form 31, p.247.). If the creditor does not request a hearing or the judge decides that the property is exempt or necessary for support, the judge will issue an ORDER that the property be returned. (see form 33, p.251.)

Warning: Following is a schedule of exempt property. Please note that the list is not complete and that an official list of exemptions can be found in the EXEMPTIONS FROM THE ENFORCEMENT OF JUDGMENTS. (see form 18, p.221.) If you have substantial property, you may want to see an attorney to ascertain whether your property can be converted into *exempt property* using the schedule.

1. Homestead, California Code of Civil Procedure, Sections 704.710-704.995 — $50,000 to $100,000 in equity. "Dwelling" can include a house, condo, community apartment project, a mobile home, motor home or boat. (Cal. Code of Civ. Pro., Sec.704.710.) Exemption amount is $50,000 for an individual, $75,000 for a head of household, $100,000 for those over 65, those over 55 with gross annual income of less than $15,000, or the disabled.

2. Motor Vehicles, California Code of Civil Procedure, Section 704.010 — $1,900.

3. Household furnishings, wearing apparel and other personal effects, California Code of Civil Procedure, Section 704.020 "ordinarily and reasonably necessary to" and used by the debtor/spouse.

4. Jewelry, heirlooms & works of art, California Code of Civil Procedure, Section 704.040 — $5,000.

5. Tools of trade, California Code of Civil Procedure, Section 704.060 — $5,000 per spouse.

6. Personal earnings (earned pre-bankruptcy), California Code of Civil Procedure, Section 704.070 — 75%.

7. Life insurance policies, California Code of Civil Procedure, Section 704.100.8. Public retirement benefits are entirely exempt, California Code of Civil Procedure, Section 704.110.

9. Vacation credits are entirely exempt. California Code of Civil Procedure, Section 704.113.

10. Private Retirement Plans (except IRA's) are completely exempt, California Code of Civil Procedure, Section 704.115. IRA's are exempt only to the extent necessary for the support of the debtor at the time of anticipated retirement.

11. Unemployment insurance and compensation, California Code of Civil Procedure, Section 704.120, disability and health insurance payments, California Code of Civil Procedure, Section 704.130,

worker's compensation claims and awards California Code of Civil Procedure, Section 704.160, and welfare payments California Code of Civil Procedure, Section 704.170, are exempt.

12. Personal injury and wrongful death causes of action are exempt; after payment of an award or settlement, they are exempt to the extent reasonably necessary for support, California Code of Civil Procedure, Sections 704.140, 704.150.

13. Cemetery plots (unless held for resale) are exempt, California Code of Civil Procedure, Section 104.200.

DRIVER'S LICENSE SUSPENSION

If you obtain a judgment for $500 or less in an auto accident case, you can file CERTIFICATE OF FACTS RE UNSATISFIED JUDGMENT (DMV FORM DL 30) (see form 26, p.237.) The debtor's driver's license will be suspended. This is one of the best ways to get paid because a driver's license is more precious than property to many people. The judgment creditor asks the small claims clerk to provide a Certified copy of the NOTICE OF ENTRY OF JUDGMENT. (see form 17, p.219.) The box on the certified copy that states "This judgment results from a motor vehicle accident..." must be checked. Send the CERTIFICATE OF FACTS RE UNSATISIFIED JUDGMENT (DMV FORM DL 30) signed by the creditor and Small Claims Clerk, certified copy of the judgment and a $20 check made payable to DMV to:

Department of Motor Vehicles
Attn: Civil Judgment Unit
P.O. Box 942884
Sacramento, CA 94284-0884
916-657-7573

VALIDITY

A judgment is good for ten years and can be renewed for ten more. In the meantime, they earn interest in the amount of ten percent each year.

AFTER THE JUDGMENT IS PAID

When the judgment is paid, the creditor is required to sign a form called ACKNOWLEDGMENT OF SATISFACTION OF JUDGMENT. (see form 34, p.253.) After it is signed, the debtor should file it with the court, just to make sure it gets filed. If an ABSTRACT OF JUDGMENT–CIVIL (form 16) has been recorded in any county by the creditor, the debtor will not be able to buy or sell property in that county unless an ACKNOWLEDGMENT OF SATISFACTION OF JUDGMENT is also filed. (see form 34, p.253.)

APPEALING YOUR CASE 10

If you are the defendant and you lose, or if you are a plaintiff who has been countersued by the defendant, and you lose on the countersuit, you are permitted to appeal. You will need to file the NOTICE OF APPEAL. (see form 19, p.223.) Insurance companies for the defendant can also appeal a judgment in excess of $2,500. The appeal will include a rehearing on all of the claims heard in small claims court, even if an appeal on that specific claim was not made. The purpose is to avoid the possibility that the superior court's decision will conflict with the small claims decision. Enforcement of the judgment is *stayed* while the appeal is pending. This means no other action can be taken on it.

You must file your NOTICE OF APPEAL with the small claims clerk within thirty days of the date the judgment was mailed to you by the court clerk. (see form 19, p.223.) A fee for filing is charged and varies from county to county. Since it usually takes a day or two for the judgment to reach you in the mail, you will not have a full thirty days. Watch your deadlines carefully. (Do not mail it. An attorney once mailed a NOTICE OF APPEAL of a superior court case where the verdict was over $2,000,000. The mail was slow and he missed the deadline.)

The appeal will be heard by a superior court judge. You will have to start from scratch, presenting all of your evidence and witnesses again. This is called a *trial de novo*. The same rules and informality regarding evidence govern the hearing.

The amount of damages requested in the small claims suit will be the amount of damages requested in the appeal, even if the judgment against you was for less.

Example: If the plaintiff won $250 after having requested $2,500, an appeal puts the defendant at risk of losing the entire $2,500 if the appeal is lost.

While some superior court judges treat small claims matters with the same importance of other matters that come before them, there are other judges who do not favor small claims appeals and make their distaste very obvious. They may rush the parties through their presentations, after they have made them wait in the courtroom for hours. They may use the opportunity to do other paperwork while they pretend to be giving the case their full attention. They may become impatient with the questioning and take it over themselves. Extraordinary requests will be denied. For these reasons, you may find it worthwhile to hire an attorney to represent you since most attorneys already have learned to deal with the idiosyncrasies of the judiciary. The sad truth is that many attorneys are not treated very well by judges either.

Another reason to consider hiring an attorney is that a judge can award the plaintiff an extra $1,000, plus lost wages if convinced that the appeal was not taken in good faith. This is in addition to the amount of the judgment, plus interest and costs that include attorney's fees in the amount of $150 if actually incurred, any lost earnings, transportation, and lodging expenses.

After the hearing, a new NOTICE OF ENTRY OF JUDGMENT will be mailed to the parties. (see form 17, p.219.)

GLOSSARY

A

abstract of judgment. A document issued by the County Clerk which when recorded at the county recorder's office places a lien on any real property owned by the debtor in that particular county.

accord and satisfaction. An agreement to accept less than the amount that is legally due.

acknowledgment of satisfaction of judgment. A Judicial Council form that the judgment creditor must complete, sign, and file when the judgment is fully paid or "satisfied."

act of god. A natural catastrophe that no one can prevent such as an earthquake, a tidal wave, a volcanic eruption, a hurricane or a tornado.

adhesion contract. A contract so imbalanced in favor of one party over the other (usually but not always on a form with a lot of very small print) that there is a strong implication it was not freely bargained.

advisory arbitration. A procedure, much like a mini, informal trial held in front of a neutral person called an arbitrator whose decision is not binding on the parties. Even if the parties decide not to accept the decision, they still have the advantage of an opportunity to reassess their positions based on the analysis and decision of the arbitrator.

age of majority. The age at which a person has capacity to enter into a contract which is enforceable by the other party for damages for negligence or intentional wrongs without a parent being liable. In California, the age of majority is 18.

admonish. To advise or caution. For example the court may caution or admonish counsel for objecting too much or berating the witness.

adversary proceeding. One having opposing parties such as a plaintiff and a defendant, a claimant and cross-claimant, petitioner and respondent, appellant and appellee.

affidavit. A written statement of facts confirmed by the oath of the party making it, before a notary or officer having authority to administer oaths.

agent for service of process. An individual (or another corporation) designated by a corporation to accept service of process if the corporation is sued. California residency is the only requirement for an individual to be named as an agent for service of process.

a.k.a. The abbreviation for "also known as" when someone is known by more than one name due to use of different initials, a nickname, an alias, a maiden or married name.

allegation. A statement of the issues in a written document (a pleading) that a person says they are prepared to prove in court.

alternative dispute resolution (ADR). Consists of several less formal methods of resolving disputes than having a judge decide the issues in a courtroom setting. These procedures are generally faster and less expensive than going to court but in the small claims setting (which is generally pretty fast and inexpensive anyway,) the main advantages are privacy and a resulting compromise between the parties, especially helpful when there are ongoing relationships to preserve.

appeal. In the small claims setting, it is a request to the Superior Court by the defendant (or by the plaintiff on the claim of the defendant) for a new hearing. The appeal is also called a "trial de novo" which is a fancy way of saying that the Superior Court hears the entire matter as though there was no small claims action. The parties are permitted to have attorneys represent them in an appeal.

appearance. The act of showing up in court and letting the court officials know you are there.

application for waiver of court fees and costs. A Judicial Council Form that permits a plaintiff to apply for a court order waiving fees and costs if the plaintiff's income comes within certain guidelines.

arbitration. A procedure where a neutral party listens to both sides of a dispute, reviews the evidence and makes a decision based on principles of law and evidence.

assumption of risk. A doctrine often used as a defense under which a person may not recover for an injury received when he has voluntarily exposed himself to a known danger.

attachment. The taking of a person's property to satisfy a court-ordered debt

B

bad faith. Dishonesty or fraud in a transaction or knowingly misrepresenting the facts

bailiff. An officer of the court responsible for keeping order and maintaining appropriate courtroom decorum.

bankruptcy: Refers to federal statutes and judicial proceedings involving persons or businesses that cannot pay their debts and seek the assistance of the court in getting a fresh start. There are several types of procedures under the protection of the bankruptcy court where debtors may discharge their debts, perhaps by paying a portion of each debt. .

bench. Refers to the judge while court is in session

binding arbitration. A procedure, much like a mini, informal trial held in front of a neutral person called an arbitrator whose decision is binding on the parties. Some contracts require the parties to submit disputes to binding arbitration. Some parties choose to have binding arbitration because it is final decision. The prevailing party may use the court to enforce the arbitrators' decision.

best evidence. Primary evidence; the best evidence available. Evidence short of this is "secondary." For example, an original letter is "best evidence," and a photocopy is "secondary evidence."

boilerplate. Provisions in a contract, form or legal pleading which are apparently routine and/or "standard" terms, some of which may not apply to every situation.

bonded. A bonding company, also known as a surety or guarantor, issues a bond in the amount of at least $7,500.00 (in the case of a home improvement contractor) so that a homeowner has another resource besides the contractor to turn to for defective work. After the bonding company denies your claim, which happens more often than not, they can be sued for a maximum of $2,500.00 in small claims court. Furthermore, if you win the case against the contractor and collect, you must refund the money to the bonding company.

breach of contract. A failure to comply with the terms of a contract.

burden of proof. The amount of evidence required to prove a fact in court. In small claims court, the burden is called a preponderance of evidence which merely means that something was more likely than not.

C

calendar. A list of cases, some times posted, scheduled for hearing in court.

calendar year. January 1 through December 31 of a particular year.

caption. The heading or introductory part of a pleading.

case law. The principles of law that come from the written opinions of judges in published cases.

cause of action. The legal theory upon which damages are requested in a lawsuit.

caveat emptor. A Latin phrase meaning "let the buyer beware." The buyer buys at his own risk and therefore should examine and test a product himself/for obvious defects and imperfections.

chambers. A judge's office.

change of venue. The act of moving a lawsuit to another place for trial. (See venue.)

chronological. A list of events arranged in the order in which events happened; according to date.

circumstantial evidence. Includes all evidence except eyewitness testimony.

civil procedure. The rules and processes by which a civil case is tried and appealed, including the preparations for trial, the rules of evidence and trial conduct, and the procedure for pursuing appeals.

claim, defendant's. The defendant's counter-claim against the plaintiff.

claim of exemption. The Judicial Council form filed by the judgment debtor that lists the exempt property that cannot be taken from him to pay the judgment (if approved by the court).

claim, plaintiff's. A combination of facts, evidence and legal arguments showing why the plaintiff should recover damages.

claim-splitting. This situation occurs when the plaintiff divides a claim and files them as separate claims to stay below the monetary jurisdictional limits.

class action. Several people join their lawsuits against the same defendant because the facts and circumstances are similar. This procedure is not formally established in small claims court but there have been situations where several individual claims have been heard collectively to deal with neighborhood problems such as drug houses.

clean hands doctrine The theory that a person coming to court with a lawsuit must be free from unfair conduct, ie "clean hands" in regard to the subject matter of his claim.

closing argument The closing statement, by the parties or by their counsel, to the trier of facts after all parties have concluded their presentation of evidence.

commissioner. An attorney who is an employee of the court whose job is to take on many of the duties of a judge. Although not a judge, this person is usually addressed as "your honor" while sitting on the bench.

common law. The legal system that originated in England and is now in use in the United States. It is based on judicial decisions rather than legislative action.

comparative negligence. A procedure where a plaintiff sues the defendant for wrongdoing and then the award is reduced by the percentage of wrongdoing attributable to the plaintiff.

compensatory damages. An award of money, including a nominal amount, made to compensate a claimant for a legally recognized injury.

complaint. A written statement by the plaintiff stating the wrongs allegedly committed by the defendant.

conformed copy. An exact copy of a document filed in court.

consumer protection laws. Federal, state and local laws enacted to protect the consumer from inferior, adulterated, hazardous or deceptively advertised products and deceptive or fraudulent sales practices.

contempt of court. Willful disobedience of a judge's command or of an official court order.

contingency fee. A fee arrangement where the lawyer is paid a percentage of the settlement or award.

continuance. Postponement of a legal proceeding to a later date.

contract. An agreement between two or more parties in which an offer is made by one party and accepted by the other for their mutual benefit. Although some contracts are required to be in writing, contracts can be oral, written on a napkin or sealed by a handshake.

costs. The money actually spent by one of the parties to file, serve, subpoena and otherwise present the case and enforce a judgment against the losing party.

counsel. Legal advice or a term used to refer to lawyers in a case.

counterclaim. A claim that a defendant makes against a plaintiff.

court reporter. A person who makes a word-for-word record of what is said in court and produces a transcript of the proceedings upon request.

court rules. The regulations governing practice and procedure in the various courts.

creditor. The person to whom a debtor owes money, goods or services.

cross-examination. The questioning of a witness produced by the other side.

D

decision. The opinion of the court in concluding a case.

damages. The amount of money ordered by the court to be paid as compensation on a claim.

debtor. The person who owes money, goods or services to a creditor.

default. If a party does not attend the small claims action; the judge may still permit the other party to present their case.

default judgment. A judgment entered upon one party proving their case in the absence of the other party.

defective service. As applied to serving the Notice of Claim (see above) on the defendant, defective service occurs when for one reason or another (for example, incorrect or incomplete address) the notice could not be delivered to the defendant and was returned to the court clerk. Defective service may also refer to the service of other documents such as subpoenas.

defendant. The person or business defending the claim in a lawsuit. A defense is a combination of facts, evidence and legal arguments made by the defendant showing why the plaintiff is not entitled to recover damages.

defunct. A corporation no longer operative; having ceased to exist.

demand letter. A letter written by the plaintiff to the defendant asking for payment of damages, usually before the lawsuit is filed but sometimes before the hearing. A demand letter is required, if possible, before filing a small claims action.

direct evidence. Proof of facts by witnesses who saw acts done or heard words spoken.

direct examination. The first questioning of witnesses by the party on whose behalf they are called.

dismissal. A document notifying the court that the parties have ended the lawsuit.

discovery. An examination before trial, of facts and documents in possession of the opponents to prepare for trial.

dismiss with prejudice. The formal ending of a lawsuit where the plaintiff is not permitted to file the case again.

dismiss without prejudice. The end of a lawsuit where the plaintiff is permitted to file the case again later.

docket. A log containing brief entries of court proceedings.

E

enjoin. An order by the court telling a person to stop performing a specific act.

equity. Justice administered according to fairness.

escrow. An account where money or written instruments such as a deeds are held by a neutral third party (held in escrow) until all conditions of the agreement are met.

esquire. In the United States the title commonly appended after the name of an attorney. For example, Royce Orleans Hurst, Esq.

evidence. The proof of a fact or facts presented in court to prove a case. Evidence can be written (e.g. a contract or receipt,) oral (e.g. an eye witness), or circumstantial (e.g. fingerprints).

execution. The completion of the legal process of enforcing (by a sheriff, marshal, or constable) the collection of the monetary award granted in the judgment.

expert witness. A witness with specialized knowledge of a particular subject who is called to testify about an event even though they were not present when the event occurred.

exhibit. Tangible items such as photographs, documents or charts shown to the judge or jury.

F

fair market value. The value for which a reasonable seller would sell an item of property and for which a reasonable buyer would buy it.

file. The act of placing a paper in the official custody of the clerk of the court to enter into the record of a case.

filing fee. The fee required for filing various documents.

fraud. Deceitful conduct, including but not limited to concealment of facts, cheating and lying, which is designed to cause a person to take detrimental action.

G

garnishment. A court-ordered method of collection where a percentage of wages or property are attached to pay a judgment.

good faith. The act of being honest and without deception.

governmental claim. A claim filed against a government agency within 6 months of the incident as a prerequisite to filing a lawsuit against the government.

government entity. An aspect of government operations such as states, cities, counties, and other agencies or units.

governmental immunity. The exemption given to government entities such as cities, school districts, counties, and their employees for certain acts for which they would otherwise be held liable

guardian ad litem. A person appointed by the court to look after the best interests of a minor in a lawsuit.

H

hearing. A formal proceeding in front of a trier of fact. Hearings are used extensively by legislative and administrative agencies.

hearsay. An extremely complicated set of rules of evidence designed to keep certain indirect items of evidence out of the record based on their unreliability. In its most simple form it is usually a statement or writing based on what someone told the witness about something or someone else.

I

impeachment. The process of using evidence to prove that a person was not telling the truth.

implied contract. A contract not created or evidenced by the explicit agreement of the parties but one inferred by law based on expectations of normal behavior.

implied warranty. The protection against defects which comes with a product.

implied warranty of fitness for a particular purpose. The warranty that exists when the buyer is relying upon the promises or statements made by the seller.

implied warranty of habitability. The warranty by landlord that the premises meet certain basic standards of fitness for occupancy.

implied warranty of merchantability. The protection that guarantees that a product will do what it is intended to do.

inadmissible. That which, under the rules of evidence, cannot be admitted or received as evidence.

incapacity. Lack of legal ability to act due to age, disability, incompetence or other disqualifying attributes.

injunction. An order of the court prohibiting or compelling the performance of a specific act to prevent irreparable damage or injury.

issue. The disputed point between parties in a lawsuit.

J

joint and several liability. A legal doctrine that makes each of the parties who are responsible for an injury, liable for all the damages awarded in a lawsuit if the other parties responsible cannot pay.

judge pro tem. Now called a temporary judge. A volunteer attorney who is "judge for the day". You have the right to refuse to have this attorney hear your case but it can take a long time to find a real judge to hear the case.

judgment. A formal decision by the court

judgment debtor hearing - An examination of the defendant by the plaintiff under court in order to discover the amount and location of the defendant's assets.

jurisdiction. This word has several meanings but in terms of small claims court means either the upper limits for which a claim can be made or that the claim is made in the correct geographical location.

K

keeper. A method of collection where the sheriff or marshal goes to the defendant's business and waits for customers to come in and pay for services and/or goods and collects the cash, checks and credit card payments.

L

latent defect. A defect that is not apparent through reasonable inspection

levy. A means of collection where the funds in the defendant's bank account are taken to satisfy a judgment

liability. The legal responsibility or obligation to pay damages.

lien. A property right that attaches to a particular piece of personal or real property (such as a car or a house) that is given to a creditor until the property is sold and the creditor can collect the money owed.

litigant. A party to a lawsuit.

litigation. A lawsuit or a legal action, including all proceedings therein.

M

malicious prosecution. An action instituted with intention of injuring the defendant and without probable cause, which terminates in favor of the person prosecuted.

malpractice. Professional misconduct that sometimes causes damages.

memorialized. The act of putting something in writing.

minor, a. A person who is under 18 years and therefore too young to file a lawsuit in his own name unless the minor is legally emancipated. The suit must be brought by a "guardian ad litem."

mitigation of damages The act of taking steps to minimize the amount of damages (e.g. if a tenant breaks a lease, the landlord has a duty to reasonably attempt to rent to someone else.)

motion. A set of papers requesting a judge to make an order.

N

negligence. The failure to act as a reasonable person would under the same or similar circumstances, which causes damages to another person. Gross negligence is a more serious level of negligence which specifies that the negligent person acted recklessly and without regard for the rights of others. Comparative negligence (formerly known as contributory negligence) is the amount of negligence by the plaintiff.

neutral. An individual or panel that facilitates mediation or negotiation sessions and who does not favor one side or the other.

notary public. A public officer whose function it is to administer oaths, to attest and certify documents, and to take acknowledgments.

notice. Formal notification to the party that has been sued in a civil case of the fact that the lawsuit has been filed. Also, any form of notification of a legal proceeding.

novation. An agreement of the parties to a contract to substitute a new contract for the old one. canceling the old agreement. It is usually made when the parties find that payments or performance under the old contract cannot reasonable be made.

nuisance. The unreasonable or unlawful use of property causing damages to another.

O

oath. A solemn pledge made under a sense of responsibility in attestation of the truth of a statement or in verification of a statement made.

objection. The process by which one party takes exception to some statement or procedure. An objection is either sustained (allowed) or overruled by the judge.

opening statement. The initial statement made by the parties or attorneys for each side, outlining the facts each intends to establish during the hearing

opinion. A judge's written explanation of a decision of the court.

oral argument. An opportunity for each party to a lawsuit to summarize their position before the court and also to answer the judges' questions.

order. Direction of a court or judge, usually made in writing.

overrule. A judge's decision not to permit an objection.

P

pain and suffering damages. Non economic emotional and physical pain that cannot be restored.

paralegal. A person with legal skills who works under the supervision of a lawyer.

parol evidence. Oral or verbal evidence; evidence given by word of mouth in court.

partnership. An agreement between two or more individuals to share the profits and losses of a business.

patent defect. A defect which is apparent through reasonable inspection.

plaintiff. The person who files the complaint in a civil lawsuit.

pleadings. Written statements of the parties in a civil case stating the issues and their position on the issues.

post-trial. Refers to procedures happening after the trial, including post-trial motions or collection procedures.

precedent. A court decision in an earlier case with facts and law similar to a dispute currently before a court. Precedent will ordinarily govern the decision of a later similar case, unless a party can show that it was wrongly decided or that it differed in some significant way.

preponderance of evidence. The level of proof needed to prevail in a civil action where the judge is convinced more for one side or the other.

presumption. A rule determining that one side has proved the issue unless the other side has evidence to refute the facts.

prima facie case. A case that has satisfied the requirements of proof necessary to allow it to continue in the judicial process.

procedure. The rules for the conduct of a lawsuit.

product liability. Legal responsibility of manufacturers and sellers to buyers, users, and bystanders for damages or injuries suffered because of defects in goods.

promisee. An individual to whom a promise is made.

promisor. An individual that makes a promise.

proof of service. A document proving that a person or business was served.

pro se or pro per. A Latin term meaning "on one's own behalf"; in courts, it refers to persons who present their own cases without lawyers.

punitive damages. Damages meant to make an example of or to punish the defendant or wrongdoer.

R

rescind. To cancel a contract, sometimes by agreement of the parties but usually based on fraud, duress or misrepresentation

reasonable person. A phrase used to denote a hypothetical person who exercises qualities of attention, knowledge, intelligence, and judgment that society requires of its members for the protection of their own interest and the interests of others. Thus, the test of negligence is based on either a failure to do something that a reasonable person, guided by considerations that ordinarily regulate conduct, would do, or on the doing of something that a reasonable and prudent (wise) person would not do.

rebut. Evidence disproving other evidence previously given or reestablishing the credibility of challenged evidence.

record. A written or recorded account of all the acts and proceedings in a lawsuit.

remedy. Legal or judicial means by which a right or privilege is enforced or the violation of a right or privilege is prevented, redressed, or compensated.

rescission. The unmaking or undoing of a contract

rest. A party is said to "rest" or "rest its case" when it has presented all the evidence it intends to offer.

rules of evidence. Standards governing whether evidence is admissible.

S

service of process. The act of formally notifying a party that a claim has been filed against the person or business. In the Small Claims Court, this can be accomplished by certified mail, personal service or "substituted service."

settlement. Parties to a lawsuit resolve their difference without having a trial.

statute. A legislative enactment

statute of frauds. A statutory requirement that certain contracts must be in writing.

statute of limitations. The time limit for filing a case usually calculated from the day that the incident occurred.

stipulation. An agreement between both parties about facts, principles of law or procedures.

stop payment. When a customer or user of services requests and authorizes the bank to withhold payment on a check.

strict liability. Liability is determined by some means without proof of negligence. For example, a dog owner is liable for damages caused by his dog biting someone, whether or not he or the dog was negligent.

subpoena. The request to the court and the court's act of requiring a person to appear at a hearing or suffer a penalty. Adding the words " Duces Tecum" means that the subpoenaed person must bring something with him to the hearing.

substituted service. The act of serving a person by leaving the papers at his home with a competent adult, or at a business by leaving the papers at the business address, during business hours with the person in charge of the office and then mailing a copy of the papers to the same address.

summons. A written document issued by the court which commences a civil action or special proceeding.

T

temporary restraining order. Prohibits a person from an action that is likely to cause irreparable harm. This differs from an injunction in that it may be granted immediately, without notice to the opposing party, and without a hearing. It is intended to last only until a hearing can be held.

testimony. The evidence given by a witness under oath.

till tap. A method of collection where the sheriff or marshall goes to the defendant's business and takes money out of the cash register to pay the judgment.

torts. The set of principles and law that establishes a person's right to be compensated by a person who caused injury to them. The tortfeaser is the person who causes the injury.

trial. A judicial examination of issues between parties to an action.

trial brief. A written document prepared for and used by a party at trial. It contains the issues to be tried, a synopsis of evidence to be presented and the relevant law to substantiate the position.

U

unlawful detainer. Remaining in possession of real estate without the consent of the owner or other person entitled to its possession. Unlawful detainer cases are not heard in Small Claims court

unlawful consumer practices. Deceptive, unfair and abusive business practices including false advertising and marketing, failure to comply with consumer protection statutes, and requests for unauthorized personal information.

uphold. The decision of an higher court not to reverse a lower court decision.

usury. Requiring interest on a loan above the maximum rate permitted by statute.

V

vacate. To set aside, as "to vacate a judgment."

venue. Authority of a court to hear a matter based on geographical location.

vicarious liability. The act of being held responsible for the acts of someone else, such as an employer being held liable for negligent acts of employees.

void. Invalidity for which there is no remedy.

voidable. Capable of being declared invalid; a voidable contract is one where a person may avoid his obligation under certain circumstances. , as a contract between an adult and a minor.

W

waiver. Voluntarily giving up a right such as agreeing to have a small claims action heard by a commissioner or temporary judge.

witness. A person called upon by either side in a lawsuit to give testimony before the court or jury.

writ of execution. An order of the court evidencing debt of one party to another and commanding the court officer to take property in satisfaction of the debt.

writ of garnishment. An order of the court whereby property, money, or credits in the possession of another person may be seized and applied to pay a debtor's debt. It is used as an incident to or auxiliary of a judgment rendered in a principal action.

APPENDIX A

SMALL CLAIMS ADVISORS (AND COUNTY COURT WEBSITES)

California requires each county to provide free help to all plaintiffs and defendants in small claims actions. Also provided are the addresses and contact numbers for the small claims court in each county. The list below also contains the name, address, phone number, and where available, email address of the Small Claims Court Advisor for each county. Although almost all of them offer help by telephone, some counties provide walk-in service or help by appointment. Two or three have small group workshops, videos or "mock court." Some have very limited hours, others are available during regular business hours, at night and on weekends.

The advisors are not permitted to dispense legal advice, however they will provide general information about preparing for the hearing. They will also explain how to collect your money after you've won or how to make periodic payments. The Advisor cannot act as your attorney; and their services are not intended to replace those of your own attorney. Also, the Advisor will not be able to tell you whether you "have a case," whether you will win, or what your chances are of winning. The Advisor's main purpose is to explain how to prepare for and use the small claims court, how to complete the forms, explain what you can do if you can't afford to pay, refer you to an attorney or other agencies who may be able to help you and to inform you about the small claims law, and about general California law and well as common consumer problems.

The advisors are also an invaluable source of information on how to use the law library, where you can find an attorney to advise you, where you can find a typewriter, copy or fax machine, and the location of the best coffee close to the courthouse.

The best way to avail yourself of the services of the advisor is to first call the county where you plan to file your lawsuit to find out the full extent of services offered and whether there are procedures unique to that county. Plan to spend some time on the phone wending your way through voice mail options or finding the information you requested.

Since there is probably more than one county that provides the correct venue for your lawsuit it makes sense to contact the advisor from all of them to determine whether there are any advantages to filing in one county over the other. For example, one county may convene small claims court at night so you won't have to miss work on the day of the hearing. One county's small claims advisor may be more knowledgeable or helpful than another. Maybe you want to choose the county that has a better mediation program, or one where the Advisor speaks Spanish, Vietnamese or other languages.

Alameda County

http://www.co.alameda.ca.us/courts/divs/small/index.shtml/

NOTE: *Legal advice is available to all parties in SMALL CLAIMS COURT. The telephone number is 510-763-9282*

OaklandSmall Claims Advice Room
Allen E. Broussard Justice Center
600 Washington St
5th floor, Dept 141
Oakland, California

HaywardCounty Offices Building
224 West Winton, Room 160
Hayward, California
(by Alameda County Law Library)

Alpine County

http://alpine.courts.ca.gov/

For Small Claims Advisor: Call County Clerk's Office
530-694-2281

Amador County

http://www.amadorcourt.org/SmallCl/smallclaims.asp

Steve Cilenti, Attorney at Law, Small Claims Advisor
35 Court Street
Jackson, CA 95642
209-223-5550
Fax: 209-223-5552

Butte County

http://www.courtinfo.ca.gov/courts/trial/butte/

Doug Day, Small Claims Advisor Program
530-873-0558

Calaveras County

http://www.co.calaveras.ca.us/departments/courts.html#claims

Calaveras Legal Assistance Service, Small Claims Advisor
P.O. Box 919
San Andreas, CA 95249
209-754-1443
Clas@goldrush.com

Colusa County

http://www.courtinfo.ca.gov/courts/trial/colusa/main.htm

Law Office of Bonnie MacFarlane, Small Claims Advisor
P.O. Box 60374
Sacramento, CA 95860-0314
888-683-6707
Bonniem@ns.net

Contra Costa County

http://www.cc-courts.org/smallcl.htm

Scott D. Reep, Small Claims Advisor
Contra Costa County Coordinated Courts
725 Court Street
Martinez, CA 94553
888-676-7277 (County of Contra Costa)
925-646-6109 (Outside of County)

NOTE: *Free seminars entitled "How to Use the Small Claims Court" are held at several locations in Contra Costa County. the two-hour seminars provide general information about the small claims process (including appeals) and are held weekly. Call for information.*

Del Norte County

http://www.courtinfo.ca.gov/courts/trial/delnorte/

Currently no Small Claims Advisor

El Dorado County

http://co.el-dorado.ca.us/superiorcourts/small-claims.html

NOTE: *Placerville–Cameron Park Area: THere is a one hour clinic that is free to the puplic. The toll free number for the small claims advisor is 800-696-8757 or 530-541-8757. South Lake Taho Area: A one hour clinic is free to the public. The number for the small calims advisor is 800-696-8757 or 530-541-8757.*

Renate H. Schauble, El Dorado Small Claims Advisor
P.O. Box 13086
South Lake Tahoe, CA 96151
530-541-8757
Ea1040@aol.com

Fresno County

http://www.fresno.ca.gov/2810/default.htm

Denise Kerner, Small Claims Advisor's Office
Del Webb Downtown Plaza Building
2220 Tulare Street, 8th Floor
Fresno, CA 93721
559-262-4291
dkerner@sjcl.org

Glenn County

http://www.courtinfo.ca.gov/courts/trial/glenn/

Norman Y. Herring and Penny Arnold, Small Claims Advisors
Glenn County Counsel
525 W. Sycamore Street
Willows, CA 95988
530-934-6455
NHerring1@prodigy.net

Humboldt County

http://www.courtinfo.ca.gov/courts/trial/humboldt/

Christopher Metzger, Small Claims Advisor
930 3rd Street, Suite 207
Eureka, CA 95501
707-441-1185
eurmetzger@aol.com

Imperial County

http://www.courtinfo.ca.gov/courts/trial/imperial/

Nancy Kizziah, Small Claims Advisor
Imperial Superior Courtt
939 West Main Street
El Centro, CA 92243
760-482-4359
Nancykizziah@imperialcounty.net

Inyo County

http://www.inyocourt.ca.gov

Law Office of Bonnie MacFarlane, Small Claims Advisor
P.O. Box 60374
Sacramento, CA 95860-0314
888-683-6707
Bonniem@ns.net

Kern County

http://www.co.kern.ca.us/courts/smlclaim.htm

Kendra Roberts, Small Claims Advisor
1215 Truxtun Avenue
Bakersfield, CA 93301
661-868-2532

Kings County

http://www.courtinfo.ca.gov/courts/trial/kings/

Cheryll Lehn, Small Claims Advisor
Kings County Law Library
1400 West Lacey Boulevard
Hanford, CA 93230
559-582-3211 Ext. 4430
Clehn@co.kings.ca.us

Lake County

http://www.courtinfo.ca.gov/courts/trial/lake/
        #smallclaims

Law Office of Bonnie MacFarlane, Small Claims Advisor
P.O. Box 60374
Sacramento, CA 95860-0314
888-683-6707
Bonniem@ns.net

Lassen County

http://www.co.lassen.ca.us/contact.htm

Janice M. Heid, Small Claims Advisor
County Counsel's Office
221 South Roop
Susanville, CA 96130
530-251-8334
janheid@hotmail.com

Los Angeles County

http://www.lasuperiorcourt.org/SmallClaims/

Los Angeles County Department of Consumer Affairs,
Small Claims Advisor
http://consumer-affairs.co.la.ca.us/
        SmallClaims/Frame.htm
500 West Temple Street, Room B-96
Los Angeles, CA 90012
213-974-9759

Madera County

http://www.courtinfo.ca.gov/courts/trial/madera/

Law Office of Bonnie MacFarlane, Small Claims Advisor
P.O. Box 60374
Sacramento, CA 95860-0314
888-683-6707
Bonniem@ns.net

Marin County

http://www.co.marin.ca.us/depts/MC/main/smallclaims

Stanley Pierce, Small Claims Advisor
3501 Civic Center Drive, Room 266
San Rafael, CA 94903
415-499-6246
spierce@marin.org

Mariposa County

http://www.courtinfo.ca.gov/courts/trial/mariposa/

Richard Gimlin, Small Claims Advisor
P.O. Box 105
Mariposa, CA 95338
209-966-3627

Mendocino County

http://www.co.mendocino.ca.us/courts/small.html

Doug O'Brien, Small Claims Advisor
Redwood Legal Assistance
P.O. Box 747
Ukiah, CA 95482
707-462-24551
800-956-5575
Ukiah@lsnc.net

Merced County

http://www.courtinfo.ca.gov/courts/trial/merced/

Jack Uren
P.O. Box 1047
Merced, CA 95341
209-385-7549

Modoc County

http://www.courtinfo.ca.gov/courts/trial/modoc/

Wendy Dier, Small Claims Advisor
201 S. Court Street #28
Alturas, CA 96101
530-233-2008
Wendy@hdo.net

Mono County

http://www.courtinfo.ca.gov/courts/trial/mono/

Law Office of Bonnie MacFarlane, Small Claims Advisor
P.O. Box 60374
Sacramento, CA 95860-0314
888-683-6707
Bonniem@ns.net

Monterey County

http://www.co.monterey.ca.us/court/small_claims.html

Candice C. Chin
Consumer Protection Coordinator
District Attorney Consumer Protection Division
P.O. Box 1131
Salinas, CA 93902

NOTE: *If you have a question about a Small Claims problem, you can get help through the Monterey College of Law's Small Claims Advisory Clinic, a program designed to serve the community. Law students are a vailable to answer questions and advise you on small claims presentations and procedures. There is no charge for this service.*

Napa County

http://www.napa.courts.ca.gov/common/content

Napa County Small Claims Advisor 707-253-4524

Nevada County

http://www.courts.co.nevada.ca.us/smallclaims.htm

Connie Crockett, Small Claims Adviser
206 Sacramento Street, Suite 207
Nevada City, CA 95959
530-470-0595
Fax: 530-265-0197
Ccrock@oro.net

NOTE: *The Small Claims Advisor does not meet with the litigants in person, as all information can be provided over the telephone. Additional written information requested will be provided via facsimile or mail. An answering machine will take your message in the event the Small Claims Advisor is not available.*

Orange County

http://www.legal-aid.com/smlclms.html

Bill Tanner, Small Claims Advisor
Legal Aid Society of Orange County
902 North Main Street
Santa Ana, CA 92701
800-963-7717
714-571-5277
btanner@legal-aid.com

NOTE: *The Small Claims Advisor provides free assistance to anyone who is suing or being sued in Orange County Small Claims Court. The Advisor is available to explain the Small Claims Court rules and procedures. To access the Advisor call the Hotline at 800-963-7717. Community*

Education Clinics use video and live presentation to explain the Small Claims court rules and procedure to help you with your case. Call the Hotline and find out when clinics are held.

Placer County

http://www.placer.ca.gov/courts/smallclaims.htm

Mark Campbell
Mark Campbell & Associates
916-652-5426

Plumas County

http://www.plumascourt.ca.gov/new_page_18.htm

Liz Cortez
Small Claims Adviser Program County Counsel
520 Main Street, Room 302
Quincy, CA 95971-6010
530-283-6240
Liz@countyofplumas.com

Riverside County

http://www.co.riverside.ca.us/depts/courts/Smallcla.htm

Albert Johnson Jr., Small Claims Advisor
4166 Almond Street
Riverside, CA 92501
800-244-8898
ajj-atty@pacbell.net

Sacramento County

http://www.saccourt.com/index/smallclaims.asp

Rick Uno, Small Claims Advisory Clinic
The Human Rights/Fair Housing Commission
of the City and County of Sacramento
301 Bicentennial Circle, Room 330
Sacramento, CA 95826
916-875-7846

NOTE: *The Human Rights/Fair Housing Commission also provides Mediation Services for Small Claims cases on site at the Carol Miller Justice Center on the day of trial. Further information is available at the Carol Miller Justice Center, or by calling 916-875-7843.*

San Benito County

http://www.superior-court.co.san-benito.ca.us/general.htm

Frank Hespe
Monterey College of Law
404 West Franklin Street
Monterey, CA 93940
831-373-1959

San Bernadino County

Cecelia Lowe
San Bernardino Superior Court
351 North Arrowhead, 1st Floor
San Bernardino, CA 92415-0215
909-387-3880
from outlying areas: 800-634-9085

San Diego County

www.sandiego.courts.ca.gov/superior/courts

San Diego - Claremont
Jay Brian Sacks
San Diego Superior Court
8950 Claremont Mesa Blvd.
San Diego, CA 92123
619-236-2471
Recorded Information: 619-236-2700

San Diego - El Cajon
Donna Morrell
250 East Main Street
El Cajon, CA 92020
619-441-4461

San Diego - South
Marilyn Wiczniski
Helen D. Fortson
500 Third Avenue
Chula Vista, CA 91910
619-691-4866
mwiczms@co-san-diego.ca.us
hfortsms@co-san-diego.ca.us

San Diego - North
Judith CokerTom McDougall
325 South Melrose Drive
Vista, CA 92083
619-236-2471

San Francisco

http://www.ci.sf.ca.us/courts/muni/smclaim.htm

San Francisco County, Small Claims Legal Advisor
Small Claims Division
575 Polk Street
San Francisco, CA 94102

Public Recorded Messages: 415-551-4000

Small Claims Legal Advisor's Office Information
415-292-2121

Small Claims Legal Advisor's Office Information
415-292-2121

How to present a case in small claims court
415-241-1302 x731

How to collect a small claims court judgment
415-292-2124

San Joaquin County

http://www.dca.ca.gov/smallclaims/sanjoaqu.htm

Kathy Ewing, Small Claims Advisor
445 West Weber Street, Suite 130
Stockton, CA 95203
209-943-8490
800-834-2201
kewing568@aol.com

San Luis Obispo County

http://www.slocourts.net/general_info.htm

Anita Wilcox, Small Claims Advisor
Office of the District Attorney
County Government Center, Room 235
San Luis Obispo, CA 93408
805-781-5856
Awilcox@co.slo.ca.us

San Mateo County

http://www.co.sanmateo.ca.us/smclaims.dir/

Central Branch
800 North Humboldt Street
San Mateo, CA 94401
650-573-2605

Attorney Allen Capeloto, Small Claims Advisor
ajc.esq@att.net

Santa Barbara County

http://www.sbcourts.org/general_info/case_types/
small_claims.ht

Figueroa Division
Small Claims Advisor's Message Line: 805-568-2984

Lompoc Division:
Small Claims Advisor's Message Line: 805-737-7756

Miller Division:
Small Claims Advisor's Message Line: 805-346-7424

Toni Lorien, Deputy County Counsel
Small Claims Advisor
Office of the County Counsel
1105 East Anapamu Street, Room 201
Santa Barbara, CA 93101
805-568-2984
lorien@co.santa-barbara.ca.us

Santa Clara County

http://www.scselfservice.org/small/index.jsp

Myrna Cohen
Small Claims Adviser of the District Attorney's Office
70 West Hedding Street, 4th Floor, Westwing
San Jose, CA 95110
408-792-288
1mcohen@dageneral.da.co.santa-clara.ca.us

Santa Cruz County

http://sccounty01.co.santa-cruz.ca.us/supct/courtweb1/
831-458-1086

Small Claims Advisor
California Rural Legal Assistance
21 Carr Street
Watsonville, CA 95076
831-724-2253
831-688-6535

Shasta County

http://www.shastacourts.com/generalinfo.shtml

Gerry L. Larrea, Small Claims Advisor
915 L Street, Suite 241
Sacramento, CA 95814
916-961-3136
800-795-8136
larreag@tomatoweb.com

Sierra County

http://www.courtinfo.ca.gov/courts/trial/sierra/

For Small Claims Advisor: Call County Clerk's Office.

Siskiyou County

http://www.co.siskiyou.ca.us/courts/index.htm

For Small Claims Advisor: Call County Clerk's Office.

Solano County

http://www.solanocourts.com/

Mary Anne Brayton, Small Claims Advisor
County Counsel's Office
580 Texas Street
Fairfield, CA 94533
707-421-7478

Sonoma County

http://www.sonomasuperiorcourt.com/Pages/
civil_smcl_div.html

E. Gregory Schrader, Attorney at Law
600 Administration Drive, Room 107
Santa Rosa, CA 95403
707-524-7349

Stanislaus County

http://www.co.stanislaus.ca.us/courts/Courts/smallclaims

Kathleen Aguilar, Small Claims Advisor
City Hall
2260 Floyd Avenue
Modesto, CA 95355
209-558-6000

Sutter County

http://www.suttercourts.com/pages/traffic/smallclaims.htm

Susan Townsend, Small Claims Advisor
Yuba-Sutter Legal Center for Seniors
725 D Street
Marysville, CA 95901
530-742-8289

Tehama County

http://www.courtinfo.ca.gov/courts/trial/tehama/

Gerry L. Larrea, Small Claims Advisor
915 L Street, Suite 241
Sacramento, CA 95814
916-961-3136

800-795-8136
larreag@tomatoweb.com

Trinity County

http://www.courtinfo.ca.gov/courts/trial/trinity/

Peter A. Navarro, Small Claims Advisor
1350 Placer Street
Redding, CA 95001-1013
530-242-1485

Tulare County

http://www.tularesuperiorcourt.ca.gov/

Walter McArthur, Small Claims Advisor
1809 West Main Street, Suite F
P.O. Box 2563728
Visalia, CA 93279
559-625-4300

Tuolumne County

http://www.courtinfo.ca.gov/courts/trial/tuolumne/

Law Office of Bonnie MacFarlane
Small Claims Advisor
P.O. Box 60374
Sacramento, CA 95860-0314
888-683-6707
Bonniem@ns.net

Ventura County

http://courts.countyofventura.org/
venturaMasterFrames3.htm

Martin Cobos, Small Claims Advisor
District Attorney's Office
Consumer Protection Unit
800 South Victoria Avenue
Ventura, CA 93009
805-644-5054
martin.cobos@mail.co.ventura.ca.us

Yolo County

http://www.yolocourts.com/faq_smallclaims.html

Law Office of Bonnie MacFarlane
Small Claims Advisor
P.O. Box 60374
Sacramento, CA 95860-0314
888-683-6707
Bonniem@ns.net

Yuba County

http://www.co.yuba.ca.us/departments.html

Susan Townsend
Yuba-Sutter Legal Center for Seniors
725 D
CA 95901
530-742-8289

APPENDIX B
MEDIATION PROGRAMS
BY COUNTY

This appendix contains the names and addresses of the mediation services available throughout the state. These can help you settle your dispute without going through with the trial.

Complaint Mediation Program

The Complaint Mediation Program, run by the California Department of Consumer affairs, provides mediators to promote mutually acceptable resolutions for consumer complaints against California businesses that are regulated by the following bureaus:

These include Automotive Repair, Smog Check, Burglar Alarm Companies, Cemetery/Funeral, Electronic and Appliance Repair, Firearms/Baton Training Facilities/Instructors, Home Furnishings and Thermal Insulation, Locksmith Companies, Private Investigators, Private Patrol Operators, Repossession Agencies, Security Guards, and many others.

Sacramento:

400 R St, Suite 5200
Sacramento, CA 95814
(916) 322-3400

Hayward:

2030 West Winton Avenue
Hayward, CA 94545
(510) 785-755

El Monte:

1180 Durfee Avenue, Suite125
South El Monte, CA 91733
(626) 575-7037

Riverside:

3737 Main Street, Suite
Riverside, CA 92501
(909) 782-4263

DRPA Mediation Programs by County

The Dispute Resolution Programs Act of 1986 provides funding of a statewide system of dispute resolution programs that meet certain requirements. In general, these programs provide either low cost or free services. For those of you who are interested in becoming volunteer mediators, you may be interested to know that many of them provide the state required training.

Alameda

Alameda County Bar Association
ADR Placement Service
Bari S. Robinson, Executive Director
360 22nd Street, Suite 800
Oakland, CA 94612
510-893-7160
FAX: 510 893-3119

Berkeley Dispute Resolution Service
Laura Bresler, Executive Director
1769 Alcatraz Avenue
Berkeley, CA 94703
510-428-1811
Fax: 510-428-1943

Center for Community Dispute Settlement
Diane Jeronimo, Executive Director
291 McLeod Street
Livermore, CA 94550
925-373-1035
Fax: 925-449-0945

California Lawyers for the Arts
Arts Arbitration & Mediation Services
Alma Robinson, Executive Director
Fort Mason Center C-255
San Francisco, CA 94123
415-775-7200

Conciliation Forums of Oakland
Benjamin Murdock, Executive Director
663 13th Street Oakland, CA 94612
510-763-2117
Fax: 510-763-7098

Mediation Resolution Services
Tina Walda-Jackson, Executive Director
22227 Redwood Road
Castro Valley, CA 94546
510-733-4940
Fax: 510-317-0781

Catholic Charities
Barbara Terrezas, Executive Director
433 Jefferson Street
Oakland, CA 94607
510-768-3139
Fax: 510-451-6998

West Oakland Health Council, Inc.
Student Conflict Resolution Program
Robert Cooper, M.D., Executive Director
1222 Preservation Park Way
Oakland, CA 94612
510-835-9610
Fax: 510-465-1508

Berkeley Dispute Resolution Program Service
1769 Alcatraz
Berkeley, CA 94703
510-834-5656

Family Violence Law Center
P.O. Box 2529
Berkeley, CA 94702
510-540-5370

Victim Offender Reconciliation Program
443 Jefferson Street
Oakland, CA 94607
510-8345656

Butte County
Mediation Center of the North Valley
Margaret Gunnell, Executive Director
341 Broadway, Suite 200
Chico, CA 95928
530-899-2277
Fax: 530-899-2270

Contra Costa County
Battered Women's Alternatives
Gloria Sandoval, Executive Director
P.O. Box 6406
Concord, CA 94524
510-676-2845
Fax: 510-676-0274

CA Community Dispute Services
Tom Bateman, Executive Director
705 7th Street
San Francisco, CA 94103
415-865-2520
Fax: 415-865-2538

The Center for Human Development
Marlene G. Morris, Project Director
391 Taylor Boulevard, Suite 120
Pleasant Hill, CA 94523
925-798-6132
Fax: 925-687-6903

Fresno County

Better Business Bureau Dispute Settlement Center
Dan DeSantis, ADR Administrator
1100 Van Ness Avenue
Fresno, CA 93724-0002
559-488-2778
Fax: 559-488-1976

Fresno Pacific University Center for Peacemaking
and Conflict Studies
Ron Claassen, Director
1717 South Chestnut Avenue
Fresno, CA 93702

San Joaquin College of Law
Regional Family Law and Mediation Center
Richard Cartier, Director
901 Fifth Street
Clovis, CA 93612
559-323-2100
Fax: 559-323-5566

Humboldt County

Humboldt Mediation Services
Mark Schaffner, Program Director
819 Seventh Street
Eureka. CA 95501
707-445-2505
Fax: 707-443-3293

Inyo County

Center for Settlement Services
Patricia Struckman, Executive Director
P.O. Box 3034
Mammoth Lakes, CA 93546
760-934-7539
Fax: 760-924-8049

Lake County

Lake County Dispute Resolution Services
Priscilla Day, Program Director
201 Smith Street
Lakeport, CA 95453
Mailing address:
P.O. Box 1173
Lakeport, CA 95453
707-263-1545

Los Angeles County

Milton Miller Memorial Fund
dba Western Law Center for Disability Rights
Loyola Law School
Lynne S. Bassis, Director
919 S. Albany Street
Los Angeles, CA 90015–0019
213-736-8104
Fax: 213-383-2854
Lynne.Bassis@LLS.edu

Asian Pacific American Legal Center of
Southern California,Dispute Resolution Center
Steve Chang, Executive Director
1145 Wilshire Boulevard, Suite 100
Los Angeles, CA 90017
213-250-8190
Fax: 213-250-8195
apadrc@netzero.net

California Academy of Mediation Professionals
Jeffrey Krivis, Executive Director
16501 Ventura Blvd., Suite 606
Encino, CA 91436
818-377-7250
Fax: 818-784-1836
jkrivis@mediation.com

Center for Conflict Resolution
Kin Wright, Director of Mediation Services
3750 E. Foothill Boulevard, Suite C
Pasadena, CA 91107-2201
626-585-9729
Fax: 626-585-1619
ccr4peace@loop.com

Centinela Valley Juvenile Diversion Program
(VORS, FARS, STARS)
Steve Goldsmith, Director
One Manchester Blvd.
Inglewood, CA 90301
310-412-5578
Fax: 310-330-5705
CVJDP@CITYOFINGLEWOOD.ORG

City of Monrovia (pending funding)
Alana Knaster, President TMI
22231 Mulholland Hwy #213
Calabasas, CA 91302
818-591-9526
Fax: 818-591-0980
ASKNASTER@AOL.COM

City of Norwalk Consumer-Rental Mediation Board
(NCRMB)
Takafumi Hamabata, Director
11929 Alondra Boulevard
Norwalk, CA 90650
562-929-5544
Fax: 562-929-5515

Claremont Dispute Resolution Center
Shauna O. Reimer, Executive Director
114 N. Indian Hill, Suite F
Claremont, CA 91711-4642
909-625-6632
Fax: 909-624-8186

Inland Valley Justice Center
Honorable James H. Piatt, Project Director
300 South Park Avenue, Suite 780
Pomona, CA 91766
909-629-6301
Fax: 909-629-1607

Korean American Coalition
Charles Kim, Executive Director
Alice Lee, Program Director
3421 West 8th Street, 2nd Floor
Los Angeles, CA 90005
213-365-5999
Fax: 213-380-7990

L.A. County Bar Assn.
Dispute Resolution Services, Inc.
Deborah Thomas, Director of Operations
261 S. Figueroa, Suite 310
P.O. Box 55020
Los Angeles, CA 90055
213-896-6564
Fax: 213-613-1299
nblacker@lacba.org

L. A. County Community &
Senior Citizens Services, Voluntary
Mediation Services (VMS)
Herb Oberman, Program Coordinator
11243 Glenoaks Boulevard, #1
Pacoima, CA 91331
818-897-2909
Fax: 818-896-1534
hoberman@co.la.ca.us

L. A. County Department of Consumer Affairs
Dispute Settlement Service
Timothy Bissell, Assistant Director
Kenneth Hahn Hall of Administration

500 W. Temple Street, Room B-96
Los Angeles, CA 90012
213-974-9774
Fax: 213-687-0233

Los Angeles Superior and Municipal Court
Julie Bronson, ADR Administrator
111 North Hill Street, Room 113
Los Angeles, CA 90012
213-974-0558
Fax: 213-620-7136
JBronson@lasc.co.la.ca.us

Martin Luther King Legacy Assn., Inc.
Martin Luther King Dispute Resolution Center
Rev. Norman S. Johnson, Interim Executive Director
4182 S. Western Avenue
Los Angeles, CA 90062
213-290-4100
Fax: 213-296-4742 or 213-295-7783
wsmoot@hotmail.com

Office of the Los Angeles City Attorney Dispute
Resolution Program
Avis Ridley Thomas, Administrative Coordinator
200 North Main Street, Suite 1600 City Hall
East Los Angeles, CA 90012
213-485-8324
213-237-2744 (24 hour access)
Fax: 213-237-0402
TDD (213-485-8334
aridley@atty.ci.la.ca.us

Loyola Law School Center for Conflict Resolution
Bill Hobbs, Director
919 S. Albany Street
Los Angeles, CA 90015-0019
213-736-1145
Fax: 213-382-5403
Bill.Hobbs@LLS.edu

California Lawyers for the Arts
Arts Arbitration and Mediation Services
Dorian Dawson, Associate Director
1641 18th Street
Santa Monica, CA 90404
310-998-5590
Fax: 310-998-5594
UserCLA@aol.com

Marin County

Marin County Mediation Services
Barbara Kob/Eleanor Spater, Coordinators
4 Jeanette Prandi Way
San Rafael, CA 94903
415-499-7454
Fax: 415-499-6978

Fair Housing of Marin
Nancy Kenyon, Executive Director
615 B Street
San Rafael, CA 94901-3884
415-457-5025
Fax: 415-457-6382

Northern California Mediation Center
Joan B. Kelly, Executive Director
100 Drake's Landing Road, Suite 150
Greenbrae, CA 94904
415-461-6392
Fax: 415-925-1144
www.ncmc-mediate.org

Mendocino County

Mendocino Dispute Resolution Services
Michael Kisslinger, Director
200 South School Street P.O. Box 205
Ukiah, CA 95482
707-462-7265
Fax: 707-462-2088

Mono County

Center for Settlement Services
Patricia Struckman, Executive Director
P.O. Box 3034
Mammoth Lakes, CA 93546
760-934-7539
Fax: 760-924-8049

Monterey County

Conflict Resolution & Mediation Center of
Monterey County
Dorene L. Matthews, Executive Director
2560 Garden Road, Suite 109
Monterey, CA 93940
831-649-6219; 408-424-4694
Fax: 831-424-6551

Nevada County

Mediation Services of Nevada County
JoAnne Stone, President
P.O. Box 2044
Nevada City, CA 95959
530-478-9107
Fax: 530-478-0318

Orange County

Human Relations Commission
Tina Fernandez, Program Director
Alfonso Clarke, Program Coordinator
Community Services Agency
1300 S Grand, Building B
Santa Ana, CA 92705
714-567-7470
Fax: 714-567-7474

Society of St. Vincent de Paul
Institute For Conflict Management
Scott Mather, Program Director
2525 N. Grand, Suite N
Santa Ana, CA 92705
714-288-5600
Fax: 714-288-5619

Fair Housing Council of Orange County
David Quezada, Program Director
Margaret Elder, Program Coordinator
1666 North Main, Suite 500
Santa Ana, CA 92701
714-569-0825
Fax: 714-835-0281

Placer County

Placer County Dispute Resolution Service
Pat Malberg and Cynthia Spears, Program Managers
P.O. Box 4944
Auburn, CA 95604-4944
530-645-9260
Fax: 530-645-9260
cds@2xtreme.net

Riverside County

Dispute Resolution Center
Rosetta Runnels, Program Coordinator
Department of Community Action
2038 Iowa Avenue, Suite B102
Riverside, CA 92507
909-955-4903
Fax: 909-955-6506

Riverside County Bar Association
County Coordinator: Ron Hulbert
Larson Justice Center
Indio, CA 92201
760-863-8935
rhulbert@co.riverside.ca.us

Sacramento County

Citizenship & Law Related Education Center (CLR)
Joseph P. Maloney, Executive Director
9738 Lincoln Village Drive
Sacramento, CA 95827
916-228-2322
Fax: 916-228-2493

Sacramento Mediation Center
Kathleen Stanbrough, Executive Director
2131 Capitol Avenue, Suite 205
Sacramento, CA 95816
916-441-7979
Fax: 916-441-3645

Arts, Arbitration & Mediation Services
California Lawyers for the Arts (CLA)
Ellen Taylor, Program Coordinator
926 J Street, Suite 811
Sacramento, CA 95814
916-442-6210
Fax: 916-442-6281

San Bernadino County

Inland Fair Housing and Mediation Board
Betty Davidow, Executive Director
1005 Begonia Avenue
Ontario, CA 91762
909-984-2254
Fax: 909-460-0274

Inland Valleys Justice Center, Inc.
J. C. Tambe, Program Administrator
401 S. Main Street, Suite 211
Pomona, CA 91766
909-629-6301
Fax: 909-629-1607

San Diego

San Diego Mediation Center
Liz O'Brien, President
625 Broadway Street, Suite 1221
San Diego, CA 92110
619-238-2400
Fax: 619-238-8041

North County Lifeline
Shirley Cole, Director
Pete Rivas, Supervisor
200 Jefferson Street
Vista, CA 92084
760-726-6396
Fax: 760-726-6102
privas@nclifeline.com

Peacemaking Institute
Clive Gill, Executive Director
1845 Ithaca Drive
Vista, California 92083
760-727-0537
clivegill@aol.com

San Francisco County

California Community Dispute Services
Charles Boneck, Program Director
Thom Bateman, Chairman
502 7th Street
San Francisco, CA 94103
415-865-2520
Fax: 415-865-2538

California Lawyers for the Arts
Alma Robinson, Executive Director
Fort Mason Center
Building C-255
San Francisco, CA 94123
415-775-7200 ext 762
Fax: 415-775-1143

San Joaquin County

Mediation Center of San Joaquin County
www.mediatorsrus.org

San Luis Obispo County

The Conflict Resolution Program
of the Central Coast
Kimberly Rosa, Director
265 South Street, Suite B
San Luis Obispo, CA 93401
805-549-0442

San Mateo County

Small Claims Mediation Program
Ana Navarro, Coordinator
520 S. El Camino Real, Suite 640
San Mateo, CA 94402
650-373-3496
Fax: 650-373-3495

Peninsula Conflict Resolution Center
Patricia Brown, Executive Director
520 S. El Camino Real, Suite 640
San Mateo, CA 94402
650-373-3490
Fax: 650-373-3495

Santa Barbara County

City of Santa Barbara Rental Housing
Mediation Task Force
423 West Victoria Street
Santa Barbara, CA 93101
805-730-1523

Isla Vista Mediation Project
970 Embarcadero Del Mar, Suite C
Isla Vista, CA 93117
805-968-5158

Community Mediation Program
906 Garden Street
Santa Barbara, CA 93101
805-963-6765

Santa Clara County

Office of Human Relations of Santa Clara County
Dispute Resolution Program Services
James P. McEntee, Director
70 West Hedding Lower Level, West Wing
San Jose, CA 95110
408-299-2206
Fax: 408-297-2463

Project Sentinel Rental Housing Mediation Program
Ann Marquart, Executive Director
Anika Stevensl, Dispute Resolution
1055 Sunnyvale Saratoga Road, Suite 3
Sunnyvale, CA 94087
408-720-9888
Fax: 408-720-0810

Pro Bono Project
John D. Hedges, ADR Coordinator
P.O. Box 103
San Jose, CA 95103-0103
408-998-5298
Fax: 408-971-9672

Court-Based Alternative Dispute Resolution
Mark Nance, Director, ADR Project Manager
Superior Court of California,County of Santa Clara
191 North First Street
San Jose, CA 95113
408-299-3232 ext 516
Fax: 408-885-9527

Santa Cruz County

Conflict Resolution Center
(Pre-filing and Small Claims Mediation Programs)
Nancy Heishman, Program Director
783 Rio Del Mar Boulevard, Suite 65
Aptos, CA 95003
408-685-3403
Fax: 408-685-1254

Santa Cruz County Bar Association
(Civil Mediation Program)
Gary Haraldsen, Administrator
340 Soquel Ave., Suite 209
Santa Cruz, CA 95062
831-662-8111
Fax: 831-768-0461

Solano County

Dispute Resolution Service
Solano County Bar Association (Small Claims)
Carol Lucas, Executive Director
744 Empire Street, Suite 100
Fairfield, CA 94533
707-422-5087
Fax: 707-422-3860

Sonoma County

Redwood Empire Conflict Resolution
Services-Recourse
Dorri Safford, Program Administrator
1212 4th Street, Suite I
Santa Rosa, CA 95404
707-525-8545

Ventura County

Ventura Center for Dispute Settlement
Claudia Young, Executive Director
4475 Market Street, Suite C
Ventura, CA 93003-7756
805-650-9202
Fax: 805-650-9243

Yolo County

Community Mediation Service
Elvia Garcia-Ayala, Program Director
604 2nd Street
Davis, CA 95616
530-757-5623
Fax: 530-757-6628

Appendix C
California Small
Claims Statutes
and Rules

The statutory law that governs the small claims court is found in the Small Claims Act, covered in CCP Sections 116.110–116.950. It is also covered under California Rules of Court 151–156,244, 1701–1706, 1725–1727.

116.110. This chapter shall be known and may be cited as "The Small Claims Act."

116.120. The Legislature hereby finds and declares as follows:

(a) Individual minor civil disputes are of special importance to the parties and of significant social and economic consequence collectively.

(b) In order to resolve minor civil disputes expeditiously, inexpensively, and fairly, it is essential to provide a judicial forum accessible to all parties directly involved in resolving these disputes.

(C) The small claims divisions have been established to provide a forum to resolve minor civil disputes, and for that reason constitute a fundamental element in the administration of justice and the protection of the rights and property of individuals.

(d) The small claims divisions, the provisions of this chapter, and the rules of the Judicial Council regarding small claims actions shall operate to ensure that the convenience of parties and witnesses who are individuals shall prevail, to the extent possible, over the convenience of any other parties or witnesses.

116.130. In this chapter, unless the context indicates otherwise:

(a) "Plaintiff" means the party who has filed a small claims action; the term includes a defendant who has filed a claim against a plaintiff.

(b) "Defendant" means the party against whom the plaintiff has filed a small claims action; the term includes a plaintiff against whom a defendant has filed a claim.

(c) "Judgment creditor" means the party, whether plaintiff or defendant, in whose favor a money judgment has been rendered.

(d) "Judgment debtor" means the party, whether plaintiff or defendant, against whom a money judgment has been rendered.

(e) "Person" means an individual, corporation, partnership, limited liability company, firm, association, or other entity.

(f) "Individual" means a natural person.

(g) "Party" means a plaintiff or defendant.

(h) "Motion" means a party's written request to the court for an order or other action; the term includes an informal written request to the court, such as a letter.

(I) "Declaration" means a written statement signed by an individual which includes the date and place of signing, and a statement under penalty of perjury that its contents are true and correct.

(j) "Good cause" means circumstances sufficient to justify the requested order or other action, as determined by the judge.

(k) "Mail" means first-class mail with postage fully prepaid, unless stated otherwise.

116.140. The following do not apply in small claims actions:

(a) Subdivision (a) of Section 1013 and subdivision (b) of Section 1005, on the extension of the time for taking action when notice is given by mail.

(b) Title 6.5 (commencing with Section 481.010) of Part 2, on the issuance of prejudgment attachments.

116.210. In each municipal court and each superior court in a county in which there is no municipal court, there shall be a small claims division. The small claims division may be known as the small claims court.

116.220.

(a) The small claims court shall have jurisdiction in the following actions:

(1) Except as provided in subdivisions (c), (e), and (f), for recovery of money, if the amount of the demand does not exceed five thousand dollars ($5,000).

(2) Except as provided in subdivisions (c), (e), and (f), to enforce payment of delinquent unsecured personal property taxes in an amount not to exceed five thousand dollars ($5,000), if the legality of the tax is not contested by the defendant.

(3) To issue the writ of possession authorized by Sections 1861.5 and 1861.10 of the Civil Code if the amount of the demand does not exceed five thousand dollars ($5,000).

(4) To confirm, correct, or vacate a fee arbitration award not exceeding five thousand dollars ($5,000) between an attorney and client that is binding or has become binding, or to conduct a hearing de novo between an attorney and client after nonbinding arbitration of a fee dispute involving no more than five thousand dollars ($5,000) in controversy, pursuant to Article 13(commencing with Section 6200) of Chapter 4 of Division 3 of the Business and Professions Code.

(b) In any action seeking relief authorized by subdivision (a), the court may grant equitable relief in the form of rescission, restitution, reformation, and specific performance, in lieu of, or in addition to, money damages. The court may issue a conditional judgment. The court shall retain jurisdiction until full payment and performance of any judgment or order.

(c) Notwithstanding subdivision (a), the small claims court shall have jurisdiction over a defendant guarantor who is required to respond based upon the default, actions, or omissions of another, only if the demand does not exceed (1) two thousand five hundred dollars ($2,500), or (2) on and after January 1, 2000, four thousand dollars ($4,000), if the defendant guarantor charges a fee for its guarantor or surety services or the defendant guarantor is the Registrar of the Contractors' State License Board.

(d) In any case in which the lack of jurisdiction is due solely to an excess in the amount of the demand, the excess may be waived, but any waiver shall not become operative until judgment.

(e) Notwithstanding subdivision (a), in any action filed by a plaintiff incarcerated in a Department of Corrections facility or a Youth Authority facility, the small claims court shall have jurisdiction over a defendant only if the plaintiff has alleged in the complaint that he or she has exhausted his or her administrative remedies against that department, including compliance with Sections 905.2 and 905.4 of the Government Code. The final administrative adjudication or determination of the plaintiff's administrative claim by the department may be attached to the complaint at the time of filing in lieu of that allegation.

(f) In any action governed by subdivision (e), if the plaintiff fails to provide proof of compliance with the requirements of subdivision (e) at the time of trial, the judicial officer shall, at his or her discretion, either dismiss the action or continue the action to give the plaintiff an opportunity to provide such proof.

(g) For purposes of this section, "department" includes an employee of a department against whom a claim has been filed under this chapter arising out of his or her duties as an employee of that department.

116.230.

(a) A fee of twenty dollars ($20) shall be charged and collected for the filing of a claim if the number of claims previously filed by the party in each court within the previous 12 months is 12 or less; and a fee of thirty-five dollars ($35) shall be collected for the filing of any additional claims.

(b) A fee to cover the actual cost of court service by mail, adjusted upward to the nearest dollar, shall be charged and collected for each defendant to whom the court clerk mails a copy of the claim under Section 116.340.

(c) The number of claims filed by a party during the previous 12 months shall be determined by a declaration by the party stating the number of claims so filed and submitted to the clerk with the current claim.

(d) Five dollars ($5) of the fees authorized in subdivision (a) shall be deposited upon collection in the special account in the county treasury established pursuant to subdivision (b) of Section 68085 of the Government Code, and transmitted therefrom monthly to the Controller for deposit in the Trial Court Trust Fund.

116.231.

(a) Except as provided in subdivision (d), no person may file more than two small claims actions in which the amount demanded exceeds two thousand five hundred dollars ($2,500), anywhere in the state in any calendar year.

(b) Except as provided in subdivision (d), if the amount demanded in any small claims action exceeds two thousand five hundred dollars ($2,500), the party making the demand shall file a declaration under penalty of perjury attesting to the fact that not more than two small claims actions in which the amount of the demand exceeded two thousand five hundred dollars ($2,500) have been filed by that party in this state within the calendar year.

(c) The Legislature finds and declares that the pilot project conducted under the authority of Chapter 1196 of the Statutes of 1991 demonstrated the efficacy of the removal of the limitation on the number of actions public entities may file in the small claims courts on claims exceeding two thousand five hundred dollars ($2,500).

(d) The limitation on the number of filings exceeding two thousand five hundred dollars ($2,500) does not apply to filings where the claim does not exceed five thousand dollars ($5,000) that are filed by a city, county, city and county, school district, county office of education, community college district, local district, or any other local public entity. If any small claims action is filed by a city, county, city and county, school district, county office of education, community college district, local district, or any other local public entity pursuant to this section, and the defendant informs the court either in advance of the hearing by written notice or at the time of the hearing, that he or she is represented in the action by legal counsel, the action shall be transferred out of the small claims division. A city, county, city and county, school district, county office of education, community college district, local district, or any other local public entity may not file a claim within the small claims division if the amount of the demand exceeds five thousand dollars ($5,000).

116.240. With the consent of the parties who appear at the hearing, the court may order a case to be heard by a temporary judge who is a member of the State Bar, and who has been sworn and empowered to act until final determination of the case.

116.250.

(a) Sessions of the small claims court may be scheduled at any time and on any day, including Saturdays, but excluding other judicial holidays. They may also be scheduled at any public building within the judicial district, including places outside the courthouse.

(b) Each small claims division of a municipal court with four or more judicial officers, and each small claims division of a superior court with seven or more judicial officers, shall conduct at least one night session or Saturday session each month for the purpose of hearing small claims cases other than small claims appeals. The term "session" includes, but is not limited to, a proceeding conducted by a member of the State Bar acting as a mediator or referee.

116.260. In each county, individual assistance shall be made available to advise small claims litigants and potential litigants without charge as provided in Section 116.940 and by rules adopted by the Judicial Council.

116.270. Any small claims division may use law clerks to assist the judge with legal research of small claims cases.

116.310.

(a) No formal pleading other than the claim described in Section 116.320 or 116.380, is necessary to initiate a small claims action.

(b) The pretrial discovery procedures described in subdivision (a) of Section 2019 are not permitted in small claims actions.

116.320.

(a) A plaintiff may commence an action in the small claims court by filing a claim under oath with the clerk of the small claims court in person or by mail.

(b) The claim form shall be a simple nontechnical form approved or adopted by the Judicial Council. The claim form shall set forth a place for (1) the name and address of the defendant, if known; (2) the amount and the basis of the claim; (3) that the plaintiff, where possible, has demanded payment and, in applicable cases, possession of the property; (4) that the defendant has failed or refused to pay, and, where applicable, has refused to surrender the property; and (5) that the plaintiff understands that the judgment on his or her claim will be conclusive and without a right of appeal.

(c) The form or accompanying instructions shall include information that the plaintiff (1) may not be represented by an attorney, (2) has no right of appeal, and (3) may ask the court to waive fees for filing and serving the claim on the ground that the plaintiff is unable to pay them, using the forms approved by the Judicial Council for that purpose.

116.330.

(a) When a claim is filed, the clerk shall schedule the case for hearing in accordance with subdivision (c) and shall issue an order directing the parties to appear at the time set for the hearing with witnesses and documents to prove their claim or defense.

(b) In lieu of the method of setting the case for hearing described in subdivision (a), at the time a claim is filed the clerk may do all of the following:

(1) Cause a copy of the claim to be mailed to the defendant by any form of mail providing for a return receipt.

(2) On receipt of proof that the claim was served as provided in paragraph (1), issue an order scheduling the case for hearing in accordance with subdivision (c) and directing the parties to appear at the time set for the hearing with witnesses and documents to prove their claim or defense.

(3) Cause a copy of the order setting the case for hearing and directing the parties to appear, to be served upon the parties by any form of mail providing for a return receipt.

(c) If the defendant resides in the county in which the action is filed, the case shall be scheduled for hearing at least 15 days but not more than 40 days from the date of the order. If the defendant besides outside the county in which the action is filed, the case shall be scheduled for hearing at least 30 days but not more than 70 days from the date of the order.

(d) If there are two or more defendants and one or more of them resides outside the county in which the action is filed, the date for the appearance of all the defendants shall be at least 30 days but not more than 70 days from the date of the order.

(e) A public entity, as defined in Section 811.2 of the Government Code, which files more than 10 claims at one time may request a date for the appearance of the defendant later than that otherwise specified in this section, and the clerk may set the case for hearing at that later date subject to the following limits:

(1) If all defendants reside in the county in which the action is filed, the date for appearance shall not be more than 70 days from the date of the order.

(2) In other cases, the date for appearance shall not be more than 90 days from the date of the order.

116.340.

(a) Service of the claim and order on the defendant may be made by any one of the following methods:

(1) The clerk may cause a copy of the claim and order to be mailed to the defendant by any form of mail providing for a return receipt.

(2) The plaintiff may cause a copy of the claim and order to be delivered to the defendant in person.

(3) The plaintiff may cause service of a copy of the claim and order to be made by substituted service as provided in subdivision (a) or (b) of Section 415.20 without the need to attempt personal service on the defendant. For these purposes, substituted service as provided in subdivision (b) of Section 415.20 may be made at the office of the sheriff or marshal who shall deliver a copy of the claim and order to any person authorized by the defendant to receive service, as provided in Section 416.90, who is at least 18 years of age, and thereafter mailing a copy of the claim and order to the defendant's usual mailing address.

(4) The clerk may cause a copy of the claim to be mailed, the order to be issued, and a copy of the order to be mailed as provided in subdivision (b) of Section 116.330.

(b) Service of the claim and order on the defendant shall be completed at least 10 days before the hearing date if the defendant resides within the county in which the action is filed, or at least 15 days before the hearing date if the defendant resides outside the county in which the action is filed.

(c) Service by the methods described in subdivision (a) shall be deemed complete on the date that the defendant signs the mail return receipt, on the date of the personal service, as provided in Section 415.20, or as established by other competent evidence, whichever applies to the method of service used.

(d) Service shall be made within this state, except as provided in subdivisions (e) and (f).

(e) The owner of record of real property in California who resides in another state and who has no lawfully designated agent in California for service of process may be served by any of the methods described in this section if the claim relates to that property.

(f) A nonresident owner or operator of a motor vehicle involved in an accident within this state may be served pursuant to the provisions on constructive service in Sections 17450 to 17461,inclusive, of the Vehicle Code without regard to whether the defendant was a nonresident at the time of the accident or when the claim was filed. Service shall be made by serving both the Director of the California Department of Motor Vehicles and the defendant, and may be made by any of the methods authorized by this chapter or by registered mail as authorized by Section 17454 or 17455 of the Vehicle Code.

(g) If an action is filed against a principal and his or her guaranty or surety pursuant to a guarantor or suretyship agreement, a reasonable attempt shall be made to complete service on the principal. If service is not completed on the principal, the action shall be transferred to the court of appropriate jurisdiction.

116.360.

(a) The defendant may file a claim against the plaintiff in the same action in an amount not to exceed the jurisdictional limits stated in Sections 116.220 and 116.231. The claim need not relate to the same subject or event as the plaintiff's claim.

(b) The defendant's claim shall be filed and served in the manner provided for filing and serving a claim of the plaintiff under
Sections 116.330 and 116.340.

(c) The defendant shall cause a copy of the claim and order to be served on the plaintiff at least five days before the hearing date, unless the defendant was served 10 days or less before the hearing date, in which event the defendant shall cause a copy of the defendant's claim and order to be served on the plaintiff at least one day before the hearing date.

116.370.

(a) Venue in small claims actions shall be the same as in other civil actions.

(b) A defendant may challenge venue by writing to the court and mailing a copy of the challenge to each of the other parties to the action, without personally appearing at the hearing.

(c) In all cases, including those in which the defendant does not either challenge venue or appear at the hearing, the court shall inquire into the facts sufficiently to determine whether venue is proper, and shall make its determination accordingly.

(1) If the court determines that the action was not commenced in the proper venue, the court, on its own motion, shall dismiss the action without prejudice unless all defendants are present and agree that the action may be heard.

(2) If the court determines that the action was commenced in the proper venue, the court may hear the case if all parties are present. If the defendant challenged venue and all parties are not present, the court shall postpone the hearing for at least 15 days and shall notify all parties by mail of the court's decision and the new hearing date, time, and place.

116.390.

(a) If a defendant has a claim against a plaintiff that exceeds the jurisdictional limits stated in Sections 116.220 and 116.231, and the claim relates to the contract, transaction, matter, or event which is the subject of the plaintiff's claim, the defendant may commence an action against the plaintiff in a court of competent jurisdiction and request the small claims court to transfer the small claims action to that court.

(b) The defendant may make the request by filing with the small claims court in which the plaintiff commenced the action, at or before the time set for the hearing of that action, a declaration stating the facts concerning the defendant's action against the plaintiff with a true copy of the complaint so filed by the defendant against the plaintiff and the sum of one dollar ($1) for a transmittal fee. The defendant shall cause a copy of the declaration and complaint to be personally delivered to the plaintiff at or before the time set for the hearing of the small claims action.

(c) In ruling on a motion to transfer, the small claims court may do any of the following: (1) render judgment on the small claims case prior to the transfer; (2) not render judgment and transfer the small claims case; (3) refuse to transfer the small claims case on the grounds that the ends of justice would not be served. If the small claims action is transferred prior to judgment, both actions shall be tried together in the transferee court.

(d) When the small claims court orders the action transferred, it shall transmit all files and papers to the transferee court.

(e) The plaintiff in the small claims action shall not be required to pay to the clerk of the transferee court any transmittal, appearance, or filing fee unless the plaintiff appears in the transferee court, in which event the plaintiff shall be required to pay the filing fee and any other fee required of a defendant in the transferee court. However, if the transferee court rules against the plaintiff in the action filed in that court, the court may award to the defendant in that action the costs incurred as a consequence of the transfer, including attorney's fees and filing fees.

CALIFORNIA CODES
CODE OF CIVIL PROCEDURE
SECTION 116.410-116.430

116.410.

(a) Any person who is at least 18 years of age and mentally competent may be a party to a small claims action.

(b) A minor or incompetent person may appear by a guardian ad litem appointed by a judge of the court in which the action is filed.

116.420.

(a) No claim shall be filed or maintained in small claims court by the assignee of the claim.

(b) This section does not prevent the filing or defense of an action in the small claims court by (1) a trustee in bankruptcy in the exercise of the trustee's duties as trustee, or (2) by the holder of a security agreement, retail installment contract, or lien contract subject to the Unruh Act (Chapter 1 (commencing with Section 1801) of Title 2 of Part 4 of Division 3 of the Civil Code) or the Automobile Sales Finance Act (Chapter 2b (commencing with Section 2981) of Title 14 of Part 4 of Division 3 of the Civil Code), purchased by the holder for the holder's portfolio of investments, provided that the holder is not an assignee for the purpose of collection.

(c) This section does not prevent the filing in small claims court by a local government which is self-insured for purposes of workers' compensation and is seeking subrogation pursuant to Section 3852 of the Labor Code.

116.430.

(a) If the plaintiff operates or does business under a fictitious business name and the claim relates to that business, the claim shall be accompanied by the filing of a declaration stating that the plaintiff has complied with the fictitious business name laws by executing, filing, and publishing a fictitious business name statement as required.

(b) A small claims action filed by a person who has not complied with the applicable fictitious business name laws by executing, filing, and publishing a fictitious business name statement as required shall be dismissed without prejudice.

(c) For purposes of this section, "fictitious business name" means the term as defined in Section 17900 of the Business and Professions Code, and "fictitious business name statement" means the statement described in Section 17913 of the Business and Professions Code.

CALIFORNIA CODES
CODE OF CIVIL PROCEDURE
SECTION 116.510-116.570

116.510. The hearing and disposition of the small claims action shall be informal, the object being to dispense justice promptly, fairly, and inexpensively.

116.520.

(a) The parties have the right to offer evidence by witnesses at the hearing or, with the permission of the court, at another time.

(b) If the defendant fails to appear, the court shall still require the plaintiff to present evidence to prove his or her claim.

(c) The court may consult witnesses informally and otherwise investigate the controversy with or without notice to the parties.

116.530.

(a) Except as permitted by this section, no attorney may take part in the conduct or defense of a small claims action.

(b) Subdivision (a) does not apply if the attorney is appearing to maintain or defend an action (1) by or against himself or herself, (2) by or against a partnership in which he or she is a general partner and in which all the partners are attorneys, or (3) by or against a professional corporation of which he or she is an officer or director and of which all other officers and directors are attorneys.

(c) Nothing in this section shall prevent an attorney from (1) providing advice to a party to a small claims action, either before or after the commencement of the action; (2) testifying to facts of which he or she has personal knowledge and about which he or she is competent to testify; (3) representing a party in an appeal to the superior court; and (4) representing a party in connection with the enforcement of a judgment.

116.531. Nothing in this article shall prevent a representative of an insurer or other expert in the matter before the small claims court from rendering assistance to a party in the litigation except during the conduct of the hearing, either before or after the commencement of the action, unless otherwise prohibited by law; nor shall anything in this article prevent those individuals from testifying to facts of which they have personal knowledge and about which they are competent to testify.

116.540.

(a) Except as permitted by this section, no individual other than the plaintiff and the defendant may take part in the conduct or defense of a small claims action.

(b) A corporation may appear and participate in a small claims action only through a regular employee, or a duly appointed or elected officer or director, who is employed, appointed, or elected for purposes other than solely representing the corporation in small claims court.

(c) A party who is not a corporation or a natural person may appear and participate in a small claims action only through a regular employee, or a duly appointed or elected officer or director, or in the case of a partnership, a partner, engaged for purposes other than solely representing the party in small claims court.

(d) If a party is an individual doing business as a sole proprietorship, the party may appear and participate in a small claims action by a representative and without personally appearing if both of the following conditions are met:

(1) The claim can be proved or disputed by evidence of an account that constitutes a business record as defined in Section 1271 of the Evidence Code, and there is no other issue of fact in the case.

(2) The representative is a regular employee of the party for purposes other than solely representing the party in small claims actions and is qualified to testify to the identity and mode of preparation of the business record.

(e) A plaintiff is not required to personally appear, and may submit declarations to serve as evidence supporting his or her claim or allow another individual to appear and participate on his or her behalf, if

(1) the plaintiff is serving on active duty in the United States armed forces outside this state,

(2) the plaintiff was assigned to his or her duty station after his or her claim arose,

(3) the assignment is for more than six months,

(4) the representative is serving without compensation, and

(5) the representative has appeared in small claims actions on behalf of others no more than four times during the calendar year.

The defendant may file a claim in the same action in an amount not to exceed the jurisdictional limits stated in Sections 116.220 and 116.231.

(f) A party incarcerated in a county jail, a Department of Corrections facility, or a Youth Authority facility is not required to personally appear, and may submit declarations to serve as evidence supporting his or her claim, or may authorize another individual to appear and participate on his or her behalf if that individual is serving without compensation and has appeared in small claims actions on behalf of others no more than four times during the calendar year.

(g) A defendant who is a nonresident owner of real property may defend against a claim relating to that property without personally appearing by (1) submitting written declarations to serve as evidence supporting his or her defense, (2) allowing another individual to appear and participate on his or her behalf if that individual is serving without compensation and has appeared in small claims actions on behalf of others no more than four times during the calendar year, or (3) taking the action described in both (1) and (2).

(h) A party who is an owner of rental real property may appear and participate in a small claims action through a property agent under contract with the owner to manage the rental of that property, if (1) the owner has retained the property agent principally to manage the rental of that property and not principally to represent the owner in small claims court, and (2) the claim relates to the rental property.

(I) At the hearing of a small claims action, the court shall require any individual who is appearing as a representative of a party under subdivisions (b) to (h), inclusive, to file a declaration stating (1) that the individual is authorized to appear for the party, and (2) the basis for that authorization. If the representative is appearing under subdivision (b), (c), (d), or (h), the declaration also shall state that the individual is not employed solely to represent the party in small claims court. If the representative is appearing under subdivision (e), (f), or (g), the declaration also shall state that the representative is serving without compensation, and has appeared in small claims actions on behalf of others no more than four times during the calendar year.

(j) A husband or wife who sues or who is sued with his or her spouse may appear and participate on behalf of his or her spouse if (1) the claim is a joint claim, (2) the represented spouse has given his or her consent, and (3) the

court determines that the interests of justice would be served.

(k) If the court determines that a party cannot properly present his or her claim or defense and needs assistance, the court may in its discretion allow another individual to assist that party.

(l) Nothing in this section shall operate or be construed to authorize an attorney to participate in a small claims action except as expressly provided in Section 116.530.

116.541.

(a) Notwithstanding Section 116.540 or any other provision of law, the Department of Corrections or the Department of the Youth Authority may appear and participate in a small claims action through a regular employee, who is employed or appointed for purposes other than solely representing that department in small claims court.

(b) Where the Department of Corrections or the Department of the Youth Authority is named as a defendant in small claims court, the representative of the department is not required to personally appear to challenge the plaintiff's compliance with the pleading requirements and may submit pleadings or declarations to assert that challenge.

(c) At the hearing of a small claims action, the court shall require any individual who is appearing as a representative of the Department of Corrections or the Department of the Youth Authority under subdivision (a) to file a declaration stating (1) that the individual is authorized to appear for the party, (2) the basis for that authorization, and (3) that the individual is not employed solely to represent the party in small claims court.

(d) Nothing in this section shall operate or be construed to authorize an attorney to participate in a small claims action except as expressly provided in Section 116.530.

(e) For purposes of this section, all references to the Department of Corrections or the Department of the Youth Authority include an employee thereof, against whom a claim has been filed under this chapter arising out of his or her duties as an employee of that department.

116.550.

(a) If the court determines that a party does not speak or understand English sufficiently to comprehend the proceedings or give testimony, and needs assistance in so doing, the court may permit another individual (other than an attorney) to assist that party.

(b) Each small claims court shall make a reasonable effort to maintain and make available to the parties a list of interpreters who are able and willing to aid parties in small claims actions either for no fee, or for a fee which is reasonable considering the nature and complexity of the claims. The list shall include interpreters for all languages that require interpretation before the court, as determined by the court in its discretion and in view of the court's experience.

(c) Failure to maintain a list of interpreters, or failure to include an interpreter for a particular language, shall not invalidate any proceedings before the court.

(d) If a court interpreter or other competent interpreter is not available to aid a party in a small claims action, at the first hearing of the case the court shall postpone the hearing one time only to allow the party the opportunity to obtain another individual (other than an attorney) to assist that party. Any additional continuances shall be at the discretion of the court.

116.560.

(a) Whenever a claim that is filed against a person operating or doing business under a fictitious business name relates to the defendant's business, the court shall inquire at the time of the hearing into the defendant's correct legal name and the name or names under which the defendant does business. If the correct legal name of the defendant, or the name actually used by the defendant, is other than the name stated on the claim, the court shall amend the claim to state the correct legal name of the defendant, and the name or names actually used by the defendant.

(b) The plaintiff may request the court at any time, whether before or after judgment, to amend the plaintiff's claim or judgment to include both the correct legal name and the name or names actually used by the defendant. Upon a showing of good cause, the court shall amend the claim or judgment to state the correct legal name of the defendant, and the name or names actually used by the defendant.

(c) For purposes of this section, "fictitious business name" means the term as defined in Section 17900 of the Business and Professions Code.

116.570.

(a) Any party may submit a written request for postponement of a hearing date.

(1) The written request may be made either by letter or on a form adopted or approved by the Judicial Council.

(2) On the date of making the written request, the requesting party shall mail or personally deliver a copy to each of the other parties to the action.

(3) (A) If the court finds that the interests of justice would be served by postponing the hearing, the court shall postpone the hearing, and shall notify all parties by mail of the new hearing date, time, and place. (B) On one occasion, upon the written request of a defendant guarantor, the court shall postpone the hearing for at least 30 days, and the court shall take this action without a hearing. Nothing in this subparagraph, however, shall limit the discretion of the court to grant additional postponements under subparagraph (A).

(4) The court shall provide a prompt response by mail to any person making a written request for postponement of a hearing date under this subdivision.

(b) If service of the claim and order upon the defendant is not completed within the number of days before the hearing date required by subdivision (b) of Section 116.340, and the defendant has not personally appeared and has not requested a postponement, the court shall postpone the hearing for at least 15 days. If a postponement is ordered under this subdivision, the clerk shall promptly notify all parties by mail of the new hearing date, time, and place.

(c) Nothing in this section limits the inherent power of the court to order postponements of hearings in appropriate circumstances.

(d) A fee of ten dollars ($10) shall be charged and collected for the filing of a request for postponement and rescheduling of a hearing date after timely service pursuant to subdivision (b) of Section 116.340 has been made upon the defendant.

CALIFORNIA CODES
CODE OF CIVIL PROCEDURE
SECTION 116.610-116.630

116.610.

(a) The small claims court shall give judgment for damages, or equitable relief, or both damages and equitable relief, within the jurisdictional limits stated in Sections 116.220 and116.231, and may make such orders as to time of payment or otherwise as the court deems just and equitable for the resolution of the dispute.

(b) The court may, at its discretion or on request of any party, continue the matter to a later date in order to permit and encourage the parties to attempt resolution by informal or alternative means.

(c) The judgment shall include a determination whether the judgment resulted from a motor vehicle accident on a California highway caused by the defendant's operation of a motor vehicle, or by the operation by some other individual, of a motor vehicle registered in the defendant's name.

(d) If the defendant has filed a claim against the plaintiff, or if the judgment is against two or more defendants, the judgment, and the statement of decision if one is rendered, shall specify the basis for and the character and amount of the liability of each of the parties, including, in the case of multiple judgment debtors, whether liability of each is joint or several.

(e) If specific property is referred to in the judgment, whether t be personal or real, tangible or intangible, the property shall be identified with sufficient detail to permit efficient implementation or enforcement of the judgment.

(f) In an action against several defendants, the court may, in its discretion, render judgment against one or more of them, leaving the action to proceed against the others, whenever a several judgment is proper.

(g) The prevailing party is entitled to the costs of the action, including the costs of serving the order for the appearance of the defendant.

(h) When the court renders judgment, the clerk shall promptly deliver or mail notice of entry of the judgment to the parties, and shall execute a certificate of personal delivery or mailing and place it in the file.

(l) The notice of entry of judgment shall be on a form approved or adopted by the Judicial Council.

116.620.

(a) The judgment debtor shall pay the amount of the judgment either immediately or at the time and upon the terms and conditions, including payment by installments, which the court may order.

(b) The court may at any time, for good cause, upon motion by a party and notice by the clerk to all affected parties at their last known address, amend the terms and conditions for payment of the judgment to provide for payment by installment. The determination shall be made without regard to the nature of the underlying debt and without regard to whether the moving party appeared before entry of the judgment.

(c) In determining the terms and conditions of payment, the court may consider any factors which would be relevant to a claim of exemption under Chapter 4 (commencing with Section 703.010) of Division 2 of Title 9 of Part 2.

116.630. The court may, at any time after judgment, for good cause, upon motion by a party and notice by the clerk to all affected parties at their last known address, amend the name of any party to include both the correct legal name and the actually used name or names of that party.

CALIFORNIA CODES
CODE OF CIVIL PROCEDURE
SECTION 116.710-116.795

116.710.

(a) The plaintiff in a small claims action shall have no right to appeal the judgment on the plaintiff's claim, but a plaintiff who did not appear at the hearing may file a motion to vacate the judgment in accordance with Section 116.720.

(b) The defendant with respect to the plaintiff's claim, and a plaintiff with respect to a claim of the defendant, may appeal the judgment to the superior court in the county in which the action was heard.

(c) With respect to the plaintiff's claim, the insurer of the defendant may appeal the judgment to the superior court in the county in which the matter was heard if the judgment exceeds two thousand five hundred dollars ($2,500) and the insurer stipulates that its policy with the defendant covers the matter to which the judgment applies.

(d) A defendant who did not appear at the hearing has no right to appeal the judgment, but may file a motion to vacate the judgment in accordance with Section 116.730 or 116.740 and also may appeal the denial of that motion.

116.720.

(a) A plaintiff who did not appear at the hearing in the small claims court may file a motion to vacate the judg-

ment with the clerk of the small claims court. The motion shall be filed within 30 days after the clerk has mailed notice of entry of the judgment to the parties.

(b) The clerk shall schedule the hearing on the motion to vacate for a date no earlier than 10 days after the clerk has mailed written notice of the date, time, and place of the hearing to the parties.

(c) Upon a showing of good cause, the small claims court may grant the motion. If the defendant is not present, the court shall hear the motion in the defendant's absence.

(d) If the motion is granted, and if all parties are present and agree, the court may hear the case without rescheduling it. If the defendant is not present, the judge or clerk shall reschedule the case and give notice in accordance with Section 116.330.

116.725. Nothing in this chapter shall be construed to prevent a court from correcting a clerical error in a judgment or from setting aside and vacating a judgment on the ground of an incorrect or erroneous legal basis for the decision.

116.730.

(a) A defendant who did not appear at the hearing in the small claims court may file a motion to vacate the judgment with the clerk of the small claims court. The motion shall be filed within 30 days after the clerk has mailed notice of entry of the judgment to the parties.

(b) The defendant shall appear at any hearing on the motion, or submit written justification for not appearing together with a declaration in support of the motion.

(c) Upon a showing of good cause, the court may grant the motion to vacate the judgment. If the plaintiff is not present, the court shall hear the motion in the plaintiff's absence.

(d) If the motion is granted, and if all parties are present and agree, the court may hear the case without rescheduling it. If the plaintiff is not present, the judge or clerk shall reschedule the case and give notice in accordance with Section 116.330.

(e) If the motion is denied, the defendant may appeal to the superior court only on the denial of the motion to vacate the judgment. The defendant shall file the notice of appeal with the clerk of the small claims court within 10 days after the small claims court has mailed or delivered notice of the court's denial of the motion to vacate the judgment.

(f) If the superior court determines that the defendant's motion to vacate the judgment should have been granted, the superior court may hear the claims of all parties without rescheduling the matter, provided that all parties are present and the defendant has previously complied with this article, or may order the case transferred to the small claims court for a hearing.

116.740.

(a) If the defendant was not properly served as required by Section 116.330 or 116.340 and did not appear at the hearing in the small claims court, the defendant may file a motion to vacate the judgment with the clerk of the small claims court. The motion shall be accompanied by a supporting declaration, and shall be filed within 180 days after the defendant discovers or should have discovered that judgment was entered against the defendant.

(b) The court may order that the enforcement of the judgment shall be suspended pending a hearing and determination of the motion to vacate the judgment.

(c) Upon a showing of good cause, the court may grant the motion to vacate the judgment. If the plaintiff is not present, the court shall hear the motion in the plaintiff's absence.

(d) Subdivisions (d), (e), and (f) of Section 116.730 apply to any motion to vacate a judgment.

116.745. The clerk shall charge and collect fees for the filing of a motion to vacate, as provided by Section 26830 of the Government Code.

116.750.

(a) An appeal from a judgment in a small claims action is taken by filing a notice of appeal with the clerk of the small claims court.

(b) A notice of appeal shall be filed not later than 30 days after the clerk has delivered or mailed notice of entry of the judgment to the parties. A notice of appeal filed after the 30-day period is ineffective for any purpose.

(c) The time for filing a notice of appeal is not extended by the filing of a request to correct a mistake or by virtue of any subsequent proceedings on that request, except that a new period for filing notice of appeal shall begin on the delivery or mailing of notice of entry of any modified judgment.

116.760.

(a) The appealing party shall pay the same fees that are required for an appeal of a limited civil case.

(b) A party who does not appeal shall not be charged any fee for filing any document relating to the appeal.

116.770.

(a) The appeal to the superior court shall consist of a new hearing before a judicial officer other than the judicial officer who heard the action in the small claims division.

(b) The hearing on an appeal to the superior court shall be conducted informally. The pretrial discovery procedures described in subdivision (a) of Section 2019 are not permitted, no party has a right to a trial by jury, and no tentative decision or statement of decision is required.

(c) Article 5 (commencing with Section 116.510) on hearings in the small claims court applies in hearings on appeal in the superior court, except that attorneys may participate.

(d) The scope of the hearing shall include the claims of all parties who were parties to the small claims action at the time the notice of appeal was filed. The hearing shall include the claim of a defendant that was heard in the small claims court.

(e) The clerk of the superior court shall schedule the hearing for the earliest available time and shall mail written notice of the hearing to the parties at least 14 days prior to the time set for the hearing.

(f) The Judicial Council may prescribe by rule the practice and procedure on appeal and the time and manner in which the record on appeal shall be prepared and filed.

116.780.

(a) The judgment of the superior court after a hearing on appeal is final and not appealable.

(b) Article 6 (commencing with Section 116.610) on judgments of the small claims court applies to judgments of the superior court after a hearing on appeal, except as provided in subdivisions (c) and(d).

(c) For good cause and where necessary to achieve substantial justice between the parties, the superior court may award a party to an appeal reimbursement of (1) attorney's fees actually and reasonably incurred in connection with the appeal, not exceeding one hundred fifty dollars ($150), and (2) actual loss of earnings and expenses of transportation and lodging actually and reasonably incurred in connection with the appeal, not exceeding one hundred fifty dollars ($150).

(d) Upon the expiration of 10 days following the completion of the appeal process, the superior court shall order the appeal and any judgment transferred to the small claims court in which the action was originally filed for purposes of enforcement and other proceedings under Article 8 (commencing with Section 116.810) of this chapter.

116.790. If the superior court finds that the appeal was without substantial merit and not based on good faith, but was intended to harass or delay the other party, or to encourage the other party to abandon the claim, the court may award the other party (a) attorney's fees actually and reasonably incurred in connection with the appeal, not exceeding one thousand dollars ($1,000), and (b) any actual loss of earnings and any expenses of transportation and lodging actually and reasonably incurred in connection with the appeal, not exceeding one thousand dollars ($1,000), following a hearing on the matter.

116.795.

(a) The superior court may dismiss the appeal if the appealing party does not appear at the hearing or if the appeal is not heard within one year from the date of filing the notice of appeal with the clerk of the small claims court.

(b) Upon dismissal of an appeal by the superior court, the small claims court shall thereafter have the same jurisdiction as if no appeal had been filed.

116.810.

(a) Enforcement of the judgment of a small claims court, including the issuance or recording of any abstract of the judgment, is automatically suspended, without the filing of a bond by the defendant, until the expiration of the time for appeal.

(b) If an appeal is filed as provided in Article 7 (commencing with Section 116.710), enforcement of the judgment of the small claims court is suspended unless (1) the appeal is dismissed by the superior court pursuant to Section 116.795, or (2) the superior court determines that the small claims court properly denied the defendant's motion to vacate filed under Section 116.730 or 116.740. In either of those events, the judgment of the small claims court may be enforced.

(c) The scope of the suspension of enforcement under this section and, unless otherwise ordered, of any suspension of enforcement ordered by the court, shall include any enforcement procedure described in Title 9 (commencing with Section 680.010) of Part 2 and in Sections 674 and 1174.

CALIFORNIA CODES
CODE OF CIVIL PROCEDURE
SECTION 116.810-116.880

116.820.

(a) The judgment of a small claims court may be enforced as provided in Title 9 (commencing with Section 680.010) of Part 2 and in Sections 674 and 1174 on the enforcement of judgments of other courts. A judgment of the superior court after a hearing on appeal, and after transfer to the small claims court under subdivision (d) of Section 116.780, may be enforced like other judgments of the small claims court, as provided in Title 9 (commencing with Section 680.010) of Part 2 and in Sections 674 and 1174 on the enforcement of judgments of other courts.

(b) Fees as provided in Sections 26828, 26830, and 26834 of the Government Code shall be charged and collected by the clerk for the issuance of a writ of execution, an order of examination of a judgment debtor, or an abstract of judgment.

(c) The prevailing party in any action subject to this chapter is entitled to the costs of enforcing the judgment and accrued interest.

116.830.

(a) At the time judgment is rendered, or notice of entry of the judgment is mailed to the parties, the clerk shall deliver or mail to the judgment debtor a form containing questions regarding the nature and location of any assets of the judgment debtor.

(b) Within 30 days after the clerk has mailed notice of entry of the judgment, unless the judgment has been satisfied, the judgment debtor shall complete the form and cause it to be delivered to the judgment creditor.

(c) In the event a motion is made to vacate the judgment or a notice of appeal is filed, a judgment debtor shall complete and deliver the form within 30 days after the clerk has delivered or mailed notice of denial of the motion to vacate, or notice of dismissal of or entry of judgment on the appeal, whichever is applicable.

(d) In case of the judgment debtor's willful failure to comply with subdivision (b) or (c), the judgment creditor may request the court to apply the sanctions, including arrest and attorney's fees, as provided in Section 708.170, on contempt of court.

(e) The Judicial Council shall approve or adopt the form to be used for the purpose of this section.

116.840.

(a) At the option of the judgment debtor, payment of the judgment may be made either (1) to the judgment creditor in accordance with Section 116.850, or (2) to the court in which the judgment was entered in accordance with Section 116.860.

(b) The small claims court may order entry of satisfaction of judgment in accordance with subdivisions (c) and (d) of Section 116.850, or subdivision (b) of Section 116.860.

116.850.

(a) If full payment of the judgment is made to the judgment creditor or to the judgment creditor's assignee of record, then immediately upon receipt of payment, the judgment creditor or assignee shall file with the clerk of the court an acknowledgment of satisfaction of the judgment.

(b) Any judgment creditor or assignee of record who, after receiving full payment of the judgment and written demand by the judgment debtor, fails without good cause to execute and file an acknowledgment of satisfaction of the judgment with the clerk of the court in which the judgment is entered within 14 days after receiving the request, is liable to the judgment debtor or the judgment debtor's grantees or heirs for all damages sustained by reason of the failure and, in addition, the sum of fifty dollars ($50).

(c) The clerk of the court shall enter a satisfaction of judgment at the request of the judgment debtor if the judgment debtor either (1) establishes a rebuttable presumption of full payment under subdivision (d), or (2) establishes a rebuttable presumption of partial payment under subdivision (d) and complies with subdivision (c) of Section 116.860.

(d) A rebuttable presumption of full or partial payment of the judgment, whichever is applicable, is created if the judgment debtor files both of the following with the clerk of the court in which the judgment was entered:

(1) Either a canceled check or money order for the full or partial amount of the judgment written by the judgment debtor after judgment and made payable to and endorsed by the judgment creditor, or a cash receipt for the full or partial amount of the judgment written by the judgment debtor after judgment and signed by the judgment creditor.

(2) A declaration stating that (A) the judgment debtor has made full or partial payment of the judgment including accrued interest and costs; (B) the judgment

creditor has been requested to file an acknowledgment of satisfaction of the judgment and refuses to do so, or refuses to accept subsequent payments, or the present address of the judgment creditor is unknown; and (c) the documents identified in and accompanying the declaration constitute evidence of the judgment creditor's receipt of full or partial payment.

116.860.

(a) A judgment debtor who desires to make payment to the court in which the judgment was entered may file a request to make payment, which shall be made on a form approved or adopted by the Judicial Council.

(b) Upon the filing of the request to make payment and the payment to the clerk of the amount of the judgment and any accrued interest and costs after judgment, plus any required fee authorized by this section, the clerk shall enter satisfaction of the judgment and shall remit payment to the judgment creditor as provided in this section.

(c) If partial payment of the judgment has been made to the judgment creditor, and the judgment debtor files the declaration and evidence of partial payment described in subdivision (d) of Section 116.850, the clerk shall enter satisfaction of the judgment upon receipt by the clerk of the balance owing on the judgment, including any accrued interest and costs after judgment, and the fee required by this section.

(d) If payment is made by means other than money order, certified or cashier's check, or cash, entry of satisfaction of the judgment shall be delayed for 30 days.

(e) The clerk shall notify the judgment creditor, at his or her last known address, that the judgment debtor has satisfied the judgment by making payment to the court. The notification shall explain the procedures which the judgment creditor has to follow to receive payment.

(f) For purposes of this section, "costs after judgment" consist of only those costs itemized in a memorandum of costs filed by the judgment creditor or otherwise authorized by the court.

(g) Payments that remain unclaimed shall go to the local agency pursuant to Sections 50050 to 50056, inclusive, of the Government Code.

(h) The board of supervisors shall set a fee, not to exceed the actual costs of administering this section, up to a maximum of twenty-five dollars ($25), which shall be paid by the judgment debtor.

116.870. Sections 16250 to 16381, inclusive, of the Vehicle Code, regarding the suspension of the judgment debtor's privilege to operate a motor vehicle for failing to satisfy a judgment, apply if the judgment (1) was for damage to property in excess of five hundred dollars ($500) or for bodily injury to, or death of, any person in any amount, and (2) resulted from the operation of a motor vehicle upon a California highway by the defendant, or by any other person for whose conduct the defendant was liable, unless the liability resulted from the defendant's signing the application of a minor for a driver's license.

116.880.

(a) If the judgment

(1) was for five hundred dollars ($500) or less,

(2) resulted from a motor vehicle accident occurring on a California highway caused by the defendant's operation of a motor vehicle, and

(3) has remained unsatisfied for more than 90 days after the judgment became final, the judgment creditor may file with the Department of Motor Vehicles a notice requesting a suspension of the judgment debtor's privilege to operate a motor vehicle.

(b) The notice shall state that the judgment has not been satisfied, and shall be accompanied by

(1) a fee set by the department,

(2) the judgment of the court determining that the judgment resulted from a motor vehicle accident occurring on a California highway caused by the judgment debtor's operation of a motor vehicle, and

(3) a declaration that the judgment has not been satisfied. The fee shall be used by the department to finance the costs of administering this section and shall not exceed the department's actual costs.

(c) Upon receipt of a notice, the department shall attempt to notify the judgment debtor by telephone, if possible, otherwise by certified mail, that the judgment debtor's privilege to operate a motor vehicle will be suspended for a period of 90 days, beginning 20 days after receipt of notice by the department from the judgment creditor, unless satisfactory proof, as provided in subdivision (e), is provided to the department before that date.

(d) At the time the notice is filed, the department shall give the judgment creditor a copy of the notice, which shall indicate the filing fee paid by the judgment creditor, and shall include a space to be signed by the judgment creditor acknowledging payment of the judgment by the judgment debtor. The judgment creditor shall mail or deliver a signed copy of the acknowledgment to the judgment debtor once the judgment is satisfied.

(e) The department shall terminate the suspension, or the suspension proceedings, upon the occurrence of any of the following:

(1) Receipt of proof that the judgment has been satisfied, either

(A) by a copy of the notice required by this section signed by the judgment creditor acknowledging satisfaction of the judgment, or (

B) by a declaration of the judgment debtor stating that the judgment has been satisfied.

(2) Receipt of proof that the judgment debtor is complying with a court-ordered payment schedule.

(3) Proof that the judgment debtor had insurance covering the accident sufficient to satisfy the judgment.

(4) A deposit with the department of the amount of the unsatisfied judgment, if the judgment debtor presents proof, satisfactory to the department, of inability to locate the judgment creditor.

(5) At the end of 90 days.

(f) When the suspension has been terminated under subdivision (e), the action is final and may not be reinstituted. Whenever the suspension is terminated, Section 14904 of the Vehicle Code shall apply. Money deposited with the department under this section shall be handled in the same manner as money deposited under subdivision (d) of Section 16377 of the Vehicle Code.

(g) No public agency is liable for any injury caused by the suspension, termination of suspension, or the failure to suspend any person's privilege to operate a motor vehicle as authorized by this section.

CALIFORNIA CODES
CODE OF CIVIL PROCEDURE
SECTION 116.910-116.950

116.910.

(a) Except as provided in this chapter (including, but not limited to, Section 116.230), no fee or charge shall be collected by any officer for any service provided under this chapter.

(b) All fees collected under this chapter shall be deposited with the treasurer of the city and county or county in whose jurisdiction the court is located.

(c) Six dollars ($6) of each fifteen dollar ($15) fee and fourteen dollars ($14) of each thirty dollar ($30) fee charged and collected under subdivision (a) of Section 116.230 shall be deposited by each county in a special account. Of the money deposited in this account:

(1) In counties with a population of less than 4,000,000, a minimum of 50 percent shall be used to fund the small claims adviser service described in Section 116.940. The remainder of these funds shall be used for court and court-related programs. Records of these moneys shall be available for inspection by the public on request.

(2) In counties with a population of at least 4,000,000, not less than five hundred thousand dollars ($500,000) shall be used to fund the small claims adviser service described in Section 116.940. That amount shall be increased each fiscal year by an amount equal to the percentage increase in revenues derived from small claims court filing fees over the prior fiscal year. The remainder of these funds shall be used for court and court-related programs. Records of these moneys shall be available for inspection by the public on request.

(d) This section and Section 116.940 shall not be applied in any manner that results in a reduction of the level of services, or the amount of funds allocated for providing the services described in Section 116.940, that are in existence in each county during the fiscal year 1989-90. Nothing in this section shall preclude the county from procuring other funding, including state court block grants, to comply with the requirements of Section 116.940.

116.920.

(a) The Judicial Council shall provide by rule for the practice and procedure and for the forms and their use in small claims actions. The rules and forms so adopted shall be consistent with this chapter.

(b) The Judicial Council, in consultation with the Department of Consumer Affairs, shall adopt rules to ensure that litigants receive adequate notice of the availability of assistance from small claims advisors, to prescribe other qualifications and the conduct of advisors, to prescribe training standards for advisors and for temporary judges hearing small claims matters, to prescribe, where appropriate, uniform rules and procedures regarding small claims actions and judgments, and to address other matters that are deemed necessary and appropriate.

116.930.

(a) Each small claims division shall provide in each courtroom in which small claims actions are heard a current copy of a publication describing small claims court law and the procedures that are applicable in the small claims courts, including the law and procedures that apply to the enforcement of judgments. The Small Claims Court and Consumer Law California Judge's Bench Book developed by the California Center for Judicial Education and Research is illustrative of a publication that satisfies the requirement of this subdivision.

(b) Each small claims division may formulate and distribute to litigants and the public a manual on small claims court rules and procedures. The manual shall explain how to complete the necessary forms, how to determine the proper court in which small claims actions may be filed, how to present and defend against claims, how to appeal, how to enforce a judgment, how to protect property that is exempt from execution, and such other matters that the court deems necessary or desirable.

(c) If the Department of Consumer Affairs determines there are sufficient private or public funds available in addition to the funds available within the department's current budget, the department, in cooperation with the Judicial Council, shall prepare a manual or information booklet on small claims court rules and procedures. The department shall distribute copies to the general public and to each small claims division.

(d) If funding is available, the Judicial Council, in cooperation with the Department of Consumer Affairs, shall prepare and distribute to each judge who sits in a small claims court a bench book describing all state and federal consumer protection laws reasonably likely to apply in small claims actions.

116.940.

(a) Except as otherwise provided in this section or in rules adopted by the Judicial Council, the characteristics of the small claims advisory service required by Section 116.260 shall be determined by each county in accordance with local needs and conditions.

(b) Each advisory service shall provide the following services:

(1) Individual personal advisory services, in person or by telephone, and by any other means reasonably calculated to provide timely and appropriate assistance.

(2) Recorded telephone messages may be used to supplement the individual personal advisory services, but shall not be the sole means of providing advice available in the county.

(3) Adjacent counties may provide advisory services jointly.

(c) In any county in which the number of small claims actions filed annually is 1,000 or less as averaged over the immediately preceding two fiscal years, the county may elect to exempt itself from the requirements set forth in subdivision (b). This exemption shall be formally noticed through the adoption of a resolution by the board of supervisors. If a county so exempts itself, the county shall nevertheless provide the following minimum advisory services in accordance with rules adopted by the Judicial Council:

(1) Recorded telephone messages providing general information relating to small claims actions filed in the county shall be provided during regular business hours.

(2) Small claims information booklets shall be provided in the court clerk's office of each municipal court, the court clerk's office of each superior court in a county in which there is no municipal court, the county administrator's office, other appropriate county offices, and in any other location that is convenient to prospective small claims litigants in the county.

(d) The advisory service shall operate in conjunction and cooperation with the small claims division, and shall be administered so as to avoid the existence or appearance of a conflict of interest between the individuals providing the advisory services and any party to a particular small claims action or any judicial officer deciding small claims actions.

(e) Advisors may be volunteers, and shall be members of the State Bar, law students, paralegals, or persons experienced in resolving minor disputes, and shall be familiar with small claims court rules and procedures. Advisors shall not appear in court as an advocate for any party.

(f) Advisors and other court employees and volunteers have the immunity conferred by Section 818.9 of the Government Code with respect to advice provided under this chapter.

116.950.

(a) This section shall become operative only if the Department of Consumer Affairs determines that sufficient private or public funds are available in addition to the funds available in the department's current budget to cover the costs of implementing this section.

(b) There shall be established an advisory committee, constituted as set forth in this section, to study small claims practice and procedure, with particular attention given to the improvement of procedures for the enforcement of judgments.

(c) The members of the advisory committee shall serve without compensation, but shall be reimbursed for expenses actually and necessarily incurred by them in the performance of their duties.

(d) The advisory committee shall be composed as follows:

(1) The Attorney General or a representative.

(2) Two consumer representatives from consumer groups or agencies, appointed by the Secretary of the State and Consumer Services Agency.

(3) One representative appointed by the Speaker of the Assembly and one representative appointed by the President pro Tempore of the Senate.

(4) Two representatives appointed by the Board of Governors of the State Bar.

(5) Two representatives of the business community, appointed by the Secretary of the Trade and Commerce Agency.

(6) Six judicial officers who have extensive experience presiding in small claims court, appointed by the Judicial Council. Judicial officers appointed under this subdivision may include judicial officers of the superior court, judicial officers of the municipal court, judges of the appellate courts, retired judicial officers, and temporary judges.

(7) One representative appointed by the Governor.

(8) Two clerks of the court appointed by the Judicial Council.

(e) Staff assistance to the advisory committee shall be provided by the Department of Consumer Affairs, with the assistance of the Judicial Council, as needed.

2002 California Rules of Court

Rule 151. Scope

1. This chapter applies to appeals to the superior court from municipal and justice courts in small claims cases.

Rule 152. Filing notice of appeal

1. (a) [Small claims case] A notice of appeal shall be signed by the appellant or by appellant's attorney and shall be sufficient if it states in substance that the appellant appeals from a specified judgment or, in the case of a defaulting defendant, from the denial of a motion to vacate the judgment. A notice of appeal shall be liberally construed in favor of its sufficiency.

(b) [Notification by clerk] When a notice of appeal is filed pursuant to subdivision (a) of this rule, the clerk of the trial court shall promptly mail a notification of the filing of the notice to each other party at the party's last known address. The notification shall state the number and title of the action or proceeding and the date the notice of appeal was filed. In the event of the death of a party prior to the court's giving notice, the mailing is a sufficient performance of the clerk's duty. The failure of the clerk to give notice of judgment or notification of the filing of notice of appeal shall not extend the time for filing notice of appeal or affect the validity of the appeal.

(c) [Premature notice] A notice of appeal filed prior to entry of the judgment, but after its rendition, shall be valid and shall be deemed to have been filed immediately after entry. A notice of appeal filed prior to rendition of the judgment, but after the judge has announced an intended ruling, may, in the discretion of the reviewing court for good cause, be treated as filed immediately after entry of the judgment.

Rule 153. Record on appeal

1. Upon the filing of the notice of appeal and the payment of any fees required by law, the clerk of the trial court shall within five days transmit to the clerk of the superior court a certified copy of the entries in the register of actions or docket relating to the action, together with the pleadings, exhibits, notices, motions, other papers and documents filed in the action, and the notice of appeal.

Rule 154. Continuances

1. Continuances of the trial in the superior court may be granted for good cause but, except in cases of extreme hardship, shall not be granted, on application of the appellant alone, for a period of time which in the aggregate exceeds 30 days. If after trial anew or new trial a new trial is ordered, there shall be a similar limitation on continuances

Rule 155. Abandonment, dismissal, and judgment for failure to bring to trial

1. (a) [Before appeal filed] At any time before the filing of the appeal in the superior court, the appellant may file in the office of the clerk of the trial court a written abandonment of the appeal; or the parties may file in that office a stipulation for abandonment. The filing of either document shall operate to dismiss the appeal and to restore the jurisdiction of the trial court.

(b) [After record filed] After the filing of an appeal in the superior court it may be dismissed by that court on written request of the appellant or stipulation of the parties filed with the clerk of the superior court.

(c) [Dismissal or judgment by court] The appeal shall be dismissed if not brought to trial within one year from the date of filing the appeal in the superior court. If after trial anew a new trial is ordered, the appeal in the case shall be dismissed if the case is not brought to trial within one year from the date of entry of the order for the new trial. Notwithstanding the foregoing provisions, dismissal shall not be ordered or judgment entered if there was in effect a written stipulation extending the time for the trial or if the appellant shows that he or she exercised reasonable diligence to bring the case to trial. In any event the appeal shall be dismissed, if the case is not brought to trial within three years after either the appeal is filed in the superior court or the most recent new trial order is entered in the superior court.

(d) [Notification by clerk] When an appellant files an abandonment of appeal, the clerk of the court in which the abandonment is filed shall immediately notify the adverse party or parties of the filing. The clerk of the superior court shall immediately notify the parties of any order of dismissal or of any judgment for defendant pursuant to subdivision (c) made by that court.

(e) [Return of papers] Upon dismissal by the superior court of an appeal from a municipal or a justice court, the clerk of the superior court shall transmit to the trial court a copy of the order of dismissal and all original papers and exhibits transmitted to the superior court. The trial court shall thereafter have the same jurisdiction as if no appeal had been taken.

(f) [Approval of compromise] Whenever the guardian of a minor or of an insane or incompetent person seeks approval of a proposed compromise of a case on appeal required to be tried anew or in which a new trial has been ordered, the superior court may hear and determine whether the proposed compromise is for the best interest of the ward.

Rule 156. Definitions

In this chapter, unless the context or subject matter otherwise requires:

(a) The past, present, and future tenses each include the other; the masculine, feminine, and neuter genders each include the other; and the singular and plural numbers each include the other.

(b) "Shall" is mandatory and "may" is permissive.

(c) "Trial court" means the municipal or justice court from which the appeal is taken.

(d) "Appellant" means the party appealing; "plaintiff" and "defendant" refer to the parties as they were designated in the trial court.

(e) Designation of a party by any terminology includes such party's attorney of record. Whenever under this chapter notice is required to be given to or served on a party, the notice or service shall be made upon the attorney of record if the party has one.

(f) "Clerk" with respect to a justice court means the judge if there is no clerk.

(g) Rule and subdivision headings do not in any manner affect the scope, meaning, or intent of the provisions of these rules.

Rule 244. Temporary judge-stipulation, order, oath, assignment, compensation, and other matters

1. (a) [Stipulation] Except as provided in rule 1727, the stipulation of the parties that a case may be tried by a temporary judge must be in writing and must state the name and office address of the member of the State Bar agreed upon. It must be submitted for approval to the presiding judge or to the supervising judge of a branch court. This subdivision does not apply to the selection of a court commissioner to act as a temporary judge. (Subd (a) amended effective July 1, 2001; previously amended and relettered effective July 1, 1993; previously amended effective January 1, 2001.)

(b) [Order and oath] The order designating the temporary judge must be endorsed upon the stipulation, which must then be filed. The temporary judge must take and subscribe the oath of office and certify that he or she is aware of and will comply with applicable provisions of canon 6 of the Code of Judicial Ethics and these rules. The oath and certification must be attached to the stipulation and order of designation, and the case will then be assigned to the temporary judge for trial. After the oath is filed, the temporary judge may proceed with the hearing, trial, and determination of the case. A filed oath and order, until revoked, may be used in any case in which the parties stipulate to the designated temporary judge. The stipulation must specify the filing date of the oath and order. This subdivision does not apply to the selection of a court commissioner to act as a temporary judge. (Subd (b) amended effective July 1, 2001; previously amended and relettered effective July 1, 1993.)

(c) [Disclosure to the parties] In addition to any other disclosure required by law, no later than five days after appointment as a temporary judge or, if the temporary judge is not aware of his or her appointment or of a matter subject to disclosure at that time, as soon as practicable thereafter, a temporary judge must disclose to the parties:

(1) Any matter subject to disclosure under subdivisions (D)(2)(f) and (D)(2)(g) of canon 6 of the Code of Judicial Ethics; and

(2) Any significant personal or professional relationship the temporary judge has or has had with a party, attorney, or law firm in the instant case, including the number and nature of any other proceedings in the past 24 months in which the temporary judge has been privately compensated by a party, attorney, law firm, or insurance company in the instant case for any services, including, but not limited to, service as an attorney, expert witness, or consultant or as a judge, referee, arbitrator, mediator, settlement facilitator, or other alternative dispute resolution neutral. (Subd (c) adopted effective July 1, 2001.)

(d) [Disqualification] Requests for disqualification of temporary judges are determined as provided in Code of Civil Procedure sections 170.1, 170.2, 170.3, 170.4, and 170.5. (Subd (d) amended and relettered effective July 1, 2001; adopted effective July 1, 1993, as subd (c).)

(e) [Use of court facilities, court personnel, and summoned jurors] A party who has elected to use the services of a privately compensated temporary judge is deemed to have elected to proceed outside the courthouse, and court facilities, court personnel, or summoned jurors must not be used, except upon a finding by the presiding judge that the use would further the interests of justice. For all matters pending before privately compensated temporary judges, the clerk must post a notice indicating the case name and number as well as the telephone number of a person to contact to arrange for attendance at any proceeding that would be open to the public if held in a courthouse.

2. (Subd (e) amended and relettered effective July 1, 2001; adopted effective July 1, 1993, as subd (d).)

(f) [Order for appropriate hearing site] The presiding judge or supervising judge, on request of any person or on the judge's own motion, may order that a case before a privately compensated temporary judge must be heard at a site easily accessible to the public and appropriate for seating those who have made known their plan to attend hearings. The request must be by letter with reasons stated and must be accompanied by a declaration that a copy of the request was mailed to each party, to the temporary judge, and to the clerk for placement in the file. The order may require that notice of trial or of other proceedings be given to the requesting party directly. An order for an appropriate hearing site is not grounds for withdrawal of a stipulation. (Subd (f) amended and relettered effective July 1, 2001; adopted effective July 1, 1993, as subd (e).)

(g) [Motion to withdraw stipulation or to seal records; complaint for intervention] A motion to withdraw a stipulation for the appointment of a temporary judge must be supported by a declaration of facts establishing good cause for permitting the party to withdraw the stipulation, and must be heard by the presiding judge or a judge designated by the presiding judge. A declaration that a ruling is based on error of fact or law does not establish good cause for withdrawing a stipulation. Notice of the motion must be served and filed, and the moving party must mail or deliver a copy to the temporary judge. If the motion is granted, the case must be transferred to the trial court docket.

A motion to seal records in a cause before a privately compensated temporary judge must be served and filed and must be heard by the presiding judge or a judge designated by the presiding judge. The moving party must mail or deliver a copy of the motion to the temporary judge and to any person or organization who has requested that the case be heard at an appropriate hearing site.

A motion for leave to file a complaint for intervention in a cause before a privately compensated temporary judge must be served and filed, and must be assigned for hearing as a law and motion matter. The party seeking intervention must mail or deliver a copy of the motion to the temporary judge. If intervention is allowed, the case must be returned to the trial court docket unless all parties stipulate in the manner prescribed in subdivision (a) to proceed before the temporary judge.

(h) [Compensation] Temporary judges must not be compensated by the parties unless the parties agree in writing on a rate of compensation to be paid by the parties. (Subd (h) amended and relettered effective July 1, 2001; adopted effective July 1, 1995, as subd (g).)

January 2001-These amendments provide an alternative means of obtaining a stipulation in small claims cases. The court must post a conspicuous sign inside or just outside the courtroom accompanied by oral, videotape, or audiotape notification by a court officer on the day of the hearing, stating that the case will be heard by a pro tem judge absent objection.

July 2001-Revised rules 244, 244.1, 244.2, 1604, and 1606 update rules relating to references to correspond to recent legislation; clarify that the reference procedure may not be used to appoint a person to conduct a mediation; enhance enforcement of and compliance with ethical standards applicable to temporary judges, referees, and court-appointed arbitrators; and clarify that courts are not prohibited from compensating temporary judges.

Rule 1701. Compliance with fictitious business name laws

1. A claimant who is required to file a declaration of compliance with the fictitious business name laws pursuant to Code of Civil Procedure section 116.430 shall file the declaration in each case filed. The clerk shall make the declaration of compliance available to the claimant in any one of the following ways:

(1) the declaration of compliance may be placed on a separate form approved by the Judicial Council;

(2) the approved Judicial Council form may be placed on the reverse of the Plaintiff's Statement to the Clerk or on the back of any Judicial Council small claims form with only one side; or

(3) the precise language of the declaration of compliance which appears on the approved Judicial Council form may be incorporated into the Plaintiff's Statement to the Clerk.

Rule 1702. Substituted service

1. If substituted service is authorized by Code of Civil Procedure section 116.340 or other provisions of law, no due diligence is required in a small claims court action

Rule 1703. Defendant's claim

1. A defendant may file a claim against the plaintiff even if the claim does not relate to the same subject or event as the plaintiff's claim, so long as the claim is within the jurisdictional limit of the small claims court.

Rule 1704. Venue challenge

1. A defendant may challenge venue by writing to the court. The defendant is not required to personally appear at the hearing on the venue challenge. If the court denies

the challenge and the defendant is not present, the hearing shall be continued to another appropriate date. The parties shall be given notice of the venue determination and hearing date.

Rule 1705. Form of judgment

1. The court shall give judgment for damages, equitable relief, or both, and may make other orders as the court deems just and equitable for the resolution of the dispute. If specific property is referred to in the judgment, whether it be personal or real, tangible or intangible, the property shall be identified with sufficient detail to permit efficient implementation or enforcement of the judgment.

Rule 1706. Role of clerk in assisting litigants

1. The clerk shall provide forms and pamphlets from the Judicial Council. The clerk shall provide materials from the Department of Consumer Affairs when available. The clerk shall inform litigants of the small claims advisory service. The clerk may answer questions relative to filing and service of the claim, designation of the parties, scheduling of hearings, and similar matters.

Rule 1725. Advisor assistance

1. (a) [Notice to parties] The clerk shall inform the parties orally or in writing

(1) that an advisor is available to assist small claims litigants at no additional charge as provided in Code of Civil Procedure sections 116.260 and 116.940, and

(2) of the provisions of Government Code section 818.9.

(b) [Training] All small claims advisors shall receive training sufficient to ensure competence in the areas of small claims court practice and procedure; alternative dispute resolution programs; consumer sales; vehicular sales, leasing, and repairs; credit and financing transactions; professional and occupational licensing; landlord-tenant law; contract, warranty, tort, and negotiable instruments law. It is the intent of this rule that the county shall provide this training.

(c) [Qualifications] In addition to the training required in subdivision (b), each county may establish additional qualifications for small claims advisors.

(d) [Conflict of interest] A small claims advisor shall disclose any known direct or indirect relationship the advisor may have with any party or witness in the action. An advisor shall not disclose information obtained in the course of the advisor's duties or use the information for financial or other advantage.

Rule 1726. Temporary judges in small claims cases

2. (a) [Qualifications] To qualify for appointment as a temporary judge hearing matters in the small claims court or on appeal of a small claims judgment, a person shall have

(1) been a member of the State Bar for at least five years immediately preceding appointment,

(2) attended and completed a training program for temporary judges provided by the appointing court, and

(3) become familiar with the publications identified in Code of Civil Procedure section 116.930.

(b) [Training program] The training program shall cover judicial ethics, substantive law,* small claims procedures (including the wording of judgments), and the conduct of small claims hearings. Judicial ethics and the conduct of small claims hearings should be taught by a judge, if possible; substantive law and procedure shall be taught by any bench officer or other person experienced in small claims law and procedure.

*Substantive areas of law are intended to include the following: consumer sales; vehicular sales, leasing, and repairs; credit and financing transactions; professional and occupational licensing; landlord-tenant law; contract, warranty, tort, and negotiable instruments law; and other subject areas deemed appropriate by the presiding judge, given local needs and conditions.

Rule 1727. Stipulation to temporary judge in small claims case

1. (a) [Stipulation] Notwithstanding rule 244, in small claims actions a party litigant shall be deemed to have stipulated to the matter being tried by a temporary judge, as defined in rule 880, if all of the following occur before the swearing in of the first witness in the hearing:

(1) The court notifies the party litigant that a temporary judge will be hearing the matters for that calendar;

(2) The court notifies the party litigant that the temporary judge is a qualified member of the State Bar;

(3) The court notifies the party litigant that he or she has a right to have the matter heard before a duly elected or appointed judicial officer of the court; and

(4) After notice, the party litigant fails to object to the matter being heard by a temporary judge.

(b) [Notice] This notice may be given in the following forms:

(1) A conspicuous sign posted inside or just outside the courtroom, accompanied by oral notification or notification by videotape or audiotape by a court officer on the day of the hearing; or

(2) A written stipulation, signed by the party litigant.

Rule 1727 adopted effective January 1, 2001.

APPENDIX D
LIST OF RELEVANT
CONSUMER STATUTES

The following is a listing of significant California and Federal Consumer Laws. There are many more than those listed below. A more complete list can be obtained from:

California Department of Consumer Affairs
400 R Street
Sacramento, CA 95814,
800-952-521

or at their web site located at:

http://www.dca.ca.gov/r-r/r-rtoc.htm

Abbreviations:

B&P = Business & Professions Code
Cal. Const. = California Constitution
CC = Civil Code
CCP = Code of Civil Procedure
CFR = Code of Federal Regulations
Com. Code = Commercial Code
PC = Penal Code
PUC = Public Utilities Code
VC = Vehicle Code
SEC. = Section

List of Relevant Consumer Statutes

Appliances and appliance repair- B&P beginning with Sec. 22410, B&P, Sec. 9800

As-is sales - CC, Sec. 1791.3, 1792.4, 1792.5, 1670.5, (unconscionability)

1770 (deception, fraud) 15 USC, Sec. 2308, 16 CFR, Sec. 455.2, Com Code, Sec. 2316 (negation of warranties)

Attorney Fee Agreements - B&P beginning with Sec. 6146

Attorneys Fees - CC, Sec. 1717, 1717.5

Automobiles financing - CC beginning with Sec. 2982

Automobile leasing - CC, Sec. 2985.7, 15 USC beginning with Sec. 1667

Automobile Rescission - CC beginning with Sec. 2986

Automobile lemon law - CC, Sec. 11793.22 - 1793.25

Bad Check Law - CC, Sec. 1719

Baggage Claims - CC beginning with Sec. 2194

Civil Liability for Petty Theft- PC, Sec. 490.5

Consumer credit contracts - CC, Sec. 1799.90(re co-signing)

California Consumer Credit Agencies Act, California. Civil Code beginning with Sec. 1785.1

Contractor's License Law - B&P beginning with Sec. 7000

Credit Repair - CC beginning with Sec. 1789.10

Dating Services - CC beginning with Sec. 1694

Dance Studio Contracts - CC beginning with Sec. 1812.50

Disasters (Home Repair) - CC beginning with Sec. 1689.6

Disasters - Price Gouging - PC 396

Door-to-Door Solicitation - B&P beginning with Sec. 17510 et sec., 16 CFR Part 429

Employment Agencies - CC beginning with Sec. 1812.500,

Fair Debt Collection Practices - CC beginning with Sec. 1788 , 15 USC beginning with Sec. 1692

False and Deceptive Advertising - B&P, Sec. 17500, 17508

Gender Based Price Discrimination - CC, Sec. 51.6

Health Studio Contracts - CC beginning with Sec. 1812.80

HMO's- Knox-Keene Health Care Service Plan Act and Regulations - H&SF beginning with Sec. 1342

Identification for paying by check or credit card - CC, Sec. 1725 and CC, Sec. 1747.8

Inducements to visit Locations or Attend Sales Presentations - B&P, Sec. 17537.1

Layaways - CC, Sec. 1749

Made in U.S.A. - B&P, Sec. 17537.1

Magnuson-Moss (Federal Warranty) Act - 15 USC, Sec. 2301-2301-2312, 16 CFR Part 703

Misrepresentation - CC, Sec. 1770

Mobile home warranties - CC, Sec. 1797-1797.5

Parking Lots - CC, Sec. 1630, 1630.5

Rent to own - CC beginning with Sec. 1812.600

Return Policies - CC, Sec. 1723

Scalping Tickets - PC, Sec. 346

Security Deposits CC, Sec. 1950.5

Self-Service Storage - B&P beginning with Sec. 21700

Seminar Sales - CC, Sec. 1689.24

Senior Citizens (enhanced penalties) - CC, Sec. 1780 (b), 3345, B&P, Sec. 17206.1

Service Contracts - CC, Sec. 1794.41 B&P beginning with Sec. 9855.1

Song-Beverly Consumer Warranty Act -

Song-Beverly Credit Card Act CC, Sec. 1747-1748.7

Sports Memorabilia - B&P beginning with Sec. 21670 , CC 1739.7

Structural Pest Control Operators - B&P beginning with Sec. 8500

Swap Meets - B&P beginning with Sec. 21660

Swimming Pool Construction - B&P, Sec. 7165-7168

Tanning Facilities - B&P, Sec. 7165-7168

Telemarketing and Consumer Fraud and Abuse Prevention Act - 15 USC beginning with Sec. 6101 16 CFR part 310

Timeshare Contracts - B &P, Sec. 11024, 11003.5

Towing - CC beginning with Sec. 3068

Travel Consumer Restitution Fund - B&P, Sec. 17550.36, 17550.37, 17500.47

Universal Product Code - CC beginning with Sec. 7100

Unpaid Wages - LC, Sec. 203, 227.3

Unruh retail sales Act - CC, Sec. 1801-1812.20

Used Merchandise (disclosure) B&P, Sec. 17531 CC 1770 (f)

Vocational Schools - EC beginning with Sec. 94316

Warranties (express) - CC, Sec. 1791.2, 1793, 1793.1, 1793.2, Com code, Sec. 2313, 2314,2315, 2316

warranties (implied) - CC, Sec. 1791.1, 1792-1792.4, Com code, Sec. 2313, 2314,2315, 2316

Water Treatment Devices - B&P beginning with Sec. 17577

Weight Loss CC beginning with Sec. 1694.5

Statutory Cancellation Periods

Automobile Sales & leases - none

Credit Repair Services - five days

Dance Studio Services - six months

Dating Services - three business days

Dental Services - three business days

Discount Buying Services - three days

Door-to-Door Sales - three business days

Employment Counseling Services - three business days

Funeral Contracts (pre-need) - indefinite

Health Studio Services - three business days

Home Repair Services (after a disaster) seven business days

Home Security Transactions - three days

Home Solicitation Sales - three business days

Home Study or Correspondence Vocational School Courses - eight business days

Immigration Consultant Services - three days

Job Listing Services - three business days

Mail/telephone sales (when order has not been filled) - 30 days

Membership Camping Services (if buyer visits site) - three business days

Membership Camping Services (if buyer does not visit site) - ten business days

Seminar Sales - three business days

Service Contracts (used cars, home appliances and home electronic products - 30 days

Service Contracts (new cars) -60 days

Service Contracts (goods, pro-rata refund less penalty) - indefinite

Timeshares - three days

Unlawful Detainer Assistance - one day

Vocational School Courses - five business days

Water Treatment Devices - three business days

Weight-loss Services - three business days

APPENDIX E
STATUTES OF LIMITATION

The Statute of Limitations refers to the deadline a claimant has to file a lawsuit to preserve a claim. Each state has its own time clock to file suit. Typically, the time to file a civil lawsuit seeking damages against a perpetrator or other responsible person or entity ranges from one to two years from the date of the attack. However, the statute of limitations for filing a claim against a government entity or one of its employees is six months.

On the following pages is a list of the most common Statutes of Limitation. They are listed for your convenience, but understand that this is an area of the law that is extremely complicated and this list is not meant to provide a complete and exhaustive explanation, but merely to inform you that you should not delay in pursuing your claim. There are also many exceptions to the rules that follow.

Likewise, if you are a defendant and you think that the plaintiff has filed the case too late, be sure to mention this in your response to the claim and be sure to bring this argument to the judge's attention.

The safest thing to do is to file your lawsuit as soon as possible. If you think you may have missed the deadline, check with a lawyer or do the legal research yourself. In some situations, the statute may have been *tolled*. For example, California law provides that a cause of action does not accrue while a defendant is out of the state. For every day a defendant is absent from the state, the statute of limitations is tolled and the time limit is moved. There are a few exceptions to this statute. Tolling does not apply to licensed California drivers or if the cars were registered in California in automobile accident cases. However, even in an automobile case, the statute may be tolled if the plaintiff proves that reasonable efforts to locate a defendant were unsuccessful. Proving that a defendant was out of state is the task of the plaintiff, not the defendant.

Another example of tolling occurs when the defendant has filed a petition with the bankruptcy court. This operates as an automatic stay of the commencement of a lawsuit against the debtor, for the period of time between the bankruptcy filing and the dismissal of the bankruptcy.

In other situations, you may not have characterized the injury correctly. For example, it is very easy to mis-characterize patent and latent construction defects. When in doubt as to whether your missed the statute, file your case and let the judge decide.

SIX MONTHS
Government entities (from the date the claim was rejected—almost all government claims are rejected—or if you do not receive a letter of rejection, you must file within two years from the date of the incident.

ONE YEAR
Assault
Bank, forged or raised checks
Battery
False imprisonment
Forcible entry or detainers
Forfeiture or penalty statute
Libel and Slander
Notary Public, malfeasance
Personal injury (except for minors and others under specific disabilities) including false imprisonment, seduction of a person below the age of legal consent, wrongful death
Public official, bond
Seduction of person below legal age
Slander
Workers Compensation Benefits
Government claims on a contract

TWO YEARS
Oral Contract and Rescission of Oral Contract—two years from the breach
An Action on an Oral Lease—two years from the breach
Title Insurance Policy, abstract, guaranty

THREE YEARS
Action for Slander of Title to real property

Fraud and mistake (from the date of discovery)

Liability created by statute (other than penalty or forfeiture)

An action against a Notary or a notary's bond holder

Personal injury based on medical negligence (You must also provide 90 days notice to the medical provider that you plan to file a lawsuit If you fell on the steps of the hospital, that is not professional)

Damage to Real and Personal Property (from the date the damage occurred)

Theft of article of historical, interpretive, scientific, or artistic significance (from date of discovery of whereabouts of article)

Public officials' act, bond

Trespass or injury to real property

FOUR YEARS
Actions not otherwise provided for
Book account or account stated (from date of last entry)
Written Contract and Rescission of Written Contract
Demand Note, from execution
Lease, written (breach or abandonment)
Marriage (Nullity)
Construction defects causing injury to person or property—Patent defects

TEN YEARS
Construction defects causing injury to person or property—Latent Defects

19TH BIRTHDAY
Minors—the statute does not start to run until they are no longer minors. For example, if a child was injured when he was 13 years old, he could file a lawsuit until his 19th birthday

Appendix F
Questions for
Judgment Debtor

...ese questions in case you must ask the defendant about his or her property to collect
...lgment.

What is your full legal name?

Have you been known by any other names?

Social Security Number?

What is your home address?

What is your home telephone number? Business? Cellular? Fax? Email?

Driver's license number, expiration?

Spouse name, address, phone number, social security number, driver's license number, other names?

Vehicles owned or leased, including boats, motorcycles, trucks, autos, recreational vehicles, etc? Descriptions? Amount owed and to whom?

Names, addresses, telephone number and employer of any former spouse?

Do you pay any or receive child support, family support, or alimony? Details?

Is your residence owned by you?

Who lives in the home with you?

Does anyone who lives in the home pay rent or board to you? Details?

Is residence or contents insured? Details?

Do you own any other residences?

Who are the other co-owners of your residence?

Is there any equity in your residence?

Who are the mortgage holders?

How long have you lived at your current address?

Do you pay your rent by check? Cash? Money Order?

Who do you make your rent checks out to?

Who owns the residence where you live?

Who is the manager?

Are your rent payments current?

What was your prior address if less than one year?

Do you own any rental property?

Do you own any other real estate, either in California or anywhere else?

Do you own any mobile homes?

Are you a member of a partnership that owns any real property?

Property you own?

Are there any liens on any of your property? Details?

Are you or spouse employed? Name, address, location etc.?

Salary? Commission? Advances? Bonuses? Expense Accounts?

Does your employer owe you any money?

Do you have any checking accounts, savings accounts, money market accounts, CDs, stock options?

Names of banks, account numbers, balances, dates of last deposit or withdrawal? Do you own any 401, 453 or IRA accounts? Details?

Any bank accounts in children's names?

Do you have any credit cards? Details?

Have you ever filed for bankruptcy? Details?

Have you ever applied for credit and been turned down?

Do you own any stock, bonds?

Name, address, telephone number of broker?

Do you own any life insurance or disability policies? Details?

Who prepared your last income tax forms?

Have you had an accountant or service prepare your income tax return within the last three years? Details?

Do you own a business?

Name, locations, phone numbers?

In what cities do you have business licenses?

Fictitious name statements filed? Where?

Sole proprietorship, partnership, corporation, what kind?

How long have you owned it? Co-owners?

Type of accounting system used? Software?

Type of business, creditors? Main customers? Methods of payment? When?

Name of bookkeeper? Bonded?

Other bank accounts not mentioned yet?

Any credit cards not mentioned yet?

Separate tax return?

How many employees? Payroll current? When employees paid? Which account?

Professional licenses current? Details?

Own an interest in anyone else's business?

Do you owe any money other than to credit card companies and mortgage? Details?

Have you loaned any money to anyone in the last five years? Details?

Do you have any children in college? How is college paid for?

Do you own any antiques, furnishings, collections, artwork? Details?

Have you inherited anything within the last ten years?

Do you have any cash?

How much money do you have with you right now?

How much money does your spouse have right now?

APPENDIX G
CHECKLISTS

The following checklists will help you follow your case and be sure not to miss some important step. Be sure that you have read the parts of this book explaining each step. If there is anything you do not understand, check with the small claims advisor for your county (see Appendix A).

PLAINTIFF'S SMALL CLAIMS CHECKLIST

1. **DECIDE IF YOU SHOULD SUE**

   ❐ Did you determine the last day you are permitted to file your case and write it in a calendar?

   ❐ Did you calculate the exact amount of damages which are in dispute? Is there a legal theory which would make the defendant liable?

   ❐ Does the defendant have defenses that would keep you from winning?

   ❐ Did you write the required "demand letter" to the other side? (see examples in Appendix H)

   ❐ Did you try to negotiate a settlement?

   ❐ Did you attempt mediation?

   ❐ Did you find out if the defendant has money or property to collect if you win?

   ❐ Did you analyze whether the case is worth your time and effort?

2. **PREPARE YOUR CASE**

   ❐ Familiarize yourself with small claims procedures and forms (read this book).

   ❐ Determine which court has venue.

   ❐ If you are unfamiliar with small claims court, attend a session to familiarize yourself with the court procedures and to observe the progress of a hearing.

   ❐ Research the proper parties and their names.

   ❐ Decide when you want to have the hearing. Plan for plenty of time to serve the defendant and return the proof of service to the court.

   ❐ Gather your evidence and contact your witnesses.

   ❐ Prepare the **PLAINTIFF'S CLAIM AND ORDER TO DEFENDANT** (form 2 in Appendix I).

   ❐ Attempt mediation before you file your case.

   ❐ File your case(and pay filing fee).

   ❐ If you are a business, file fictitious business name statement.

   ❐ Arrange for service of process on each defendant.

   ❐ Make sure the proof of service is timely filed with the court.

3. **PREPARE FOR THE HEARING**

☐ Organize your presentation, either chronologically, or in another order which will be easy for the judge to follow. Prepare an outline that you can follow during your presentation.

☐ Write a summary of your case to give to the judge.

☐ Try to anticipate arguments and facts which the defense will present and have your own arguments and evidence ready.

4. **ATTEND THE HEARING**

☐ Be prepared to settle if the defendant makes a good offer.

☐ Be prepared to mediate if the defendant agrees.

5. **AFTER THE TRIAL**

☐ Obtain NOTICE OF ENTRY OF JUDGMENT (form 17 in Appendix I).

☐ If you did not attend the hearing for a good reason, file a NOTICE OF MOTION TO VACATE JUDGMENT AND DECLARATION (form 22) to request new hearing by small claims court

☐ If you lost on the defendant's counterclaim, decide if you want to appeal. If you decide to appeal, the NOTICE OF APPEAL (form 19) must be filed within thirty days of the date of the small claims decision or if the clerk mails the NOTICE OF ENTRY OF JUDGMENT (form 17), within thirty days of the mailing as indicated on the form.

☐ Institute collection procedures (garnishment of wage, levy on bank account, record an abstract of judgment, till tap, keeper, etc.).

☐ File ACKNOWLEDGMENT OF SATISFACTION OF JUDGMENT (form 34) with the small claims court after the judgment is satisfied.

DEFENDANT'S SMALL CLAIMS CHECKLIST

1. **AFTER YOU ARE SERVED WITH THE PLAINTIFF'S CLAIM AND ORDER TO DEFENDANT** (form _)

   ❑ Analyze whether the case is worth defending.

   ❑ Consider the possibility of initiating mediation or perhaps negotiating a settlement on your own or through a third party. Keep trying to settle throughout the lawsuit.

   ❑ Decide if you have defenses that would keep the plaintiff from winning based on improper procedures.

   ❑ Decide if you have defenses based on principles of law.

   ❑ Determine whether your homeowners, auto, or business insurance policy covers you.

   ❑ Determine whether you have a basis for a counterclaim against the Plaintiff arising from the same set of facts.

   ❑ If you want to pursue your counterclaim file the **DEFENDANT'S CLAIM AND ORDER TO PLAINTIFF** (form 11 in Appendix I) within the time limits and make sure you get it served.

   ❑ File your proof of service with the court.

2. **BEFORE THE HEARING**

   ❑ Gather all the evidence and make copies for the other parties and you to refer to while the judge looks at the original.

   ❑ Subpoena witnesses and documents if necessary (form 14).

   ❑ Prepare a concise statement of the case so you can explain the case to the judge clearly and quickly.

   ❑ Make another attempt to resolve the case.

3. **PREPARE FOR THE HEARING**

   ❑ Organize your presentation, either chronologically, or in another order which will be easy for the judge to follow. Prepare an outline that you can follow during your presentation.

   ❑ Write a summary of your case to give to the judge.

   ❑ Try to anticipate arguments and facts which the plaintiff will present and have your own arguments and evidence ready.

4. **ATTEND THE HEARING**

❑ Be prepared to settle if the plaintiff makes a reasonable demand.

❑ Be prepared to mediate if the plaintiff agrees.

5. **AFTER THE TRIAL**

❑ Obtain NOTICE OF ENTRY OF JUDGMENT (form 17).

❑ If you did not attend the hearing for a good reason, file a NOTICE OF MOTION TO VACATE JUDGMENT AND DECLARATION (form 22) to request new hearing by small claims court.

❑ If you lost on the plaintiff's claim, decide if you want to appeal. If you decide to appeal, the NOTICE OF APPEAL (form 19) must be filed within thirty days of the date of the Small Claims Decision or if the clerk mails the NOTICE OF ENTRY OF JUDGMENT (form 17), within thirty days of the mailing as indicated on the form.

❑ If you won on your counterclaim, write a letter to the plaintiff asking for payment before you start collection procedures. (You cannot start them until the appeal period is over anyway.) Sometimes, the plaintiff will not want his employer to know about the judgment, which will surely happen if you institute garnishment proceedings. Or the plaintiff (now called the *judgment debtor*) does not want to lose another day from work to appear for a judgment debtor exam. On the other hand, if you think the judgment debtor is likely to remove all his money from the only bank account you know about, or is likely to quit his job to avoid garnishment of wages, you may want to lay low until the appeal period is over, so that you can attach the property before the judgment debtor can dispose of it. The steps you take prior to collection require careful analysis of all your options.

❑ Institute collection procedures (garnishment of wage, levy on bank account, record an abstract of judgment, till tap, keeper, etc.)

❑ File ACKNOWLEDGMENT OF SATISFACTION OF JUDGMENT (form 34) with the small claims court after the judgment is satisfied.

APPENDIX H
DEMAND LETTERS AND SAMPLE CLAIM AGAINST GOVERNMENT AGENCY

The following are samples of the types of demand letters you need to send to someone before filing suit. Use these as guides for writing your own letter.

Via Certified Mail

May 1, 2001

123 Main Street
(555)555-5555

Mr. Warren Tee, Manager
Magnets R' Us
5000 Elm Street
Anytown, California

Re: defective magnets

Dear Mr. Tee:

On January 12, 2001 I purchased 12 refrigerator magnets in the shapes of various items of food from your store. I paid $3.95 for each magnet for a total of $47.40 plus $3.56 tax for a total of $50.96. I paid in cash, and received a receipt, a copy of which is enclosed. The person who sold me the magnets was wearing a name tag which said Suzanne.

While admiring the magnets, I told Suzanne that I would love to purchase them but that I was afraid that they wouldn't stick to my brushed steel refrigerator. Suzanne assured me that the refrigerator magnets will stay put on any refrigerator.

When I got home from your store, I took all of the magnets out of their wrapping and tried to put them on my refrigerator. Every one of them fell and broke into several pieces.

As you know, I returned to the store the next day to return the broken magnets and get my money back. You told me that you would only refund my money on one magnet, for a total of $3.95 plus tax. You told me that I should not have taken the 11 other magnets out of their packages or attempted to put them on the refrigerator until I was sure that the first one would stay on the refrigerator. As I told you then, I tried them all out because Suzanne had assured me that they would stay on any refrigerator.

Your salesperson sold me a product which did not work the way she said it would. This constitutes a breach of the warranty of fitness for a particular purpose.

The purpose of this letter is to let you know that I intend to file a claim against you in small claims court in the amount of $50.96 plus costs unless you refund the money I paid for the magnets within 7 days.

Please call me to discuss this matter to see if we can resolve it without the additional time and expense of a lawsuit.

Sincerely,

Dee Straught

Via Certified Mail

February 1, 2001

                                        124 Main Street
                                        (555)555-5555

Mr. Red Handid
111 Hwy 100
Anytown, California

Re: Return of Security Deposit

Dear Mr. Handid:

On November 30, 2000, I notified you by mail that I would be moving out of the premises known as 12 East 14th Street, Unit 12C in Any town, California on December 31, 2000. I had been a resident on a month-to-month rental agreement since January 12, 1995.

On December 31, 2000, I cleaned and vacated the unit. I still have not received the return of my security deposit of $400.00, nor have I received an itemized list of any deductions.

Section 1950.5 of the California Civil Code states that a landlord must return all deposits no later than three weeks after vacating. Furthermore, you may be subject to an additional $600.00 in damages if you are determined to have retained my deposit in bad faith.

I would appreciate a response and a check in the mail from you within five working days after your receipt of this letter so that there will be no need for me to institute legal proceedings.

                        Sincerely,

                        M.T. Pockets

NOTICE OF CLAIM AGAINST GOVERNMENTAL ENTITY

<u>Claim Against the City of Anytown, California</u>

Joe Tenashus hereby makes claim against Charles Blind, employee, and the City of Anytown for damages sustained when Claimant was hit by a city owned vehicle while crossing the street at the corner of Pine and 4th Street at 7 a.m. on October 31, 2001.

Claimant's address is   Joseph T. Tenashus
                         67 W. Pine Avenue
                         Anytown, California, 12345-6789
                         3-333-333-3333

Notices concerning this claim should be sent to claimant at the address above.

The occurrence giving rise to this claim is as follows:

On October 31, 2001, claimant, dressed as an escaped convict in celebration of Halloween, was walking to his job as a teller at the Bank of Anytown located at 12 Civic Center Drive from his residence at 67 W. Pine. Upon arriving at the pedestrian walkway at the intersection of Pine and 4th Street, claimant entered the crosswalk and was thereafter hit by City police vehicle license # E33333, driven by Officer Charles Blind, Shield # 3333 who negligently failed to stop at the stop sign and hit claimant as claimant was trying to move out of the path of the vehicle. Claimant was thereafter taken to City Jail for questioning.

As a result of the collision, Claimant was forced to seek medical attention for a sprained wrist and was absent from work for 3 days. Claimant is requesting compensation in the amount of $6,000.00 as follows: $ 100.00 medical treatment
            300.00 lost wages
            100.00 property damage to costume
            1000.00 for false arrest
            3500.00 pain & suffering

The names of the public employees causing this claimant's injuries are Officer Charles Blind and other unknown employees. Claimant claims that the City of Anytown failed to properly hire, supervise and train its personnel, thereby causing the above damages to claimant.

Date _____   _____
                                   Joseph T. Tenashus

Appendix 1
Judicial Council Forms

The Judicial Council of the State of California furnishes many mandatory forms to be used in the state courts. The list of forms is extensive. All of the mandated Judicial Counsel Small Claims Court forms are provided below. All of the forms in this book are perforated and can be filled in with a typewriter. The forms can also be downloaded from **http://www.courtinfo.ca.gov/forms/**, and filled in with a typewriter.

Some county courts require you to file a form called "Plaintiff's Statement to the Clerk." You must obtain this form from the Clerk's office of the court in which you intend to file your claim. In most cases, you can obtain this form by mailing the court a letter asking for the form and enclosing with your letter a self-addressed envelope with a first class stamp. Appendix B1 contains a list of the counties that have developed their own local forms. These forms may also be available on the local court's web site.

Also included is a Department of Motor Vehicle Form designated with **. You will use this form to take steps to have the driver's license of the debtor suspended. (See Chapter 9)

Some hints:

1. Make a rough draft first. This means making at least 2 copies in advance.

2. Type. Handwriting looks sloppy. Most courthouses have typewriters available and so do most libraries.

3. Most of the forms are self-explanatory. If you have questions that have not been answered by this book, call the small claims advisor in your county. Do not leave

blanks. You can also ask the small claims clerk for help in filling out the forms. Remember, they cannot give legal advice.

4. Only sign the form(s) you plan to submit to the court. If you have signed copies of drafts lying around, you will end up getting confused. Make 3 copies of the Original, and ask the court to "conform" the copies. Have an envelope prepared with sufficient postage in case the procedure in the local court is to mail the conformed copies

5. California courts require the back pages of forms to be upside down for their filing systems. That is why some pages appear upside down in this book.

NOTE: *The forms in this appendix are the most current forms available at the time of publication, even though some of the forms are dated as early as 1982.*

LIST OF FORMS

NOTE: *The back side of forms are intentionally upside down as required by California Court filing guidelines.*

INFORMATION FOR THE SMALL CLAIMS PLAINTIFF

This information sheet is written for the person who sues in the small claims court. It explains some of the rules of and some general information about the small claims court. It may also be helpful for the person who is sued.

WHAT IS SMALL CLAIMS COURT?

Small claims court is a special court where disputes are resolved quickly and inexpensively. The rules are simple and informal. The person who sues is the **plaintiff.** The person who is sued is the **defendant.** In small claims court, you may ask a lawyer for advice before you go to court, but you cannot have a lawyer in court. Your claim cannot be for more than $5,000 (*see below).* If you have a claim for more than this amount, you may sue in the civil division of the trial court or you may sue in the small claims court and give up your right to the amount over $5,000. You cannot, however, file more than two cases in small claims court for more than $2,500 each during a calendar year.

WHO CAN FILE A CLAIM?

1. You must be at least *18 years old* to file a claim. If you are not yet 18, you may ask the court to appoint a **guardian ad litem.** This is a person who will act for you in the case. The guardian ad litem is usually a parent, a relative, or an adult friend.

2. A person who sues in small claims court must first make a **demand** if possible. This means that you have asked the defendant to pay, and the defendant has refused. If your claim is for possession of property, you must ask the defendant to give you the property.

3. Unless you fall within two technical exceptions, you must be the **original owner** of the claim. This means that if the claim is assigned, the buyer cannot sue in the small claims court. **You must also appear at the small claims hearing yourself unless you filed the claim for a corporation or other entity that is not a natural person.**

4. If a corporation files a claim, an employee, officer, or director must act on its behalf. If the claim is filed on behalf of an association or other entity that is not a natural person, a regularly employed person of the entity must act on its behalf. A person who appears on behalf of a corporation or other entity must not be employed or associated solely for the purpose of representing the corporation or other entity in the small claims court. **You must file a declaration with the court to appear in any of these instances.**

WHERE CAN YOU FILE YOUR CLAIM?

You must sue in the right court and **judicial district.** This rule is called **venue.**

If you file your claim in the wrong court, the court will dismiss the claim unless all defendants personally appear at the hearing and agree that the claim may be heard.

The right district may be any of these:

1. Where the defendant lives or where the business involved is located;

2. Where the damage or accident happened;

3. Where the contract was signed or carried out;

4. If the defendant is a corporation, where the contract was broken;

5. For a retail installment account or sales contract or a motor vehicle finance sale:
   a. Where the buyer lives;
   b. Where the buyer lived when the contract was entered into;
   c. Where the buyer signed the contract;
   d. Where the goods or vehicle are permanently kept.

SOME RULES ABOUT THE DEFENDANT (including government agencies)

1. You must sue using the defendant's *exact legal name.* If the defendant is a business or a corporation and you do not know the exact legal name, check with: the state or local licensing agency; the county clerk's office; or the Office of the Secretary of State, corporate status unit. Ask the clerk for help if you do not know how to find this information. If you do not use the defendant's exact legal name, the court may be able to correct the name on your claim at the hearing or after the judgment.

2. If you want to sue a government agency, you must first file a claim with the agency before you can file a lawsuit in court. Strict time limits apply. If you are in a Department of Corrections or Youth Authority facility, you must prove that the agency denied your claim. Please attach a copy of the denial to your claim.

HOW DOES THE DEFENDANT FIND OUT ABOUT THE CLAIM?

You must make sure the defendant finds out about your lawsuit. This has to be done according to the rules or your case may be dismissed or delayed. The correct way of telling the defendant about the lawsuit is called **service of process**. This means giving the defendant a copy of the claim. **YOU CANNOT DO THIS YOURSELF**. Here are four ways to serve the defendant:

1. **Service by a law officer** — You may ask the marshal or sheriff to serve the defendant. A fee will be charged.

2. **Process server** — You may ask anyone who is *not a party* in your case and who is at least *18 years old* to serve the defendant. The person is called a **process server** and must personally give a copy of your claim to the defendant. The person must also sign a proof of service form showing when the defendant was served. Registered process servers will do this for you for a fee. You may also ask a friend or relative to do it.

3. **Certified mail** — You may ask the clerk of the court to serve the defendant by certified mail. The clerk will charge a fee. You should check back with the court prior to the hearing to see if the receipt for certified mail was returned to the court. **Service by certified mail must be done by the clerk's office except in motor vehicle accident cases involving out-of-state defendants.**

4. **Substituted service** — This method lets you serve another person instead of the defendant. You must follow the procedures carefully. You may also wish to use the marshal or sheriff or a registered process server.

* The $5,000 limit does not apply, and a $4,000 limit applies, if a "defendant guarantor . . . is required to respond based upon the default, actions, or omissions of another" ($2,500 if the defendant guarantor does not charge a fee for the service).

(Continued on reverse)

Form Adopted for Mandatory Use
Judicial Council of California
SC-150 [Rev. January 1, 2000]

INFORMATION FOR THE PLAINTIFF
(Small Claims)

Cal. Rules of Court, rule 982.7;
Code of Civil Procedure,
§§ 116.110 et seq., 116.220(c), 16.340(g)

181

4. **Substituted service** *(continued)*

A copy of your claim must be left
— at the defendant's business with the person in charge;
OR
— at the defendant's home with a competent person who is at least 18 years old. The person who receives the claim must be told about its contents. Another copy must be mailed, first class, postage prepaid, to the defendant at the address where the paper was left. The service is not complete until *10 days* after the copy is mailed.

No matter which method of service you choose, the defendant must be served by a certain date or the trial will be postponed. If the defendant lives in the county, service must be completed at least *10 days* before the trial date. This period is *15 days* if the defendant lives outside the county.

The person who serves the defendant must sign a court paper showing when the defendant was served. This paper is called a *Proof of Service* (form SC-104). It must be signed and returned to the court clerk as soon as the defendant has been served.

WHAT IF THE DEFENDANT ALSO HAS A CLAIM?

Sometimes the person who was sued (the **defendant**) will also have a claim against the person who filed the lawsuit (the **plaintiff**). This claim is called the *Defendant's Claim*. The defendant may file this claim in the same lawsuit. This helps to resolve all of the disagreements between the parties at the same time.

If the defendant decides to file the claim in the small claims court, the claim may not be for more than $5,000 (*see reverse*). If the value of the claim is more than this

amount, the defendant may either give up the amount over $5,000 and sue in the small claims court or file a motion to transfer the case to the appropriate court for the full value of the claim.

The defendant's claim must be served on the plaintiff at least *5 days* before the trial. If the defendant received the plaintiff's claim *10 days* or less before the trial, then the claim must be served at least *1 day* before the trial. Both claims will be heard by the court at the same time.

WHAT HAPPENS AT THE TRIAL?

Be sure you are on time for the trial. The small claims trial is informal. You must bring with you all witnesses, books, receipts, and other papers or things to prove your case. You may ask the witnesses to come to court voluntarily. You may also ask the clerk of the court to issue a **subpoena**. A subpoena is a court order that *requires* the witness to go to trial. The witness has a right to charge a fee for going to the trial. If you do not have the records or papers to prove your case, you may also get a court order prior to the trial date requiring the papers to be brought to

the trial. This order is called a *Small Claims Subpoena and Declaration* (form SC-107).

If you settle the case before the trial, you must file a **dismissal** form with the clerk.

The court's decision is usually mailed to you after the trial. It may also be hand delivered to you when the trial is over and after the judge has made a decision. The decision appears on a form called the *Notice of Entry of Judgment* (form SC-130).

WHAT HAPPENS AFTER JUDGMENT?

The court may have ordered one party to pay money to the other party. The party who wins the case and collects the money is called the **judgment creditor**. The party who loses the case and owes the money is called the **judgment debtor**. Enforcement of the judgment is **postponed** until the time for appeal ends or until the appeal is decided. This means that the judgment creditor cannot collect any

money or take any action until this period is over. Generally both parties may be represented by lawyers after judgment. More information about your rights after judgment is available on the back of the *Notice of Entry of Judgment* form. The clerk may also have this information on a separate sheet.

HOW TO GET HELP WITH YOUR CASE

1. **Lawyers** — Both parties may ask a lawyer about the case, but a lawyer may not represent either party in court at the small claims trial. Generally, after judgment and on appeal, both parties may be represented by a lawyer.

2. **Interpreters** — If you do not speak English, you may take a family member or friend to court with you. The court should keep a list of interpreters who will interpret for you. Some interpreters charge a reasonable or no fee. If an interpreter is not available, the court must postpone the hearing one time only so that you have time to get one.

3. **Waiver of fees** — The court charges fees for some of its procedures. Fees are also charged for serving the defendant with the claim. The court may excuse you from paying these fees if you cannot afford them. Ask the clerk for the *Information Sheet on Waiver of Court Fees and Costs* (form 982(a)(17)(A)) to find out if you meet the requirements so that you do not have to pay the fees.

4. **Night and Saturday court** — If you cannot go to court during working hours, ask the clerk if the court has trials at **night** or on **Saturdays**.

5. **Parties who are in jail** — If you are in jail, the court may excuse you from going to the trial. Instead, you may ask another person who is not an attorney to go to the trial for you. You may mail written declarations to the court to support your case.

6. **Accommodations** — If you have a disability and need assistance, please ask the court immediately to help accommodate your needs. If you are hearing impaired and need assistance, please notify the court immediately.

7. **Small claims advisors** — The law requires each county to provide assistance in small claims cases free of charge. *(Small claims advisor information)*:

INFORMATION FOR THE PLAINTIFF
(Small Claims)

Name and Address of Court: **SC-100**

SMALL CLAIMS CASE NO.:

— NOTICE TO DEFENDANT — YOU ARE BEING SUED BY PLAINTIFF	— *AVISO AL DEMANDADO* — *A USTED LO ESTAN DEMANDANDO*
To protect your rights, you must appear in this court on the trial date shown in the table below. You may lose the case if you do not appear. The court may award the plaintiff the amount of the claim and the costs. Your wages, money, and property may be taken without further warning from the court.	*Para proteger sus derechos, usted debe presentarse ante esta corte en la fecha del juicio indicada en el cuadro que aparece a continuación. Si no se presenta, puede perder el caso. La corte puede decidir en favor del demandante por la cantidad del reclamo y los costos. A usted le pueden quitar su salario, su dinero, y otras cosas de su propiedad, sin aviso adicional por parte de esta corte.*

PLAINTIFF/DEMANDANTE *(Name, street address, and telephone number of each)*:

DEFENDANT/DEMANDADO *(Name, street address, and telephone number of each)*:

Telephone No.:

Telephone No.:

Telephone No.:

Telephone No.:

Fict. Bus. Name Stmt. No.   Expires: ☐ See attached sheet for additional plaintiffs and defendants.

PLAINTIFF'S CLAIM

1. a. ☐ Defendant owes me the sum of: $ _____ , not including court costs, because *(describe claim and date)*:

   b. ☐ I have had an **arbitration of an attorney-client fee dispute.** *(Attach* Attorney-Client Fee Dispute *form (see form SC-101).)*

2. ☐ This claim is against a government agency, and I filed a claim with the agency. My claim was denied by the agency, or the agency did not act on my claim before the legal deadline. *(See form SC-150.)*

3. a. ☐ I have asked defendant to pay this money, but it has not been paid.
   b. ☐ I have NOT asked defendant to pay this money because *(explain)*:

4. This court is the proper court for the trial because ☐ *(In the box at the left, insert one of the letters from the list called "Venue Table" on the back of this sheet. If you select D, E, or F, specify additional facts in this space)*:

5. I ☐ have ☐ have not   filed more than one other small claims action anywhere in California during this calendar year in which the amount demanded is more than $2,500.

6. I ☐ have ☐ have not   filed more than 12 small claims, including this claim, during the previous 12 months.

7. I understand that
   a. I may talk to an attorney about this claim, but I cannot be represented by an attorney at the trial in the small claims court.
   b. I must appear at the time and place of trial and bring all witnesses, books, receipts, and other papers or things to prove my case.
   c. **I have no right of appeal on my claim,** but I may appeal a claim filed by the defendant in this case.
   d. If I cannot afford to pay the fees for filing or service by a sheriff, marshal, or constable, I may ask that the fees be waived.

8. I have received and read the information sheet explaining some important rights of plaintiffs in the small claims court.

9. No defendant is in the military service ☐ except *(name)*:

I declare under penalty of perjury under the laws of the State of California that the foregoing is true and correct.

Date:

▶

. . . .
(TYPE OR PRINT NAME)   (SIGNATURE OF PLAINTIFF)

ORDER TO DEFENDANT

You must appear in this court on the trial date and at the time LAST SHOWN IN THE BOX BELOW if you do not agree with the plaintiff's claim. Bring all witnesses, books, receipts, and other papers or things with you to support your case.

TRIAL DATE FECHA DEL JUICIO		DATE	DAY	TIME	PLACE	COURT USE
	1.					
	2.					
	3.					

Filed on *(date)*:   Clerk, by _____ , Deputy

— The county provides small claims advisor services free of charge. Read the information on the reverse. —

Form Adopted for Mandatory Use Judicial Council of California SC-100 [Rev. January 1, 2000]	**PLAINTIFF'S CLAIM AND ORDER TO DEFENDANT** **(Small Claims)**	Cal. Rules of Court, rule 982.7; Code of Civil Procedure, §§ 116.110 et seq., 116.220(c), 116.340(g)

INFORMATION FOR DEFENDANT

1. **What is the small claims court?** The small claims court is a special court in which disagreements are resolved quickly and cheaply. A small claim must be for $5,000 *(*see below)* or less. With some exceptions no party may file more than two small claims actions in which the amount demanded is more than $2,500 anywhere in the state in a calendar year. The party who sues is called a **plaintiff**. The party who is sued is called a **defendant**. Neither party can be represented by a lawyer at the trial, but either party may talk to a lawyer about the case.

2. **What can you do if you are sued in the small claims court?**
   a. **SETTLE** — You may settle your case before the trial. If you do, be sure that the plaintiff files a dismissal form with the court. If you would like help in settling your case, ask the small claims advisor (see No. 5, below) to refer you to an alternative dispute resolution provider.
   b. **DEFAULT** — If you do not go to the trial, it is called a **default**. The plaintiff may win the amount of the claim and costs. The plaintiff may then be able to use legal procedures to take your money or property to pay the judgment.
   c. **APPEAR AND CONTEST** — You may go to the trial and disagree with the plaintiff's claim. If you do, bring all witnesses, books, receipts, and other papers or things to prove your case. You may ask the witnesses in your case to go to the trial or, before the trial, you may ask the clerk of the court to issue a **subpoena**. A subpoena is a court order that requires the witness to go to the trial.
   d. **APPEAR AND REQUEST PAYMENTS** — You may agree with the plaintiff's claim, but you may be unable to pay the money all at once. You may then choose to go to the trial and ask the court to order payments you can afford.
   e. **POSTPONE** — If you live in the county where the claim was filed, you must be served with a copy of the claim *10 days before the trial.* If you live outside the county, you must be served *15 days before the trial.* If you did not receive the claim within these time limits, you may ask the court for a postponement. (No fee charged.)
      If you cannot attend the hearing on the date scheduled, write to the court before the hearing date and tell why, and ask the court to postpone the hearing. (Fee charged.)
   f. **CHALLENGE VENUE** — If you believe the plaintiff's claim was filed in the wrong court (see Venue Table, below), write to the court before the hearing date, explain why you think so, and ask the court to dismiss the claim. Mail a copy to the plaintiff and file a proof of mailing with the court. For information about proof of mailing, see the small claims advisor.

3. **What can you do if you also have a claim against the person who sued you?** A claim against the person who sued you is called a *Defendant's Claim* (form SC-120). Ask the clerk for this form to file your claim. The claim must not be for more than $5,000.* If you received your copy of the plaintiff's claim *less than 10 days* before the trial date, you must have the plaintiff served with your claim *at least 1 day* before the trial date. If you received your claim *more than 10 days* before the trial date, you must have the plaintiff served with your claim *at least 5 days* before the trial date. The court will hear both claims at the same time.

4. **What happens after trial?** The court will deliver or mail to you a copy of a form called the *Notice of Entry of Judgment (form SC-130). This form tells you how the case was decided. If you disagree with the court's decision, you may appeal the judgment on the plaintiff's claim. You may not appeal your own claim. If you appeared at the trial, you must begin your appeal by filing a Notice of Appeal (form SC-140) and pay the required fees within 30 days after the date the Notice of Entry of Judgment was mailed or handed to you. If you did not appear at the trial, you must first ask the court to vacate or cancel the judgment. To make this request, you must file a Motion to Vacate the Judgment (form SC-135) and pay the required fees within 30 days after the date the Notice of Entry of Judgment was mailed or handed to you. If your request is denied, you then have 10 days from the date the notice of denial was mailed or handed to you to file an appeal.*

5. **How can you get help with your case?**
   a. **MINORS** — If you are under 18 years old, you should tell the clerk. You are too young to act for yourself in the case. You must ask the court to appoint someone to act for you. That person is called a **guardian ad litem**.
   b. **INTERPRETERS** — If you do not speak English, you may take a family member or friend to court with you. The court should keep a list of interpreters who will interpret for you. Some interpreters charge a reasonable or no fee. If an interpreter is not available, the court must postpone the hearing one time only so that you have time to get one.
   c. **ACCOMMODATIONS** — If you have a disability and need assistance, please ask the court immediately to help accommodate your needs. If you are hearing impaired and need assistance, please notify the court immediately.
   d. **SMALL CLAIMS ADVISORS** — The law requires each county to provide assistance in small claims cases free of charge. *(Small claims advisor information)*:

VENUE TABLE

The plaintiff must file the claim in the proper court and geographical area. This rule is called **venue.** Below are possible reasons for filing the claim in this court. *If you are the plaintiff, insert the proper letter from the list below in item 4 on the other side of this sheet and specify additional facts for D, E, or F.* **This court is the proper court for the trial of this case because**

A. a defendant lives in this judicial district or a defendant corporation or unincorporated association has its principal place of business in this judicial district.

B. a person was injured or personal property was damaged in this judicial district.

C. a defendant signed or entered into a contract in this judicial district, a defendant lived in this judicial district when the contract was entered into, a contract or obligation was to be performed in this judicial district, or, if the defendant was a corporation, the contract was breached in this judicial district.

D. the claim is on a retail installment account or contract subject to Civil Code section 1812.10. *(Specify facts on the other side of this sheet.)*

E. the claim is on a vehicle finance sale subject to Civil Code section 2984.4. *(Specify facts on the other side of this sheet.)*

F. other. *(Specify facts on the other side of this sheet.)*

---

* The $5,000 limit does not apply, and a $4,000 limit applies, if a "defendant guarantor . . . is required to respond based upon the default, actions, or omissions of another" ($2,500 if the defendant guarantor does not charge a fee for the service).

INSTRUCTIONS TO FILL OUT FORM SC-100 PLAINTIFF'S CLAIM AND ORDER TO DEFENDANT

Fill in the form as indicated below.
This form must be typed.

A. THE HEADING SECTION.
Name of Court
Street Address of Court
City, Zip, Telephone of court   Do not fill in the case number.

PLAINTIFF/DEMANDANTE
This is where you put the name, address and telephone number of each plaintiff

DEFENDANT/DEMANDADO
This is where you put the name, address and telephone number of each defendant

Fict. Bus. Name Statement Number Expires:

If a business is filing suit then it must attest to the fact that the business has complied with fictitious business name laws by providing the fictitious business name statement number and the date it expires in the heading. Be sure to fill in form SC-103 Fictitious Business Declaration form. This form must be filed in Court with your Plaintiff's Claim and Order to Defendant form

B. PLAINTIFF'S CLAIM SECTION:

Defendant owes me the sum of $_____ , not including court costs, because *(described claim and date)*:
Provide a brief description of what the claim is about and the amount of damages you are asking for.
I have had an arbitration of an attorney-client fee dispute. (Attach Attorney -Client Fee Dispute form (see form SC-101).
Fill in this part only if you have already participated in an arbitration of an attorney-client fee dispute. There is a judicial counsel instruction sheet for filling out this part.
This claim is against a government agency, and I filed a claim with the agency. My claim was denied by the agency, or the agency did not act on my claim before the legal deadline. (*See form SC-150.*)
Before you can sue a government agency you must first file a claim with that agency. You must attach a copy of the denial by the agency.

I have asked defendant to pay this money, but it has not been paid.

> Before you bring suit in Small Claims Court make a demand on your defendant if possible

I have NOT asked defendant to pay this money because *(explain)*:

If you have not asked the defendant to pay the money, put an X in the box and briefly explain

This court is the proper court for the trial because *(In the box at the left, insert one of the letters from the list called "Venue Table" on the back of this sheet. If you select D, E, or F specify additional facts in this space)*:

> If you file your claim in the wrong Court, the judge will dismiss your claim unless all defendants agree during the hearing.

Enter:

"A" a defendant lives in this judicial district or the defendant business has its principle place of business in this judicial district.

"B" if you were injured or personal property was damaged in this judicial district.

"C" the contract was signed or entered into in this judicial district, the defendant lived in this judicial district when the contract was entered into, the contract or obligation was to be performed in this judicial district or if a corporation, the corporation breached the contract in this judicial district.

"D" if the suit is based on a retail installment account or contract.

"E" if the claim is on a vehicle finance sale.

"F" for other types of situations.

I have have not filed more than one other small claims action anywhere in California during this calendar year in which the amount demanded is more than $2,500.

> You may only file two claims for more that $2,500 per calendar year and must attest to the fact that this claim meets the rule.

I have not filed more than 12 small claims, including this claim, during the previous 12 months.

$20.00 to file; 12 claims per calendar year the filing fee is raised to $35.00.

I understand that

  I may talk to an attorney about this claim, but I cannot be represented by an attorney at the trial in the small claims court.

> Attorneys may only appear if they are plaintiffs or defendants in the claim.

 I must appear at the time and place of trial and bring all witnesses, books, receipts, and other papers or things to prove my case.

> In other words, prepare

I have no right to appeal on my claim, but I may appeal a claim filed by the defendant in this case.

> You have no right to appeal your claim, however, the defendant does have the right to appeal. However, if the defendant counter sues naming you as a defendant you may appeal if you lose the counter suit.

If I cannot afford to pay the fees for filing or service by a sheriff, marshal, or constable, I may ask that the fees be waived.

> Fill in the the Application for Waiver of Court Fees and Costs form and the Information Sheet on Waiver of Court Fees and Costs.

I have received and read the information sheet explaining some important rights of plaintiffs in the small claims court.

Rread the SC-150 Information for the Plaintiff form .

No defendant is in the military service except (*name*):

I declare under penalty of perjury under the laws of the State of California that the foregoing is true and correct.

Date:

_____   _____
(TYPE OR PRINT NAME)   (SIGNATURE OF PLAINTIFF)

C. COURT'S ORDER TO DEFENDANT SECTION.

ORDER TO DEFENDANT

You must appear in this court on the trial date and at the time LAST SHOWN IN THE BOX BELOW if you do not agree with the plaintiff's claim. Bring all witnesses, books, receipts, and other papers or things with you to support your case.

DATE DAY TIME PLACE COURT USE 1. (CHECK COURT CALENDAR FOR DIVISION) 2.   3.   4.

Filed on *(date):* Clerk, by_____,Deputy Don't fill out this part. It will be filled out by the Small Claims Court Clerk

this page intentionally left blank

ATTORNEY *(Name, state bar number, and address):*

FOR COURT USE ONLY

TELEPHONE NO.:　　　　　　　FAX NO. *(Optional):*

E–MAIL ADDRESS *(Optional):*

ATTORNEY FOR *(Name):*

SUPERIOR COURT OF CALIFORNIA, COUNTY OF

STREET ADDRESS:

MAILING ADDRESS:

CITY AND ZIP CODE:

BRANCH NAME:

PLAINTIFF/PETITIONER:

DEFENDANT/RESPONDENT:

**APPLICATION AND ORDER FOR APPOINTMENT
OF GUARDIAN AD LITEM—CIVIL
☐ EX PARTE**

CASE NUMBER:

NOTE: *This form is for use in civil proceedings in which a party is a minor, an incapacitated person, or a person for whom a conservator has been appointed. A party who seeks the appointment of a guardian ad litem in a family law or juvenile proceeding should use Form FJ-200. A party who seeks the appointment of a guardian ad litem in a probate proceeding should use Form DE-350, GC-100. An individual cannot act as a guardian ad litem unless he or she is represented by an attorney or is an attorney.*

1. Applicant *(name):*　　　　　　　　　　　　　　　　　　　　is
   a. ☐ the parent of *(name):*
   b. ☐ the guardian of *(name):*
   c. ☐ the conservator of *(name):*
   d. ☐ a party to the suit.
   e. ☐ the minor to be represented *(if the minor is 14 years of age or older).*
   f. ☐ another interested person *(specify capacity):*

2. This application seeks the appointment of the following person as guardian ad litem *(state name, address, and telephone number):*

3. The guardian ad litem is to represent the interests of the following person *(state name, address, and telephone number):*

4. The person to be represented is:
   a. ☐ a minor *(date of birth):*
   b. ☐ an incompetent person.
   c. ☐ a person for whom a conservator has been appointed.

5. The court should appoint a guardian ad litem because:
   a. ☐ the person named in item 3 has a cause or causes of action on which suit should be brought *(describe):*

☐ Continued on Attachment 5a.

(Continued on reverse)

**APPLICATION AND ORDER FOR APPOINTMENT
OF GUARDIAN AD LITEM—CIVIL**

Code of Civil Procedure,
§ 372 et seq.

PLAINTIFF/PETITIONER:	CASE NUMBER:
DEFENDANT/RESPONDENT:	

5. b. ☐ more than 10 days have elapsed since the summons in the above-entitled matter was served on the person named in item 3, and no application for the appointment of a guardian ad litem has been made by the person identified in item 3 or any other person.

c. ☐ the person named in item 3 has no guardian or conservator of his or her estate.

d. ☐ the appointment of a guardian ad litem is necessary for the following reasons (specify):

☐ Continued on Attachment 5d.

6. The proposed guardian ad litem's relationship to the person he or she will be representing is:
a. ☐ related (state relationship):
b. ☐ not related (specify capacity):

7. The proposed guardian ad litem is fully competent and qualified to understand and protect the rights of the person he or she will represent and has no interests adverse to the interests of that person. (If there are any issues of competency or qualification or any possible adverse interests, describe and explain why the proposed guardian should nevertheless be appointed):

☐ Continued on Attachment 7.

_____   ▶ _____
(TYPE OR PRINT NAME)   (SIGNATURE OF ATTORNEY)

I declare under penalty of perjury under the laws of the State of California that the foregoing is true and correct.

Date:

_____   ▶ _____
(TYPE OR PRINT NAME)   (SIGNATURE OF APPLICANT)

CONSENT TO ACT AS GUARDIAN AD LITEM

I consent to the appointment as guardian ad litem under the above petition.

Date:

_____   ▶ _____
(TYPE OR PRINT NAME)   (SIGNATURE OF PROPOSED GUARDIAN AD LITEM)

ORDER   ☐ EX PARTE

THE COURT FINDS that it is reasonable and necessary to appoint a guardian ad litem for the person named in item 3 of the application, as requested.

THE COURT ORDERS that (name):
is hereby appointed as the guardian ad litem for (name):
for the reasons set forth in item 5 of the application.

Date:

_____
JUDICIAL OFFICER
☐ SIGNATURE FOLLOWS LAST ATTACHMENT

**APPLICATION AND ORDER FOR APPOINTMENT
OF GUARDIAN AD LITEM—CIVIL**

Name and Address of Court:

SMALL CLAIMS CASE NO.:

— INSTRUCTIONS —

A. **If you regularly do business in California for profit under a fictitious business name, you must execute, file, and publish a fictitious business name statement. This is sometimes called a "dba" which stands for "doing business as." This requirement applies if you are doing business as an individual, a partnership, a corporation, or an association. The requirement does not apply to nonprofit corporations and associations or certain real estate investment trusts. You must file the fictitious business name statement with the clerk of the county where you have your principal place of business, or in Sacramento County if you have no place of business within the state.**

B. **If you do business under a fictitious business name and you also wish to file an action in the small claims court, you must declare under penalty of perjury that you have complied with the fictitious business name laws by filling out the form below.**

C. **If you have not complied with the fictitious business name laws, the court may dismiss your claim. You may be able to refile your claim when you have fulfilled these requirements.**

FICTITIOUS BUSINESS NAME DECLARATION

1. I wish to file a claim in the small claims court for a business doing business under the fictitious name of *(specify name and address of business):*

2. The business is doing business as

   ☐ an individual
   ☐ a partnership
   ☐ a corporation

   ☐ an association
   ☐ other *(specify):*

statement in the county of *(specify):*

4. The number of the statement is *(specify):*   and the statement expires on *(date):*

I declare under penalty of perjury under the laws of the State of California that the foregoing is true and correct.

Date:

▶

. . . .
(TYPE OR PRINT NAME)   (SIGNATURE OF DECLARANT)

Form Approved by the
Judicial Council of California
SC-103 [Rev. January 1, 1992]
FICTITIOUS BUSINESS NAME DECLARATION
(Small Claims)
Rule 982.7(b)
Code of Civil Procedure, § 116.430

191

this page intentionally left blank

INFORMATION SHEET ON WAIVER
OF COURT FEES AND COSTS
(California Rules of Court, rule 985)

If you have been sued or if you wish to sue someone, and if you cannot afford to pay court fees and costs, you may not have to pay them if:

1. You are receiving **financial assistance** under one or more of the following programs:

   - SSI and SSP (Supplemental Security Income and State Supplemental Payments Programs)
   - CalWORKs (California Work Opportunity and Responsibility to Kids Act, implementing TANF, Temporary Assistance for Needy Families, formerly AFDC, Aid to Families with Dependent Children Program)
   - The Food Stamp Program
   - County Relief, General Relief (G.R.), or General Assistance (G.A.)

   If you are claiming eligibility for a waiver of court fees and costs because you receive financial assistance under one or more of these programs, and you did not provide your Medi-Cal number or your social security number and birthdate, you must produce documentation confirming benefits from a public assistance agency or one of the following documents, unless you are a defendant in an unlawful detainer action:

PROGRAM	VERIFICATION
SSI/SSP	Medi-Cal Card *or* Notice of Planned Action *or* SSI Computer-Generated Printout *or* Bank Statement Showing SSI Deposit *or* "Passport to Services"
CalWORKs/TANF (formerly known as AFDC)	Medi-Cal Card *or* Notice of Action *or* Income and Eligibility Verification Form *or* Monthly Reporting Form *or* Electronic Benefit Transfer Card *or* "Passport to Services"
Food Stamp Program	Notice of Action *or* Food Stamp ID Card *or* "Passport to Services"
General Relief/General Assistance	Notice of Action *or* Copy of Check Stub *or* County Voucher

— OR —

2. Your total gross **monthly household income** is less than the following amounts:

NUMBER IN FAMILY	FAMILY INCOME		NUMBER IN FAMILY	FAMILY INCOME
1	$ 922.92		6	$ 2,527.08
2	1,243.75		7	2,847.92
3	1,564.58		8	3,168.75
4	1,885.42		Each additional	320.83
5	2,206.25			

— OR —

3. Your income is not enough to pay for the common **necessaries** of life for yourself and the people you support and also pay court fees and costs.

To apply, fill out the Application for Waiver of Court Fees and Costs (Form 982(a)(17)) available from the clerk's office. If you claim no income, you may be required to file a declaration under penalty of perjury. Prison and jail inmates may be required to pay up to the full amount of the filing fee.

If you have any questions and cannot afford an attorney, you may wish to consult the legal aid office, legal services office, or lawyer referral service in your county (listed in the Yellow Pages under "Attorneys").

If you are asking for review of the decision of an administrative body under Code of Civil Procedure section 1094.5 (administrative mandate), you may ask for a transcript of the administrative proceedings at the expense of the administrative body.

Form Adopted for Mandatory Use
Judicial Council of California
982(a)(17)(A) [Rev. March 1, 2002]

**INFORMATION SHEET ON WAIVER
OF COURT FEES AND COSTS
(In Forma Pauperis)**

Government Code, § 68511.3;
Cal. Rules of Court, rule 985

this page intentionally left blank

— THIS FORM MUST BE KEPT CONFIDENTIAL — 982(a)(17)

ATTORNEY OR PARTY WITHOUT ATTORNEY *(Name, state bar number, and address)*:	*FOR COURT USE ONLY*
TELEPHONE NO.: FAX NO. *(Optional)*: E-MAIL ADDRESS *(Optional)*: ATTORNEY FOR *(Name)*:	
NAME OF COURT: STREET ADDRESS: MAILING ADDRESS: CITY AND ZIP CODE: BRANCH NAME:	

PLAINTIFF/ PETITIONER:

DEFENDANT/ RESPONDENT:

APPLICATION FOR WAIVER OF COURT FEES AND COSTS	CASE NUMBER:

I request a court order so that I do not have to pay court fees and costs.

1. a. ☐ I am **not** able to pay any of the court fees and costs.
    b. ☐ I am able to pay **only** the following court fees and costs *(specify)*:

2. My current street or mailing address is *(if applicable, include city or town, apartment no., if any, and zip code)*:

3. a. My occupation, employer, and employer's address are *(specify)*:

    b. My spouse's occupation, employer, and employer's address are *(specify)*:

4. ☐ I am receiving financial assistance under one or more of the following programs:
    a. ☐ **SSI and SSP:** Supplemental Security Income and State Supplemental Payments Programs
    b. ☐ **CalWORKs:** California Work Opportunity and Responsibility to Kids Act, implementing TANF, Temporary Assistance for Needy Families (formerly AFDC)
    c. ☐ **Food Stamps:** The Food Stamp Program
    d. ☐ **County Relief, General Relief (G.R.), or General Assistance (G.A.)**

5. *If you checked box 4, you must check and complete **one of the three boxes below, unless you are a defendant in an unlawful detainer action. Do not check more than one box.***
    a. ☐ *(Optional)* My Medi-Cal number is *(specify)*:
    b. ☐ *(Optional)* My social security number is *(specify)*:
    ☐☐☐ – ☐☐ – ☐☐☐☐   and my date of birth is *(specify)*:
    [*Federal law does not require that you give your social security number. However, if you don't give your social security number, you must check box c and attach documents to verify the benefits checked in item 4.*]
    c. ☐ I am attaching documents to verify receipt of the benefits checked in item 4, if requested by the court.
    [*See Form 982(a)(17)(A)* Information Sheet on Waiver of Court Fees and Costs, *available from the clerk's office, for a list of acceptable documents.*]

[*If you checked box 4 above, skip items 6 and 7, and sign at the bottom of this side.*]

6. ☐ My total gross monthly household income is less than the amount shown on the *Information Sheet on Waiver of Court Fees and Costs* available from the clerk's office.

[*If you checked box 6 above, skip item 7, complete items 8, 9a, 9d, 9f, and 9g on the back of this form, and sign at the bottom of this side.*]

7. ☐ My income is not enough to pay for the common necessaries of life for me and the people in my family whom I support and also pay court fees and costs. **[*If you check this box, you must complete the back of this form.*]**

> **WARNING: You must immediately tell the court if you become able to pay court fees or costs during this action. You may be ordered to appear in court and answer questions about your ability to pay court fees or costs.**

I declare under penalty of perjury under the laws of the State of California that the information on both sides of this form and all attachments are true and correct.

Date:

▶

_____   _____
(TYPE OR PRINT NAME)   (Financial information on reverse)   (SIGNATURE)

Form Adopted for Mandatory Use
Judicial Council of California
982(a)(17) [Rev. January 1, 2001]

APPLICATION FOR WAIVER OF COURT FEES AND COSTS
(In Forma Pauperis)

Government Code,
§ 68511.3

PLAINTIFF/PETITIONER:	CASE NUMBER:
DEFENDANT/RESPONDENT:	

FINANCIAL INFORMATION

8. ☐ My pay changes considerably from month to month. **[If you check this box, each of the amounts reported in item 9 should be your average for the past 12 months.]**

9. **MY MONTHLY INCOME**
   a. My gross monthly pay is: . . . . $ _____
   b. **My payroll deductions are (specify purpose and amount):**
   (1) _____ $ _____
   (2) _____ $ _____
   (3) _____ $ _____
   (4) _____ $ _____
   My TOTAL payroll deduction amount is: $ _____
   c. My monthly take-home pay is
   (a. minus b.): . . . . $ _____
   d. Other money I get each month is *(specify **source** and **amount**; include spousal support, child support, parental support, support from outside the home, scholarships, retirement or pensions, social security, disability, unemployment, military basic allowance for quarters (BAQ), veterans payments, dividends, interest or royalty, trust income, annuities, net business income, net rental income, reimbursement of job-related expenses, and net gambling or lottery winnings):*
   (1) _____ $ _____
   (2) _____ $ _____
   (3) _____ $ _____
   (4) _____ $ _____
   The TOTAL amount of other money is: $ _____
   (If more space is needed, attach page labeled Attachment 9d.)
   e. **MY TOTAL MONTHLY INCOME IS**
   (c. plus d.): . . . . $ _____
   f. Number of persons living in my home: _____
   Below list all the persons living in your home, including your spouse, who depend in whole or in part on you for support, **or** on whom you depend in whole or in part for support:

Name	Age	Relationship	Gross Monthly Income
(1) _____	___	_____	$ _____
(2) _____	___	_____	$ _____
(3) _____	___	_____	$ _____
(4) _____	___	_____	$ _____
(5) _____	___	_____	$ _____

   The TOTAL amount of other money is: $ _____
   (If more space is needed, attach page labeled Attachment 9f.)
   g. **MY TOTAL GROSS MONTHLY HOUSEHOLD INCOME IS**
   (a. plus d. plus f.): . . . . $ _____

10. **I own or have an interest in the following property:**
   a. Cash . . . . $ _____
   b. Checking, savings, and credit union accounts *(list banks):*
   (1) _____ $ _____
   (2) _____ $ _____
   (3) _____ $ _____
   (4) _____ $ _____

   c. Cars, other vehicles, and boats *(list make, year, fair market value (FMV), and loan balance of each):*

Property	FMV	Loan Balance
(1) _____	$ _____	$ _____
(2) _____	$ _____	$ _____
(3) _____	$ _____	$ _____

   d. Real estate *(list address, estimated fair market value (FMV), and loan balance of each property):*

Property	FMV	Loan Balance
(1) _____	$ _____	$ _____
(2) _____	$ _____	$ _____
(3) _____	$ _____	$ _____

   e. Other personal property — jewelry, furniture, furs, stocks, bonds, etc. *(list separately):*
   $ _____

11. **My monthly expenses not already listed in item 9b above are the following:**
   a. Rent or house payment & maintenance $ _____
   b. Food and household supplies . . . . $ _____
   c. Utilities and telephone . . . . $ _____
   d. Clothing . . . . $ _____
   e. Laundry and cleaning . . . . $ _____
   f. Medical and dental payments . . . . $ _____
   g. Insurance (life, health, accident, etc.) . . $ _____
   h. School, child care . . . . $ _____
   i. Child, spousal support (prior marriage) $ _____
   j. Transportation and auto expenses (insurance, gas, repair) . . . . $ _____
   k. Installment payments *(specify **purpose** and **amount**):*
   (1) _____ $ _____
   (2) _____ $ _____
   (3) _____ $ _____
   The TOTAL amount of monthly installment payments is: . . . . $ _____
   l. Amounts deducted due to wage assignments and earnings withholding orders: $ _____
   m. Other expenses *(specify):*
   (1) _____ $ _____
   (2) _____ $ _____
   (3) _____ $ _____
   (4) _____ $ _____
   (5) _____ $ _____
   The TOTAL amount of other monthly expenses is: . . . . $ _____
   n. **MY TOTAL MONTHLY EXPENSES ARE**
   (add a. through m.): . . . . $ _____

12. Other facts that support this application are *(describe unusual medical needs, expenses for recent family emergencies, or other unusual circumstances or expenses to help the court understand your budget; if more space is needed, attach page labeled Attachment 12):*

WARNING: You must immediately tell the court if you become able to pay court fees or costs during this action. You may be ordered to appear in court and answer questions about your ability to pay court fees or costs.

APPLICATION FOR WAIVER OF COURT FEES AND COSTS
(In Forma Pauperis)

982(a)(18)

ATTORNEY OR PARTY WITHOUT ATTORNEY *(Name, state bar number, and address):*	FOR COURT USE ONLY

TELEPHONE NO.:   FAX NO.:

ATTORNEY FOR *(Name)*:

NAME OF COURT:

STREET ADDRESS:

MAILING ADDRESS:

CITY AND ZIP CODE:

BRANCH NAME:

PLAINTIFF/ PETITIONER:

DEFENDANT/ RESPONDENT:

ORDER ON APPLICATION FOR WAIVER OF COURT FEES AND COSTS	CASE NUMBER:

1. The application was filed on *(date):* ☐ A previous order was issued on *(date):*

2. The application was filed by *(name):*

3. ☐ IT IS ORDERED that the application is **granted** ☐ in whole ☐ in part *(see Cal. Rules of Court, rule 985).*

     a. ☐ **No payments.** Payment of all the fees and costs listed in California Rules of Court, rule 985(i), **is waived.**

     b. ☐ **The applicant shall pay** all the fees and costs listed in California Rules of Court, rule 985(i), EXCEPT the following:

         (1) ☐ Filing papers.   (6) ☐ Sheriff and marshal fees.

         (2) ☐ Certification and copying.   (7) ☐ Reporter's fees* *(valid for 60 days).*

         (3) ☐ Issuing process and certification.   (8) ☐ Telephone appearance (Gov. Code, § 68070.1(c))

         (4) ☐ Transmittal of papers.   (9) ☐ Other *(specify code section):*

         (5) ☐ Court-appointed interpreter *(small claims only).*

         * Reporter's fees are per diem pursuant to Code Civ. Proc., §§ 269, 274c, and Gov. Code, §§ 69947, 69948, and 72195.

     c. **Method of payment.** The applicant shall pay all the fees and costs when charged, EXCEPT as follows:

         (1) ☐ Pay *(specify):*   percent.   (2) ☐ Pay: $ per month or more until the balance is paid.

     d. The clerk of the court, county financial officer, or appropriate county officer is authorized to require the litigant to appear before and be examined by the court no sooner than four months from the date of this order, and not more than once in any four-month period. ☐ The applicant is ordered to appear in this court as follows for review of his or her financial status:

Date:	Time:	Dept.:	Div.:	Room:

     e. ☐ *(must be completed if application is granted in part)* Reasons for denial of a requested waiver *(specify):*

     f. ☐ The clerk is directed to mail a copy of this order to the applicant's attorney or to the applicant if unrepresented.

     g. **All unpaid fees and costs shall be deemed to be taxable costs if the applicant is entitled to costs and shall be a lien on any judgment recovered by the applicant and shall be paid directly to the clerk by the judgment debtor upon such recovery.**

4. ☐ IT IS ORDERED that the application is **denied** for the following reasons *(specify):*

     a. The applicant shall pay any fees and costs due in this action within 10 days from the date of service of this order or any paper filed by the applicant with the clerk will be of no effect.

     b. The clerk is directed to mail a copy of this order to all parties who have appeared in this action.

5. ☐ IT IS ORDERED that a **hearing** be held.

     a. The substantial evidentiary conflict to be resolved by the hearing is *(specify):*

     b. The applicant should appear in this court at the following hearing to help resolve the conflict:

Date:	Time:	Dept.:	Div.:	Room:

     c. The address of the court is *(specify):*

     d. The clerk is directed to mail a copy of this order to the applicant only.

NOTICE: If item 3d or item 5b is filled in and the applicant does not attend the hearing, the court may revoke or change the order or deny the application without considering information the applicant wants the court to consider.

WARNING: The applicant must immediately tell the court if he or she becomes able to pay court fees or costs during this action. The applicant may be ordered to appear in court and answer questions about his or her ability to pay fees or costs.

Date: _____

_____
JUDICIAL OFFICER

(Continued on reverse)

ORDER ON APPLICATION FOR WAIVER OF COURT FEES AND COSTS (In Forma Pauperis)

Government Code, §
68511.3; Cal. Rules
of Court, rule 985

PLAINTIFF/PETITIONER *(Name):*	CASE NUMBER:
DEFENDANT/RESPONDENT *(Name):*	

CLERK'S CERTIFICATE OF MAILING

I certify that I am not a party to this cause and that a true copy of the foregoing was mailed first class, postage prepaid, in a sealed envelope addressed as shown below, and that the mailing of the foregoing and execution of this certificate occurred at *(place):*   , California, on *(date):*

Clerk, by _____, Deputy

(SEAL)

CLERK'S CERTIFICATE

I certify that the foregoing is a true and correct copy of the original on file in my office.

Date: Clerk, by _____, Deputy

**ORDER ON APPLICATION FOR WAIVER OF
COURT FEES AND COSTS (In Forma Pauperis)**

PARTY ☐ PLAINTIFF ☐ DEFENDANT *(Name and Address):*		TELEPHONE NO.:	**FOR COURT USE ONLY**
NAME AND ADDRESS OF COURT:			
PLAINTIFF(S):			
DEFENDANT(S):			

PROOF OF SERVICE (Small Claims)	HEARING DATE:	DAY:	TIME:	DEPT./DIVISION:	CASE NUMBER:

1. At the time of service I was at least 18 years of age and not a party to this action, and **I served copies** of the following:

☐ Plaintiff's Claim   ☐ Order of Examination   ☐ Other *(specify):*
☐ Defendant's Claim   ☐ Subpena Duces Tecum

2. a. Party served *(specify name of party as shown on the documents served):*

   b. Person served: ☐ party in item 2.a. ☐ other *(specify name and title or relationship to the party named in item 2.a.)*

3. By delivery ☐ at home ☐ at business
   a. date:
   b. time:
   c. address:

4. **Manner of service** *(check proper box):*
   a. ☐ **Personal service.** I personally delivered to and left copies with the party served. **(C.C.P. 415.10)**
   b. ☐ **Substituted service on corporation, unincorporated association (including partnership), or public entity.** By leaving, during usual office hours, copies in the office of the person served with the person who apparently was in charge and thereafter mailing (by first-class mail, postage prepaid) copies to the person to be served at the place where the copies were left. **(C.C.P. 415.20(a))**
   c. ☐ **Substituted service on natural person, minor, incompetent, or candidate.** By leaving copies at the dwelling house, usual place of abode, usual place of business, or usual mailing address other than a U. S. Postal Service post office box of the person served in the presence of a competent member of the household or a person apparently in charge of the office or place of business, at least 18 years of age, who was informed of the general nature of the papers, and thereafter mailing (by first-class mail, postage prepaid) copies to the person to be served at the place where the copies were left. **(C.C.P. 415.20(b))**
   d. ☐ **Date of mailing:**   **From** *(city):*

> **Information regarding date and place of mailing is required for services effected in manner 4.b. and 4.c. above.**
> **Certified mail service may be performed only by the Clerk of the Court in small claims matters.**

5. **Person serving** *(name, address, and telephone number):*
   a. **Fee** for service: $
   b. ☐ Not a registered California process server
   c. ☐ **Exempt** from registration under B&P Section 22350(b)
   d. ☐ **Registered** California process server
      1. ☐ Employee or independent contractor
      2. **Registration Number:**
      3. **County:**

6. ☐ I declare under penalty of perjury under the laws of the State of California that the foregoing is true and correct.
7. ☐ I am a California sheriff, marshal, or constable and I certify that the foregoing is true and correct.

Date: ▶

_____
(SIGNATURE OF SERVER)

Form Approved by the
Judicial Council of California
SC-104 [New January 1, 1992]

PROOF OF SERVICE
(Small Claims)

Code of Civil Procedure
§§ 415.10, 415.20

199

INSTRUCTIONS FOR FILING PROOF OF SERVICE

A. Print the name and address of the person filing the Proof Of Service.

B. Print the name and address of the Court in which you are filing.

C. Print the name of the plaintiff and defendant as it appears on the Plaintiff's Claim.

D. Date of hearing.

E. Day of week.

F. Time in which your case is scheduled to be heard.

G. Division in which your case is calendared.

H. **YOUR CASE NUMBER**

1. X the appropriate box.

2. a. Print the name of the party you served (most effective service made is on the defendant directly).

    b. Print the relationship to the party named in 2a.(if the person you served was not the defendant).

3. Where the documents were delivered and the address.

4. Manner of Service (check proper box).
    Indicate how the defendant was served, i.e., personal or substituted service.

    If you subserved the defendant, **YOU MUST MAIL A COPY OF THE PLAINTIFF'S CLAIM TO THE DEFENDANT.**

5. Print the name and address of the person serving the document.
    Check the appropriate box.

6. **CHECKING THIS BOX INDICATES TO THE COURT THAT ALL YOU HAVE STATED ABOVE IS TRUE AND CORRECT.**

7. Check this box only if you are a California marshal, etc.

    DATE AND SIGN THE PROOF OF SERVICE BEFORE FILING WITH THE CLERK'S OFFICE. RETURN THE PROOF OF SERVICE TO THE COURT 5 DAYS PRIOR TO THE HEARING DATE.

Name and Address of Court:

SMALL CLAIMS CASE NO.

Names and addresses of additional plaintiffs and defendants:	*Nombres y direcciones de los demandantes y demandados adicionales:*

☐ PLAINTIFF/DEMANDANTE
(Name and address)

☐ DEFENDANT/DEMANDADO

☐ PLAINTIFF/DEMANDANTE
(Name and address)

☐ DEFENDANT/DEMANDADO

☐ PLAINTIFF/DEMANDANTE
(Name and address)

☐ DEFENDANT/DEMANDADO

☐ PLAINTIFF/DEMANDANTE
(Name and address)

☐ DEFENDANT/DEMANDADO

☐ PLAINTIFF/DEMANDANTE
(Name and address)

☐ DEFENDANT/DEMANDADO

☐ PLAINTIFF/DEMANDANTE
(Name and address)

☐ DEFENDANT/DEMANDADO

☐ PLAINTIFF/DEMANDANTE
(Name and address)

☐ DEFENDANT/DEMANDADO

☐ PLAINTIFF/DEMANDANTE
(Name and address)

☐ DEFENDANT/DEMANDADO

When space is not available on a small claims form, this form may be used to list additional plaintiffs and defendants. If this form is used, be sure to attach it to the accompanying small claims form and serve both together on the plaintiffs and defendants as provided by law.

Form Approved by the
Judicial Council of California
SC-160 [New January 1, 1985]

ADDITIONAL PLAINTIFFS AND DEFENDANTS
(Small Claims)

Rule 982.7

this page intentionally left blank

_____

_____

_____

_____

REQUEST FOR POSTPONEMENT (CCP 116.570)

Name and Address of Requesting Party	Case Number:
Telephone Number: ( )	

PLAINTIFF:	VS	DEFENDANT:

I am the Plaintiff/Defendant in the above entitled action. I declare that:

_____ A $10.00 postponement fee is attached (non-refundable)

_____ A fee waiver for the $10.00 postponement fee has been filed.

I am requesting that my small claims hearing date of _____ be postponed and rescheduled to _____ for the following reason:

I declare under the penalty of perjury under the laws of the State of California that the foregoing is true and correct.

Date:_____   _____
                                                                    SIGNATURE OF DECLARANT

REQUEST FOR POSTPONEMENT

DECLARATION OF SERVICE BY MAIL

I served a copy of the Request for Postponement by depositing a copy thereof enclosed in sealed envelope, with postage prepaid in the United States mail at (city) _____, addressed as follows (name and address of opposing party(s).

I declare under penalty of perjury that the foregoing is true and correct.

Executed on_____at_____, California.
               DATE   PLACE

_____
SIGNATURE OF DECLARANT

_____
TYPE OR PRINT NAME OF DECLARANT

_____
TYPE OR PRINT ADDRESS OF DECLARANT

Name and Address of Court:

SC-120

SMALL CLAIMS CASE NO.

— NOTICE TO PLAINTIFF — **YOU ARE BEING SUED BY DEFENDANT**	— *AVISO AL DEMANDANTE* — *A USTED LO ESTA DEMANDANDO EL*
To protect your rights, you must appear in this court on the trial date shown in the table below. You may lose the case if you do not appear. The court may award the defendant the amount of the claim and the costs. Your wages, money, and property may be taken without further warning from the court.	*Para proteger sus derechos, usted debe presentarse ante esta corte en la fecha del juicio indicada en el cuadro que aparece a continuación. Si no se presenta, puede perder el caso. La corte puede decidir en favor del deman- dado por la cantidad del reclamo y los costos. A usted le pueden quitar su salario, su dinero, y otras cosas de su propiedad, sin aviso adicional por parte de esta corte.*

PLAINTIFF/*DEMANDANTE* (Name, address, and telephone number of each):

DEFENDANT/*DEMANDADO* (Name, address, and telephone number of each):

Telephone No.:

Telephone No.:

Telephone No.:

Telephone No.:

Fict. Bus. Name Stmt. No.   Expires: ☐ See attached sheet for additional plaintiffs and defendants.

DEFENDANT'S CLAIM

1. Plaintiff owes me the sum of: $ _____ , not including court costs, because *(describe claim and date)*:

2. a. ☐ I have asked plaintiff to pay this money, but it has not been paid.
   b. ☐ I have NOT asked plaintiff to pay this money because *(explain)*:

3. I ☐ have ☐ have not   filed more than one other small claims action anywhere in California during this calendar year in which the amount demanded is more than $2,500.

4. I understand that
   a. I may talk to an attorney about this claim, but I cannot be represented by an attorney at the trial in the small claims court.
   b. I must appear at the time and place of trial and bring all witnesses, books, receipts, and other papers or things to prove my case.
   c. **I have no right of appeal on my claim,** but I may appeal a claim filed by the plaintiff in this case.
   d. If I cannot afford to pay the fees for filing or service by a sheriff or marshal, I may ask that the fees be waived.

5. I have received and read the information sheet explaining some important rights of defendants in the small claims court.

6. No plaintiff is in the military service ☐ except *(name)*:

I declare under penalty of perjury under the laws of the State of California that the foregoing is true and correct.
Date:

▶

_____   _____
(TYPE OR PRINT NAME)   (SIGNATURE OF DEFENDANT)

ORDER TO PLAINTIFF

You must appear in this court on the trial date and at the time LAST SHOWN IN THE BOX BELOW if you do not agree with the defendant's claim. Bring all witnesses, books, receipts, and other papers or things with you to support your case.

TRIAL DATE FECHA DEL JUICIO		DATE	DAY	TIME	PLACE	COURT USE
	1.					
	2.					
	3.					
	4.					

Filed on *(date)*: _____   Clerk, by _____ , Deputy

— The county provides small claims advisor services free of charge. (Advisor phone number: _____)—

Form Adopted for Mandatory Use
Judicial Council of California
SC-120 [Rev. July 1, 2000]

DEFENDANT'S CLAIM AND ORDER TO PLAINTIFF
(Small Claims)

Cal. Rules of Court, rule 982.7;
Code of Civil Procedure, § 116.110 et seq.

this page intentionally left blank

Name and Address of Court:

| | SMALL CLAIMS CASE NO. |

PLAINTIFF/DEMANDANTE *(Name, address, and telephone number of each)*:

DEFENDANT/DEMANDADO *(Name, address, and telephone number of each)*:

Telephone No.:

Telephone No.:

Telephone No.:

Telephone No.:

☐ See attached sheet for additional plaintiffs and defendants.

NOTICE TO *(Names)*:

NOTICE OF MOTION FOR *(specify)*:

1. I request the court to make an order to *(specify)*:
2. My request is based on this notice of motion and declaration, the records on file with the court, and any evidence that may be presented at the hearing.

DECLARATION SUPPORTING MY REQUEST FOR THIS MOTION

3. I am the ☐ plaintiff ☐ defendant in this action.

4. The facts supporting this motion are as follows *(specify)*:

☐ Item 4 continued on attached page.

I declare under penalty of perjury under the laws of the State of California that the foregoing is true and correct.

Date:

. . . .
(TYPE OR PRINT NAME)

▶

(SIGNATURE)

5. If you wish to oppose this request you should appear at the court on

		DATE	DAY	TIME	PLACE
HEARING DATE	1.				
FECHA DEL JUICIO	2.				
	3.				
	4.				

CLERK'S CERTIFICATE OF MAILING

I certify that I am not a party to this action. This Notice of Motion was mailed first class, postage prepaid, in a sealed envelope to the responding party at the address shown above. The mailing and this certification occurred

at *(place)*: , California,

on *(date)*:

Clerk, by _____ , Deputy

| — The county provides small claims advisor services free of charge. — |

Form Approved by the
Judicial Council of California
SC-105 [New January 1. 1992]

NOTICE OF MOTION AND DECLARATION
(Small Claims)

this page intentionally left blank

Name and Address of Court:

SMALL CLAIMS CASE NO.:

PLAINTIFF/DEMANDANTE *(Name, street address, and telephone number of each)*:

DEFENDANT/DEMANDADO *(Name, street address, and telephone number of each)*:

Telephone No.:

Telephone No.:

☐ See attached sheet for additional plaintiffs and defendants.

ORDER TO PRODUCE STATEMENT OF ASSETS AND TO APPEAR FOR EXAMINATION

1. TO JUDGMENT DEBTOR *(name)*:
2. YOU ARE ORDERED
   a. to pay the judgment and file proof of payment (a canceled check or money order or cash receipt, and a written declaration that shows full payment of the judgment, including postjudgment costs and interest) with the court before the hearing date shown in the box below, **OR**
   b. to (1) personally appear in this court on the date and time shown in the box below, and (2) bring with you a completed *Judgment Debtor's Statement of Assets* (form SC-133). (At the hearing you will be required to explain why you did not complete and mail form SC-133 to judgment creditor within 30 days after the *Notice of Entry of Judgment* (form SC-130) was mailed or handed to you by the clerk, and to answer questions about your income and assets.)

HEARING DATE / FECHA DEL JUICIO		DATE	DAY	TIME	PLACE	COURT USE
	1.					
	2.					
	3.					

If you fail to appear and have not paid the judgment, including postjudgment costs and interest, a bench warrant may be issued for your arrest, you may be held in contempt of court, and you may be ordered to pay penalties.	Si usted no se presenta y no ha pagado el monto del fallo judicial, inclusive las costas e intereses posteriores al fallo, la corte puede expedir una orden de detención contra usted, declararle en desacato y ordenar que pague multas.

3. This order may be served by a sheriff, marshal, or registered process server.

Date:

▶

_____
(SIGNATURE OF JUDGE)

APPLICATION FOR THIS ORDER

A. Judgment creditor (the person who won the case) *(name)*: applies for an order requiring
   judgment debtor (the person or business who lost the case and owes money) *(name)*:
   to (1) pay the judgment **or** (2) personally appear in this court with a completed *Judgment Debtor's Statement of Assets* (form SC-133), explain why judgment debtor did not pay the judgment or complete and mail form SC-133 to judgment creditor within 30 days after the *Notice of Entry of Judgment* was mailed or handed to judgment debtor, and answer questions about judgment debtor's income and assets.

B. Judgment creditor states the following:
   (1) Judgment debtor has not paid the judgment.
   (2) Judgment debtor either did not file an appeal or the appeal has been dismissed or judgment debtor lost the appeal.
   (3) Judgment debtor either did not file a motion to vacate or the motion to vacate has been denied.
   (4) More than 30 days have passed since the *Notice of Entry of Judgment* form was mailed or delivered to judgment debtor.
   (5) Judgment creditor has not received a completed *Judgment Debtor's Statement of Assets* form from judgment debtor.
   (6) The person to be examined resides or has a place of business in this county or within 150 miles of the place of examination.

I declare under penalty of perjury under the laws of the State of California that the foregoing is true and correct.

Date:

▶

_____   _____
(TYPE OR PRINT NAME)   (See Instructions on reverse)   (DECLARANT)

— The county provides small claims advisor services free of charge. —

Form Adopted by the
Judicial Council of California
SC-134 [Rev. January 1, 1999]

**APPLICATION AND ORDER TO PRODUCE STATEMENT
OF ASSETS AND TO APPEAR FOR EXAMINATION**
(Small Claims)

Cal. Rules of Court,
rule 982.7(a); Code of
Civil Procedure
§§ 116.820, 116.830

INSTRUCTIONS FOR JUDGMENT CREDITOR

1. To set a hearing on an *Application for Order to Produce Statement of Assets and to Appear for Examination*, you must complete this form, present it to the court clerk, and pay the fee for an initial hearing date or a reset hearing date.

2. After you file this form, the clerk will set a hearing date, note the hearing date on the form, and return two copies or an original and one copy of the form to you.

3. You must have a copy of this form and a blank copy of the *Judgment Debtor's Statement of Assets* (form SC-133) personally served on the judgment debtor by a sheriff, marshal, or registered process server at least 10 calendar days before the date of the hearing, and have a proof of service filed with the court. The law provides for a new fee if you reset the hearing.

4. If the judgment is paid, including all postjudgment costs and interest, you must immediately complete the *Acknowledgment of Satisfaction of Judgment* form on the reverse of the *Notice of Entry of Judgment* (form SC-130) and file a copy with the court.

5. You must attend the hearing unless the judgment has been paid.

6. This form is intended to be an easy tool to enforce your right to receive a completed *Judgment Debtor's Statement of Assets* (form SC-133). This form is not intended to replace the *Application and Order for Appearance and Examination* (form EJ-125), often called an "Order for Examination." The *Application and Order for Appearance and Examination* may still be used to enforce a small claims judgment if you are **not** seeking at the same time to make the debtor complete a *Judgment Debtor's Statement of Assets*.

SC-107

Name and Address of Court:

SMALL CLAIMS CASE NO.

PLAINTIFF/DEMANDANTE *(Name, address, and telephone number of each)*:

DEFENDANT/DEMANDADO *(Name, address, and telephone number of each)*:

Telephone No.:

Telephone No.:

Telephone No.:

Telephone No.:

☐ See attached sheet for additional plaintiffs and defendants.

SMALL CLAIMS SUBPOENA
FOR PERSONAL APPEARANCE AND PRODUCTION OF DOCUMENTS AND THINGS AT TRIAL OR HEARING AND DECLARATION

THE PEOPLE OF THE STATE OF CALIFORNIA, TO *(name, address, and telephone number of witness, if known)*:

1. **YOU ARE ORDERED TO APPEAR AS A WITNESS in this case at the date, time, and place shown in the box below UNLESS your appearance is excused as indicated in box 4b below or you make an agreement with the person named in item 2 below.**

   a. Date: Time: ☐ Dept.:   ☐ Div.:   ☐ Room:
   b. Address:

2. **IF YOU HAVE ANY QUESTIONS ABOUT THE TIME OR DATE YOU ARE TO APPEAR, OR IF YOU WANT TO BE CERTAIN THAT YOUR PRESENCE IS REQUIRED, CONTACT THE FOLLOWING PERSON BEFORE THE DATE ON WHICH YOU ARE TO APPEAR:**

   a. Name of subpoenaing party: b. Telephone number:

3. **Witness Fees:** You are entitled to witness fees and mileage actually traveled both ways, as provided by law, if you request them at the time of service. You may request them before your scheduled appearance from the person named in item 2.

PRODUCTION OF DOCUMENTS AND THINGS

(Complete item 4 only if you want the witness to produce documents and things at the trial or hearing.)

4. YOU ARE *(item a or b must be checked)*:

   a. ☐ Ordered to appear in person and to produce the records described in the declaration on page two. The personal attendance of the custodian or other qualified witness and the production of the original records are required by this subpoena. The procedure authorized by Evidence Code sections 1560(b), 1561, and 1562 will not be deemed sufficient compliance with this subpoena.

   b. ☐ Not required to appear in person if you produce (i) the records described in the declaration on page two and (ii) a completed declaration of custodian of records in compliance with Evidence Code sections 1560, 1561, 1562, and 1271.
   (1) Place a copy of the records in an envelope (or other wrapper). Enclose the original declaration of the custodian with the records. Seal the envelope. (2) Attach a copy of this subpoena to the envelope or write on the envelope the case name and number; your name; and the date, time, and place from item 1 in the box above. (3) Place this first envelope in an outer envelope, seal it, and mail it to the clerk of the court at the address in item 1. (4) Mail a copy of your declaration to the attorney or party listed at the top of this form.

5. **IF YOU HAVE BEEN SERVED WITH THIS SUBPOENA AS A CUSTODIAN OF CONSUMER OR EMPLOYEE RECORDS UNDER CODE OF CIVIL PROCEDURE SECTION 1985.3 OR 1985.6 AND A MOTION TO QUASH OR AN OBJECTION HAS BEEN SERVED ON YOU, A COURT ORDER OR AGREEMENT OF THE PARTIES, WITNESSES, *AND* CONSUMER OR EMPLOYEE AFFECTED MUST BE OBTAINED BEFORE YOU ARE REQUIRED TO PRODUCE CONSUMER OR EMPLOYEE RECORDS.**

> **DISOBEDIENCE OF THIS SUBPOENA MAY BE PUNISHED AS CONTEMPT BY THIS COURT. YOU WILL ALSO BE LIABLE FOR THE SUM OF FIVE HUNDRED DOLLARS AND ALL DAMAGES RESULTING FROM YOUR FAILURE TO OBEY.**

[SEAL]   Date issued:

Clerk, by _____, Deputy

(See reverse for declaration in support of subpoena)   **Page one of three**

Form Adopted for Mandatory Use
Judicial Council of California
SC-107 [Rev. January 1, 2000]

**SMALL CLAIMS SUBPOENA
AND DECLARATION**

Code of Civil Procedure,
§ 1985 et seq.

PLAINTIFF/PETITIONER:	CASE NUMBER:
DEFENDANT/RESPONDENT:	

DECLARATION IN SUPPORT OF
SMALL CLAIMS SUBPOENA FOR PERSONAL APPEARANCE
AND PRODUCTION OF DOCUMENT AND THINGS AT TRIAL OR HEARING
(Code Civil Procedure sections 1985, 1987.5)

. I, the undersigned, declare I am the ☐ plaintiff ☐ defendant ☐ judgment creditor
☐ other *(specify)*:   in the above entitled action.

!. The witness has possession or control of the following documents or other things and shall produce them at the time and place
specified on the *Small Claims Subpoena* on the first page of this form.

     a. ☐ For trial or hearing *(specify the exact documents or other things to be produced by the witness)*:

        ☐ Continued on Attachment 2a.

     b. ☐ After trial to enforce a judgment *(specify the exact documents or other things to be produced by the party who is the
judgment debtor or other witness possessing records relating to the judgment debtor)*:

        (1) ☐ Payroll receipts, stubs, and other records concerning employment of the party. Receipts, invoices, documents,
and other papers or records concerning any and all accounts receivable of the party.

        (2) ☐ Bank account statements, canceled checks, and check registers from any and all bank accounts in which the part
has an interest.

        (3) ☐ Savings account passbooks and statements, savings and loan account passbooks and statements, and credit
union share account passbooks and statements of the party.

        (4) ☐ Stock certificates, bonds, money market certificates, and any other records, documents, or papers concerning all
investments of the party.

        (5) ☐ California registration certificates and ownership certificates for all vehicles registered to the party.

        (6) ☐ Deeds to any and all real property owned or being purchased by the party.

        (7) ☐ Other *(specify)*:

!. Good cause exists for the production of the documents or other things described in paragraph 2 for the following reasons:

     ☐ Continued on Attachment 3.

!. These documents are material to the issues involved in this case for the following reasons:

     ☐ Continued on Attachment 4.

declare under penalty of perjury under the laws of the State of California that the foregoing is true and correct.

)ate:

▶

        . . . .

                (TYPE OR PRINT NAME)   (SIGNATURE OF PARTY)

PROOF OF SERVICE OF SMALL CLAIMS SUBPOENA FOR PERSONAL APPEARANCE AND PRODUCTION OF DOCUMENTS AND THINGS AT TRIAL OR HEARING AND DECLARATION

1. I served this *Small Claims Subpoena for Personal Appearance and Production of Documents and Things at Trial or Hearing and Declaration* by personally delivering a copy to the person served as follows:

   a. Person served *(name)*:

   b. Address where served:

   c. Date of delivery:

   d. Time of delivery:

   e. Witness fees *(check one)*:
      (1) ☐ were offered or demanded
          and paid. Amount: . . . . . $ _____
      (2) ☐ were not demanded or paid.

   f. Fee for service: . . . . $ _____

2. I received this subpoena for service on *(date)*:

3. Person serving:
   a. ☐ Not a registered California process server.
   b. ☐ California sheriff, marshal, or constable.
   c. ☐ Registered California process server.
   d. ☐ Employee or independent contractor of a registered California process server.
   e. ☐ Exempt from registration under Business & Professions Code section 22350(b).
   f. ☐ Registered professional photocopier.
   g. ☐ Exempt from registration under Business & Professions Code section 22451.
   h. Name, address, and telephone number and, if applicable, county of registration and number:

I declare under penalty of perjury under the laws of the State of California that the foregoing is true and correct.

Date:

▶ _____
(SIGNATURE)

(For California sheriff, marshal, or constable use only)
I certify that the foregoing is true and correct.

Date:

▶ _____
(SIGNATURE)

SC-107 [Rev. January 1, 2000]

**PROOF OF SERVICE OF SMALL CLAIMS SUBPOENA
FOR PERSONAL APPEARANCE AND PRODUCTION OF DOCUMENTS
AT TRIAL OF HEARING AND DECLARATION**

Page three of three

213

this page intentionally left blank

ATTORNEY OR PARTY WITHOUT ATTORNEY *(Name and Address):*	TELEPHONE NO.:	*FOR COURT USE ONLY*
ATTORNEY FOR *(Name):*		

Insert name of court and name of judicial district and branch court, if any:

PLAINTIFF/PETITIONER:

DEFENDANT/RESPONDENT:

REQUEST FOR DISMISSAL	CASE NUMBER:
☐ **Personal Injury, Property Damage, or Wrongful Death** ☐ **Motor Vehicle** ☐ **Other** ☐ **Family Law** ☐ **Eminent Domain** ☐ **Other** *(specify):*	

— A conformed copy will not be returned by the clerk unless a method of return is provided with the document. —

1. **TO THE CLERK: Please dismiss this action as follows:**

   a. (1) ☐ With prejudice   (2) ☐ Without prejudice

   b. (1) ☐ Complaint   (2) ☐ Petition
   (3) ☐ Cross-complaint filed by *(name):*   on *(date):*
   (4) ☐ Cross-complaint filed by *(name):*   on *(date):*
   (5) ☐ Entire action of all parties and all causes of action
   (6) ☐ Other *(specify):**

Date:

▶

(TYPE OR PRINT NAME OF ☐ ATTORNEY ☐ PARTY WITHOUT ATTORNEY)   (SIGNATURE)
* If dismissal requested is of specified parties only, of specified causes of action only, or of specified cross-complaints only, so state and identify the parties, causes of action, or cross-complaints to be dismissed.

Attorney or party without attorney for:
☐ Plaintiff/Petitioner   ☐ Defendant/Respondent
☐ Cross-complainant

2. **TO THE CLERK: Consent to the above dismissal is hereby given.****
Date:

▶

(TYPE OR PRINT NAME OF ☐ ATTORNEY ☐ PARTY WITHOUT ATTORNEY)   (SIGNATURE)
** If a cross-complaint—or Response (Family Law) seeking affirmative relief—is on file, the attorney for cross-complainant (respondent) must sign this consent if required by Code of Civil Procedure section 581(i) or (j).

Attorney or party without attorney for:
☐ Plaintiff/Petitioner   ☐ Defendant/Respondent
☐ Cross-complainant

(To be completed by clerk)

3. ☐ Dismissal entered as requested on *(date):*
4. ☐ Dismissal entered on *(date):*   as to only *(name):*
5. ☐ Dismissal **not entered** as requested for the following reasons *(specify):*

6. ☐ a. Attorney or party without attorney notified on *(date):*
   b. Attorney or party without attorney not notified. Filing party failed to provide
   ☐ a copy to conform   ☐ means to return conformed copy

Date: Clerk, by _____ , Deputy

Form Adopted by the Judicial Council of California 982(a)(5) [Rev. January 1, 1997] | **REQUEST FOR DISMISSAL** | Code of Civil Procedure, § 581 et seq. Cal. Rules of Court, rules 383, 1233

this page intentionally left blank

EJ-001

ATTORNEY OR PARTY WITHOUT ATTORNEY *(Name and Address):*   TEL NO.:

☐ Recording requested by and return to:

☐ ATTORNEY   ☐ JUDGMENT   ☐ ASSIGNEE OF
    FOR   CREDITOR   RECORD

NAME OF COURT:
STREET ADDRESS:
MAILING ADDRESS:
CITY AND ZIP CODE:
BRANCH NAME:

FOR RECORDER'S USE ONLY

PLAINTIFF:

DEFENDANT:

ABSTRACT OF JUDGMENT ☐ Amended	CASE NUMBER:

FOR COURT USE ONLY

1. The ☐ judgment creditor ☐ assignee of record
   applies for an abstract of judgment and represents the following:
   a. Judgment debtor's
                    Name and last known address

   b. Driver's license No. and state: ☐ Unknown
   c. Social security No.:   ☐ Unknown
   d. Summons or notice of entry of sister-state judgment was personally served or
      mailed to *(name and address):*

   e. ☐ Original abstract recorded in this county: f. ☐ Information on additional judgment debtors is
      (1) Date: shown on page two.
      (2) Instrument No.:

Date:

_____   ▶   _____
(TYPE OR PRINT NAME)   (SIGNATURE OF APPLICANT OR ATTORNEY)

2. a. ☐ I certify that the following is a true and correct abstract   6. Total amount of judgment as entered or last renewed:
        of the judgment entered in this action. $
   b. ☐ A certified copy of the judgment is attached.   7. ☐ An ☐ execution lien ☐ attachment lien
3. Judgment creditor *(name and address):*   is endorsed on the judgment as follows:
                                                                                 a. Amount: $
                                                                                 b. In favor of *(name and address):*

4. Judgment debtor *(full name as it appears in judgment):*

[SEAL]   5. a. Judgment entered on   8. A stay of enforcement has
                                    (date):   a. ☐ not been ordered by the court.
                                 b. Renewal entered on   b. ☐ been ordered by the court effective until
                                    (date):   *(date):*
                                 c. Renewal entered on   9. ☐ This judgment is an installment judgment.
                                    (date):

                              This abstract issued on *(date):*

                                                             Clerk, by _____, Deputy

Form Adopted for Mandatory Use
Judicial Council of California
EJ-001 [Rev. January 1, 2002]

ABSTRACT OF JUDGMENT
(CIVIL)

Page 1 of 2
Code of Civil Procedure, §§ 488.480,
674, 700.190

217

PLAINTIFF:	CASE NUMBER:
DEFENDANT:	

INFORMATION ON ADDITIONAL JUDGMENT DEBTORS

10. Name and last known address

Driver's license No. & state: ☐ Unknown
Social security No.: ☐ Unknown
Summons was personally served at or mailed to *(address):*

11. Name and last known address

Driver's license No. & state: ☐ Unknown
Social security No.: ☐ Unknown
Summons was personally served at or mailed to *(address):*

12. Name and last known address

Driver's license No. & state: ☐ Unknown
Social security No.: ☐ Unknown
Summons was personally served at or mailed to *(address):*

13. Name and last known address

Driver's license No. & state: ☐ Unknown
Social security No.: ☐ Unknown
Summons was personally served at or mailed to *(address):*

14. Name and last known address

Driver's license No. & state: ☐ Unknown
Social security No.: ☐ Unknown
Summons was personally served at or mailed to *(address):*

15. Name and last known address

Driver's license No. & state: ☐ Unknown
Social security No.: ☐ Unknown
Summons was personally served at or mailed to *(address):*

16. Name and last known address

Driver's license No. & state: ☐ Unknown
Social security No.: ☐ Unknown
Summons was personally served at or mailed to *(address):*

17. Name and last known address

Driver's license No. & state: ☐ Unknown
Social security No.: ☐ Unknown
Summons was personally served at or mailed to *(address):*

18. ☐ Continued on Attachment 18.

ABSTRACT OF JUDGMENT
(CIVIL)

SC-130

Name and Address of Court:

SMALL CLAIMS CASE NO.:

NOTICE TO ALL PLAINTIFFS AND DEFENDANTS: Your small claims case has been decided. If you lost the case, and the court ordered you to pay money, your wages, money, and property may be taken without further warning from the court. Read the back of this sheet for important information about your rights.	*AVISO A TODOS LOS DEMANDANTES Y DEMANDADOS: Su caso ha sido resuelto por la corte para reclamos judiciales menores. Si la corte ha decidido en su contra y ha ordenado que usted pague dinero, le pueden quitar su salario, su dinero, y otras cosas de su propiedad, sin aviso adicional por parte de esta corte. Lea el reverso de este formulario para obtener información de importancia acerca de sus derechos.*

PLAINTIFF/DEMANDANTE *(Name, street address, and telephone number of each)*:

DEFENDANT/DEMANDADO *(Name, street address, and telephone number of each)*:

Telephone No.:

Telephone No.:

Telephone No.:

Telephone No.:

☐ See attached sheet for additional plaintiffs and defendants.

NOTICE OF ENTRY OF JUDGMENT

Judgment was entered as checked below on *(date)*:

1. ☐ Defendant *(name, if more than one)*:
   shall pay plaintiff *(name, if more than one)*:
   $_____ principal and: $_____ costs on plaintiff's claim.
2. ☐ Defendant does not owe plaintiff any money on plaintiff's claim.
3. ☐ Plaintiff *(name, if more than one)*:
   shall pay defendant *(name, if more than one)*:
   $_____ principal and: $_____ costs on defendant's claim.
4. ☐ Plaintiff does not owe defendant any money on defendant's claim.
5. ☐ Possession of the following property is awarded to plaintiff *(describe property)*:

6. ☐ Payments are to be made at the rate of: $_____ per *(specify period)*:_____ , beginning on *(date)*:_____
   and on the *(specify day)*:_____ day of each month thereafter until paid in full. If any payment is missed, the entire balance may become due immediately.
7. ☐ Dismissed in court ☐ with prejudice ☐ without prejudice.
8. ☐ *Attorney-Client Fee Dispute (Attachment to Notice of Entry of Judgment)* (form SC-132) is attached.
9. ☐ Other *(specify)*:

10. ☐ This judgment results from a motor vehicle accident on a California highway and was caused by the judgment debtor's operation of a motor vehicle. If the judgment is not paid, the judgment creditor may apply to have the judgment debtor's driver's license suspended.
11. Enforcement of the judgment is automatically postponed for 30 days or, if an appeal is filed, until the appeal is decided.
12. ☐ This notice was personally delivered to *(insert name and date)*:
13. CLERK'S CERTIFICATE OF MAILING—I certify that I am not a party to this action. This *Notice of Entry of Judgment* was mailed first class, postage prepaid, in a sealed envelope to the parties at the addresses shown above. The mailing and this certification occurred at the place and on the date shown below.

Place of mailing: _____, California

Date of mailing: _____ Clerk, by _____, Deputy

— The county provides small claims advisor services free of charge. Read the information sheet on the reverse. —

Form Adopted for Mandatory Use
Judicial Council of California
SC-130 [Rev. January 1, 2000]

NOTICE OF ENTRY OF JUDGMENT
(Small Claims)

Cal. Rules of Court, rule 982.7;
Code of Civil Procedure, § 116.610

INFORMATION AFTER JUDGMENT	INFORMACION DESPUES DEL FALLO DE LA CORTE

Your small claims case has been decided. The **judgment** or decision of the court appears on the front of this sheet. The court may have ordered one party to pay money to the other party. The person (or business) who won the case and who can collect the money is called the **judgment creditor**. The person (or business) who lost the case and who owes the money is called the **judgment debtor**.

Enforcement of the judgment is **postponed** until the time for appeal ends or until the appeal is decided. This means that the judgment creditor cannot collect any money or take any action until this period is over. Generally, both parties may be represented by lawyers after judgment.

IF YOU LOST THE CASE . . .

1. If you lost the case on your own claim and the court did not award you any money, the court's decision on your claim is **FINAL**. You may not appeal your own claim.

2. If you lost the case and the court ordered you to pay money, your money and property may be taken to pay the claim unless you do one of the following things:

   a. **PAY THE JUDGMENT**
   The law requires you to pay the amount of the judgment. You may pay the judgment creditor directly, or pay the judgment to the court for an additional fee. You may also ask the court to order monthly payments you can afford. Ask the clerk for information about these procedures.

   b. **APPEAL**
   If you disagree with the court's decision, you may appeal the decision *on the other party's claim*. You may not appeal the decision on your own claim. However, if any party appeals, there will be a new trial on *all* the claims. If you appeared at the trial, you *must* begin your appeal by filing a form called a *Notice of Appeal* (form SC-140) and pay the required fees within *30 days* after the date this *Notice of Entry of Judgment* was mailed or handed to you. Your appeal will be in the superior court. You will have a **new trial** and you must present your evidence again. You may be represented by a lawyer.

   c. **VACATE OR CANCEL THE JUDGMENT**
   If you did not go to the trial, you may ask the court to vacate or cancel the judgment. To make this request, you must file a *Motion to Vacate the Judgment* (form SC-135) and pay the required fee *within 30 days* after the date this *Notice of Entry of Judgment* was mailed. If your request is denied, you then have *10 days* from the date the notice of denial was mailed to file an appeal.
   The period to file the *Motion to Vacate the Judgment* is 180 days if you were *not properly served* with the claim. The 180-day period begins on the date you found out or should have found out about the judgment against you.

IF YOU WON THE CASE . . .

1. If you were sued by the other party and you won the case, then the other party may not appeal the court's decision.

2. If you won the case and the court awarded you money, here are some steps you may take to collect your money or get possession of your property:

   a. **COLLECTING FEES AND INTEREST**
   Sometimes fees are charged for filing court papers or for serving the judgment debtor. These extra costs and after-judgment interest can become part of your original judgment. To claim these fees and interest, ask the clerk for a *Memorandum of Costs*.

b. **VOLUNTARY PAYMENT**
Ask the judgment debtor to pay the money. If your claim was for possession of property, ask the judgment debtor to return the property to you. **THE COURT WILL NOT COLLECT THE MONEY OR ENFORCE THE JUDGMENT FOR YOU**.

c. **STATEMENT OF ASSETS**
If the judgment debtor does not pay the money, the law requires the debtor to fill out a form called the *Judgment Debtor's Statement of Assets* (form SC-133). This form will tell you what property the judgment debtor has that may be available to pay your claim. If the judgment debtor willfully fails to send you the completed form, you may file an *Application and Order to Produce Statement of Assets and to Appear for Examination* (form SC-134) and ask the court to give you your attorney's fees and expenses and other appropriate relief, after proper notice, under Code of Civil Procedure section 708.170.

d. **ORDER OF EXAMINATION**
You may also make the debtor come to court to answer questions about income and property. To do this, ask the clerk for an *Application and Order for Appearance and Examination (Enforcement of Judgment)* (form EJ-125) and pay the required fee. There is a fee if a law officer serves the order on the judgment debtor. You may also obtain the judgment debtor's financial records. Ask the clerk for the *Small Claims Subpoena and Declaration (form SC-107) or Civil Subpoena Duces Tecum* (form 982(a)(15.1)).

e. **WRIT OF EXECUTION**
After you find out about the judgment debtor's property, you may ask the court for a *Writ of Execution* (form EJ-130) and pay the required fee. A writ of execution is a court paper that tells a law officer to take property of the judgment debtor to pay your claim. Here are some examples of the kinds of property the officer may be able to take: **wages, bank account, automobile, business property, or rental income**. For some kinds of property, you may need to file other forms. See the law officer for information.

f. **ABSTRACT OF JUDGMENT**
The judgment debtor may own land or a house or other buildings. You may want to put a lien on the property so that you will be paid if the property is sold. You can get a lien by filing an *Abstract of Judgment* (form 982(a)(1)) with the county recorder in the county where the property is located. The recorder will charge a fee for the *Abstract of Judgment*.

NOTICE TO THE PARTY WHO WON: As soon as you have been paid in full, you *must* fill out the form below and mail it to the court *immediately* or you may be fined. If an *Abstract of Judgment* has been recorded, you must use another form; see the clerk for the proper form.

SMALL CLAIMS CASE NO.:

ACKNOWLEDGMENT OF SATISFACTION OF JUDGMENT
(Do not use this form if an Abstract of Judgment *has been recorded.)*

To the Clerk of the Court:

I am the ☐ judgment creditor ☐ assignee of record.

I agree that the judgment in this action has been paid in full or otherwise satisfied.

Date:

(TYPE OR PRINT NAME)

▶

(SIGNATURE)

NOTICE OF ENTRY OF JUDGMENT
(Small Claims)

EXEMPTIONS FROM THE ENFORCEMENT OF JUDGMENTS

The following is a list of assets that may be exempt from levy.

Exemptions are found in the United States Code **(USC)** and in the California codes, primarily in the Code of Civil Procedure **(CCP)**.

Because of periodic changes in the law, the list may not include all exemptions that apply in your case. The exemptions may not apply in full or under all circumstances. Some are not available after a certain period of time. You or your attorney should read the statutes.

If you believe the assets that are being levied on are exempt, file a claim of exemption, which you can get from the levying officer.

Type of Property	Code and Section
Accounts *(See Deposit Accounts)*	
Appliances	CCP § 704.020
Art and Heirlooms	CCP § 704.040
Automobiles	CCP § 704.010
BART District Benefits	CCP § 704.110
	Pub Util C § 28896
Benefit Payments:	
BART District Benefits	CCP § 704.110
	Pub Util C § 28896
Charity	CCP § 704.170
Civil Service Retirement Benefits (Federal)	5 USC § 8346
County Employees Retirement Benefits	CCP § 704.110
	Govt C § 31452
Disability Insurance Benefits	CCP § 704.130
Fire Service Retirement Benefits	CCP § 704.110
	Govt C § 32210
Fraternal Organization Funds Benefits	CCP § 704.130
	CCP § 704.170
Health Insurance Benefits	CCP § 704.130
Irrigation System Retirement Benefits	CCP § 704.110
Judges Survivors Benefits (Federal)	28 USC § 376(n)
Legislators Retirement Benefits	CCP § 704.110
	Govt C § 9359.3
Life Insurance Benefits—	
Group	CCP § 704.100
Individual	CCP § 704.100
Lighthouse Keepers Widows Benefits	33 USC § 775
Longshore & Harbor Workers Compensation or Benefits	33 USC § 916
Military Benefits—	
Retirement	10 USC § 1440
Survivors	10 USC § 1450
Municipal Utility District Retirement Benefits	CCP § 704.110
	Pub Util C § 12337
Peace Officers Retirement Benefits	CCP § 704.110
	Govt C § 31913
Pension Plans (and Death Benefits)—	
Private	CCP § 704.115
Public	CCP § 704.110
Public Assistance	CCP § 704.170
	Welf & I C § 17409
Public Employees—	
Death Benefits	CCP § 704.110
Pension	CCP § 704.110
Retirement Benefits	CCP § 704.110
Vacation Credits	CCP § 704.113
Railroad Retirement Benefits	45 USC § 228l
Railroad Unemployment Insurance	45 USC § 352(e)

Type of Property	Code and Section
Benefit Payments (cont.)	
Relocation Benefits	CCP § 704.180
Retirement Benefits and Contributions—	
Private	CCP § 704.115
Public	CCP § 704.110
Segregated Benefit Funds	Ins C § 10498.5
Social Security Benefits	42 USC § 407
Strike Benefits	CCP § 704.120
Transit District Retirement Benefits (Alameda & Contra Costa Counties)	CCP § 704.110
	Pub Util C § 25337
Unemployment Benefits and Contributions	CCP § 704.120
Veterans Benefits	38 USC § 3101
Veterans Medal of Honor Benefits	38 USC § 562
Welfare Payments	CCP § 704.170
	Welf & I C § 17409
Workers Compensation	CCP § 704.160
Boats	CCP § 704.060
	CCP § 704.710
Books	CCP § 704.060
Building Materials (Residential)	CCP § 704.030
Business:	
Licenses	CCP § 695.060
	CCP § 699.720(a)(1)
Tools of Trade	CCP § 704.060
Cars and Trucks (including proceeds)	CCP § 704.010
Cash	CCP § 704.070
Cemeteries	
Land Proceeds	Health & S § 7925
Plots	CCP § 704.200
Charity	CCP § 704.170
Claims, Actions & Awards:	
Personal Injury	CCP § 704.140
Worker's Compensation	CCP § 704.160
Wrongful Death	CCP § 704.150
Clothing	CCP § 704.020
Condemnation Proceeds	CCP § 704.720(b)
County Employees Retirement Benefits	CCP § 704.110
	Govt C § 31452
Credit Union Shares	Fin C § 14864
Damages *(See Personal Injury and Wrongful Death)*	
Deposit Accounts:	
Escrow or Trust Funds	Fin C § 17410
Social Security Direct Deposits	CCP § 704.080
Direct Deposit Account—	
Social Security	CCP § 704.080
Disability Insurance Benefits	CCP § 704.130
Dwelling House	CCP § 704.740
Earnings	CCP § 704.070
	CCP § 706.050
	15 USC § 1673(a)
Educational Grant	Ed C § 21116

(Continued on reverse)

EXEMPTIONS FROM THE ENFORCEMENT OF JUDGMENTS
(Continued)

Type of Property	Code and Section	Type of Property	Code and Section
Employment Bonds	Lab C § 404	Peace Officers Retirement	
Financial Assistance:		Benefits	CCP § 704.110
Charity	CCP § 704.170		Govt C § 31913
Public Assistance	CCP § 704.170	Personal Effects	CCP § 704.020
	Welf & I C § 17409	Personal Injury Actions	
Student Aid	CCP § 704.190	or Damages	CCP § 704.140
Welfare *(See Public Assistance)*		Pension Plans:	
Fire Service Retirement	CCP § 704.110	Private	CCP § 704.115
	Govt C § 32210	Public	CCP § 704.110
Fraternal Organizations		Prisoner's Funds	CCP § 704.090
Funds and Benefits	CCP § 704.130	Property Not Subject to	
	CCP § 704.170	Enforcement of Money	
Fuel for Residence	CCP § 704.020	Judgments	CCP § 704.210
Furniture	CCP § 704.020	Prosthetic & Orthopedic	
General Assignment for		Devices	CCP § 704.050
Benefit of Creditors	CCP § 1801	Provisions (for Residence)	CCP § 704.020
Health Aids	CCP § 704.050	Public Assistance	CCP § 704.170
Health Insurance Benefits	CCP § 704.130		Welf & I C § 17409
Home:		Public Employees:	
Building Materials	CCP § 704.030	Death Benefits	CCP § 704.110
Dwelling House	CCP § 704.740	Pension	CCP § 704.110
Homestead	CCP § 704.720	Retirement Benefits	CCP § 704.110
	CCP § 704.730	Vacation Credits	CCP § 704.113
Housetrailer	CCP § 704.710	**R**ailroad Retirement Benefits	45 USC § 228*l*
Mobilehome	CCP § 704.710	Railroad Unemployment	
Homestead	CCP § 704.720	Insurance	45 USC § 352(e)
	CCP § 704.730	Relocation Benefits	CCP § 704.180
Household Furnishings	CCP § 704.020	Retirement Benefits &	
Irrigation System		Contributions—	
Retirement Benefits	CCP § 704.110	Private	CCP § 704.115
Insurance:		Public	CCP § 704.110
Disability Insurance	CCP § 704.130		Ins C § 10498.5
Fraternal Benefit Society	CCP § 704.110	**S**egregated Benefit Funds	Ins C § 10498.6
Group Life	CCP § 704.100	Social Security	42 USC § 407
Health Insurance Benefits	CCP § 704.130	Social Security	
Individual	CCP § 704.100	Direct Deposit Account	CCP § 704.080
Insurance Proceeds —		Soldiers & Sailors Property	50 USC § 523(b)
Motor Vehicle	CCP § 704.010	Strike Benefits	CCP § 704.120
Jewelry	CCP § 704.040	Student Aid	CCP § 704.190
Judges Survivors Benefits		**T**ools of Trade	CCP § 704.060
(Federal)	28 USC § 376(n)	Transit District Retirement	
Legislators Retirement		Benefits (Alameda & Contra	
Benefits	CCP § 704.110	Costa Counties)	CCP § 704.110
	Govt C § 9359.3		Pub Util C § 25337
Licenses	CCP § 695.060	Travelers Check Sales Proceeds	Fin C § 1875
	CCP § 720(a)(1)	**U**nemployment Benefits &	
Lighthouse Keepers Widows		Contributions	CCP § 704.120
Benefits	33 USC § 775	Uniforms	CCP § 704.060
Longshore & Harbor Workers		**V**acation Credits (Public	
Compensation or Benefits	33 USC § 916	Employees)	CCP § 704.113
Military Benefits:		Veterans Benefits	38 USC § 3101
Retirement	10 USC § 1440	Veterans Medal of Honor	
Survivors	10 USC § 1450	Benefits	38 USC § 562
Military Personnel — Property	50 USC § 523(b)	**W**ages	CCP § 704.070
Motor Vehicle (including			CCP § 706.050
proceeds)	CCP § 704.010		CCP § 706.051
	CCP § 704.060	Welfare Payments	CCP § 704.170
			Welf & I C § 17409
Municipal Utility District		Workers Compensation	
Retirement Benefits	CCP § 704.110	Claims or Awards	CCP § 704.160
	Pub Util C § 12337	Wrongful Death Actions or	
		Damages	CCP § 704.150

Name and Address of Court:

SMALL CLAIMS CASE NO.

PLAINTIFF/DEMANDANTE *(Name, address, and telephone number of each):*

DEFENDANT/DEMANDADO *(Name, address, and telephone number of each):*

Telephone No.:

Telephone No.:

Telephone No.:

Telephone No.:

☐ See attached sheet for additional plaintiffs and defendants.

NOTICE OF FILING NOTICE OF APPEAL

TO: ☐ Plaintiff *(name):*
☐ Defendant *(name):*

Your small claims case has been APPEALED to the superior court. Do not contact the small claims court about this appeal. The superior court will notify you of the date you should appear in court. The notice of appeal is set forth below.	*La decisión hecha por la corte para reclamos judiciales menores en su caso ha sido APELADA ante la corte superior. No se ponga en contacto con la corte para reclamos judiciales menores acerca de esta apelación. La corte superior le notificará la fecha en que usted debe presentarse ante ella. El aviso de la apelación aparece a continuación.*

Date: _____

Clerk, by _____, Deputy

NOTICE OF APPEAL

I appeal to the superior court, as provided by law, from
☐ the small claims judgment **or** ☐ the denial of the motion to vacate the small claims judgment.

DATE APPEAL FILED *(clerk to insert date):*

▶

. . . .
(TYPE OR PRINT NAME)

(SIGNATURE OF APPELLANT OR APPELLANT'S ATTORNEY)

☐ I am an insurer of defendant *(name)* _____ in this case. The judgment against defendant exceeds $2,500, and the policy of insurance with the defendant covers the matter to which the judgment applies.

▶

. . . .
(NAME OF INSURER)

(SIGNATURE OF DECLARANT)

CLERK'S CERTIFICATE OF MAILING

I certify that
1. I am not a party to this action.
2. This Notice of Filing Notice of Appeal and Notice of Appeal were mailed first class, postage prepaid, in a sealed envelope to
   ☐ plaintiff
   ☐ defendant
   at the address shown above.
3. The mailing and this certification occurred
   at *(place):* _____, California,
   on *(date):* _____

Clerk, by _____, Deputy

Form Adopted by the
Judicial Council of California
SC-140 [Rev. January 1, 1992]

NOTICE OF APPEAL
(Small Claims)

Rule 982.7
Code of Civil Procedure, § 116.710

this page intentionally left blank

MC-010

ATTORNEY OR PARTY WITHOUT ATTORNEY *(Name, state bar number, and address)*:	*FOR COURT USE ONLY*

TELEPHONE NO.:   FAX NO.:

ATTORNEY FOR *(Name)*:

INSERT NAME OF COURT, JUDICIAL DISTRICT, AND BRANCH COURT, IF ANY:

PLAINTIFF:

DEFENDANT:

MEMORANDUM OF COSTS (SUMMARY)	CASE NUMBER:

The following costs are requested:

                                                   TOTALS

1. Filing and motion fees .... 1. $ _____

2. Jury fees .... 2. $ _____

3. Jury food and lodging .... 3. $ _____

4. Deposition costs .... 4. $ _____

5. Service of process .... 5. $ _____

6. Attachment expenses .... 6. $ _____

7. Surety bond premiums .... 7. $ _____

8. Witness fees .... 8. $ _____

9. Court-ordered transcripts .... 9. $ _____

10. Attorney fees *(enter here if contractual or statutory fees are fixed without necessity of a court determination; otherwise a noticed motion is required)* .... 10. $ _____

11. Models, blowups, and photocopies of exhibits .... 11. $ _____

12. Court reporter fees as established by statute .... 12. $ _____

13. Other .... 13. $ _____

TOTAL COSTS .... **$** _____

I am the attorney, agent, or party who claims these costs. To the best of my knowledge and belief this memorandum of costs is correct and these costs were necessarily incurred in this case.

Date:

▶

....
(TYPE OR PRINT NAME)   (SIGNATURE)

(Proof of service on reverse)

Form Approved for Optional Use
Judicial Council of California
MC-010 [Rev. July 1, 1999]

MEMORANDUM OF COSTS (SUMMARY)

Code of Civil Procedure,
§§ 1032, 1033.5

225

SHORT TITLE:	CASE NUMBER:

PROOF OF ☐ MAILING ☐ PERSONAL DELIVERY

1. At the time of mailing or personal delivery, I was at least 18 years of age and **not a party** to this legal action.
2. My residence or business address is *(specify)*:

3. I mailed or personally delivered a copy of the *Memorandum of Costs (Summary)* as follows *(complete either a or b)*:
   a. ☐ **Mail.** I am a resident of or employed in the county where the mailing occurred.
      (1) I enclosed a copy in an envelope AND
         (a) ☐ **deposited** the sealed envelope with the United States Postal Service with the postage fully prepaid.
         (b) ☐ **placed** the envelope for collection and mailing on the date and at the place shown in items below following our ordinary business practices. I am readily familiar with this business' practice for collecting and processing correspondence for mailing. On the same day that correspondence is placed for collection and mailing, it is deposited in the ordinary course of business with the United States Postal Service in a sealed envelope with postage fully prepaid.
      (2) The envelope was addressed and mailed as follows:
         (a) Name of person served:
         (b) Address on envelope:

         (c) Date of mailing:
         (d) Place of mailing *(city and state)*:

   b. ☐ **Personal delivery.** I personally delivered a copy as follows:
      (1) Name of person served:
      (2) Address where delivered:

      (3) Date delivered:
      (4) Time delivered:

I declare under penalty of perjury under the laws of the State of California that the foregoing is true and correct.

Date:

. . . .
(TYPE OR PRINT NAME)

▶ _____
(SIGNATURE OF DECLARANT)

Name and Address of Court:

SMALL CLAIMS CASE NO. _____

PLAINTIFF/DEMANDANTE *(Name, address, and telephone number of each)*:

DEFENDANT/DEMANDADO *(Name, address, and telephone number of each)*:

Telephone No.: _____

Telephone No.: _____

Telephone No.: _____

Telephone No.: _____

[ ] See attached sheet for additional plaintiffs and defendants.

REQUEST TO CORRECT OR VACATE JUDGMENT

FILING THIS REQUEST DOES NOT INCREASE THE TIME FOR FILING A NOTICE OF APPEAL

REQUEST TO [ ] **CORRECT** [ ] **VACATE JUDGMENT**

1. I request the court to make an order to [ ] correct [ ] vacate the judgment entered on *(date)*:
2. My request is based on this declaration and the records on file with the court.

DECLARATION SUPPORTING MY REQUEST

3. I am the [ ] plaintiff [ ] defendant in this action.
4. The facts supporting this request
   a. [ ] to correct a clerical error in the judgment
   b. [ ] to set aside or vacate the judgment on the grounds of an incorrect or erroneous legal basis for the decision
   are as follows *(specify facts, statute, rule of court case law, etc.)*:

[ ] Item 4 continued on attached page.

I declare under penalty of perjury under the laws of the State of California that the foregoing is true and correct.

Date:

. . . .
(TYPE OR PRINT NAME)

▶ _____
(SIGNATURE)

5. If you wish to oppose this request, please file a response with the court within 15 days and serve a copy on the opposing side.

No hearing will be held unless ordered by the court.

CLERK'S CERTIFICATE OF MAILING

I certify that I am not a party to this action. A copy of this Request was mailed first class, postage prepaid, in a sealed envelope to the responding party at the address shown above. The mailing and this certification occurred
at *(place)*: _____, California,
on *(date)*:

Clerk, by _____, Deputy

— The county provides small claims advisor services free of charge. —

Form Approved by the
Judicial Council of California
SC-108 [New January 1, 1994]

REQUEST TO CORRECT OR VACATE JUDGMENT
(Small Claims)

Code of Civil Procedure, § 116.725

FOR COURT USE ONLY

ORDER

1. ☐ Request is granted.

2. ☐ Request is denied.

3. ☐ A hearing on this request is scheduled as follows:

DATE	DAY	TIME	PLACE

4. ☐ Other orders:

5. ☐ Comments, if any:

Date: _____

_____
(JUDGE)

Name and Address of Court:

SMALL CLAIMS CASE NO.:

PLAINTIFF/DEMANDANTE *(Name, street address, and telephone number of each)*:

DEFENDANT/DEMANDADO *(Name, street address, and telephone number of each)*:

Telephone No.:

Telephone No.:

Telephone No.:

Telephone No.:

☐ See attached sheet for additional plaintiffs and defendants.

NOTICE TO *(Name)*:

One of the parties has asked the court to CANCEL the small claims judgment in your case. If you disagree with this request, you should appear in this court on the hearing date shown below. If the request is granted, ANOTHER TRIAL may immediately be held. Bring all witnesses, books, receipts, and other papers or things with you to support your case.	*Una de las partes en el caso le ha solicitado a la corte que DEJE SIN EFECTO la decisión tomada en su caso por la corte para reclamos judiciales menores. Si usted está en desacuerdo con esta solicitud, debe presentarse en esta corte en la fecha de la audiencia indicada a continuación. Si se concede esta solicitud, es posible que se efectúe otro juicio inmediatamente. Traiga a todos sus testigos, libros, recibos, y otros documentos o cosas para presentarlos en apoyo de su caso.*

NOTICE OF MOTION TO VACATE (CANCEL) JUDGMENT

1. A hearing will be held in this court at which I will ask the court to **cancel** the judgment entered against me in this case. If you wish to oppose the motion you should appear at the court on

HEARING DATE FECHA DEL JUICIO		DATE	DAY	TIME	PLACE	COURT USE
	1.					
	2.					
	3.					

2. I am asking the court to cancel the judgment for the reasons stated in item 5 below. My request is based on this notice of motion and declaration, the records on file with the court, and any evidence that may be presented at the hearing.

DECLARATION FOR MOTION TO VACATE (CANCEL) JUDGMENT

3. Judgment was entered against me in this case on *(date)*:
4. I first learned of the entry of judgment against me on *(date)*:
5. I am asking the court to cancel the judgment for the following reason:
   a. ☐ I did not appear at the trial of this claim because *(specify facts)*:
   b. ☐ Other *(specify facts)*:
6. I understand that I must bring with me to the hearing on this motion all witnesses, books, receipts, and other papers or things to support my case.

I declare under penalty of perjury under the laws of the State of California that the foregoing is true and correct.

Date:

(TYPE OR PRINT NAME)

(SIGNATURE)

CLERK'S CERTIFICATE OF MAILING

I certify that I am not a party to this action. This Notice of Motion to Vacate Judgment and Declaration was mailed first class, postage prepaid, in a sealed envelope to the responding party at the address shown above. The mailing and this certification occurred
at *(place)*: , California,
on *(date)*:

Clerk, by _____ , Deputy

— The county provides small claims advisor services free of charge. —

* NOTE: Continued use of form SC-135 (Rev. January 1, 1992) is authorized through December 31, 1997.

Form Approved by the Judicial Council of California
SC-135 [Rev. January 1, 1997*]

NOTICE OF MOTION TO VACATE JUDGMENT AND DECLARATION
(Small Claims)

Cal. Rules of Court, rule 982.7
Code of Civil Procedure,
§§ 116.720, 116.730, 116.740

this page intentionally left blank

Name and Address of Court:

SMALL CLAIMS CASE NO.

PLAINTIFF/DEMANDANTE *(Name and address of each)*:	DEFENDANT/DEMANDADO *(Name and address of each)*:

☐ See attached sheet for additional plaintiffs and defendants.

REQUEST TO PAY JUDGMENT TO COURT

1. **Instead of paying** the judgment directly to the creditor, I want to pay it to the court.
2. Date judgment was entered *(specify)*:
3. **Judgment creditor** *(the person or business you were ordered to pay)*
   a. Full name:
   b. Address *(use last known)*:

4. **I understand** that the amount of money I must pay to get a satisfaction of judgment is the total of the
   a. principal amount of money the court ordered me to pay,
   b. costs (if awarded by the court),
   c. interest accrued on the judgment,
   d. the court's processing fee, and
   e. other charges the court has added to the judgment. *(The court will calculate the total (see reverse).)*
5. **Partial payment** *(Complete this section if you have ALREADY PAID PART of the judgment.)*
   ☐ I have already paid part of the judgment.
   Amount paid: $ *(check one or both of the boxes below)*
   a. ☐ by check or money order. *(Attach a copy of both sides of the canceled check or money order.)*
   b. ☐ by cash. *(Attach a copy of the signed, dated cash receipt.)*
6. I understand that if I pay by personal check, satisfaction of judgment will be delayed 30 days.
7. **I request the court** to calculate the total amount required to enter a satisfaction of judgment, and to enter a satisfaction of judgment after I have paid the total amount to the court.

I declare under penalty of perjury under the laws of the State of California that the foregoing is true and correct.

Date:

▶

_____
(TYPE OR PRINT NAME)

_____
(SIGNATURE OF JUDGMENT DEBTOR)

Judgment creditor: See important notice on reverse.

CERTIFICATION	SATISFACTION OF JUDGMENT (for court use only)
I certify that this document is a true and correct copy of the original on file with this court. (Seal) Clerk, by _____, Deputy	(1) ☐ Full satisfaction of judgment entered as to judgment debtor *(name)*: on *(date)*: (2) ☐ Full satisfaction of judgment NOT entered as requested *(state reason)*: Clerk, by _____, Deputy

(Continued on reverse)

Form Adopted by the
Judicial Council of California
SC-145 [New January 1, 1990]

**REQUEST TO PAY
JUDGMENT TO COURT
(Small Claims)**

Rule 982.7

PLAINTIFF:	CASE NUMBER:
DEFENDANT:	

FOR COURT USE ONLY

1. Judgment entered on *(date)*:

2. **Amount to be paid as of date of request *(specify)*:**
   - a. Unpaid principal . . . . $
   - b. Costs . . . . $
   - c. Post judgment costs . . . . $
   - d. Credits *(see receipts)* . . . . $
   - e. Interest accrued (to date in item 2, above) . . . . $
   - f. Processing fee . . . . $
   - g. Other *(specify)* . . . . $

   SUBTOTAL $

   Add interest at: $ per day *(from date in item 2)* . . . . $

   TOTAL | $ |

CLERK'S CERTIFICATE OF MAILING

I certify that I am not a party to this action. This Notice to Judgment Creditor was mailed first class, postage prepaid, in a sealed envelope to the address shown in item 3 on the reverse. The mailing and this certification occurred
at *(place)*:   California,
on *(date)*:

Clerk, by _____ , Deputy

NOTICE TO JUDGMENT CREDITOR

1. The judgment debtor has fully satisfied the judgment entered by making payment to the court in the amount shown above.

2. You may claim this money by
   - a. presenting this form in person to the court clerk during regular business hours,
     -OR-
   - b. mailing this form to the court.

3. Complete the Judgment Creditor's Request for Funds below.

4. Money not claimed within three years becomes the property of the court *(see Government Code sections 50050-50056)*.

JUDGMENT CREDITOR'S REQUEST FOR FUNDS

I request the court to pay the money to me by mail at my current address *(specify)*:

(Mail or deliver this form to the court clerk. Keep a photocopy for yourself.)

Date:

▶

. . . .
(TYPE OR PRINT NAME)   (SIGNATURE OF JUDGMENT CREDITOR)

Name and Address of Court:

SMALL CLAIMS CASE NO.

PLAINTIFF/DEMANDANTE *(Name, address, and telephone number of each)*:

DEFENDANT/DEMANDADO *(Name, address, and telephone number of each)*:

Telephone No.:

Telephone No.:

Telephone No.:

Telephone No.:

[ ] See attached sheet for additional plaintiffs and defendants.

REQUEST TO PAY JUDGMENT IN INSTALLMENTS

1. I request the court to allow me to make installment payments on the judgment entered against me in this case in the amount and manner stated below.

2. My request is based on this declaration, the court records, my completed financial declaration (Form EJ-165—*obtain from court clerk*) attached to this declaration, and any other evidence that may be presented.

   NOTE: YOU MUST ATTACH A COMPLETED FINANCIAL DECLARATION WITH THIS REQUEST TO MAKE INSTALLMENT PAYMENTS.

3. Judgment was entered against me in this matter on *(date)*:   in the amount of *(specify)*: $

4. Payment of the entire amount of the judgment at one time will be a hardship on me because *(specify)*:

5. I can and will make payments toward the judgment in the amount of *(specify)*: $ per [ ] week [ ] month.

6. I request the court to order that I make payments as specified in item 5 and that execution on the judgment be stayed as long as I make payments according to this schedule.

   I declare under penalty of perjury under the laws of the State of California that the foregoing is true and correct.

Date:

▶

. . . .
(TYPE OR PRINT NAME)   (SIGNATURE OF JUDGMENT DEBTOR)

NOTICE TO JUDGMENT CREDITOR

The judgment debtor has requested the court to allow payment of the judgment in installments. Complete the following and return this form to the court within 10 days. You will be notified of the court's order, or, if a hearing is necessary, the date of the hearing.

1. I am the judgment creditor, and I have read and considered the judgment debtor's request to make installment payments on the judgment.

2. a. [ ] I am willing to accept the payment schedule the judgment debtor has requested.

   b. [ ] I am willing to accept payments in the amount of *(specify)*: $ per [ ] week [ ] month.

   c. [ ] I am opposed to accepting installment payments because *(specify)*:

   I declare under penalty of perjury under the laws of the State of California that the foregoing is true and correct.

Date:

▶

. . . .
(TYPE OR PRINT NAME)   (SIGNATURE OF JUDGMENT CREDITOR)

| SEE REVERSE FOR HEARING DATE, IF ANY. |

(Continued on reverse)

Form Approved by the
Judicial Council of California
SC-106 [New January 1, 1992]

REQUEST TO PAY JUDGMENT IN INSTALLMENTS
(Small Claims)

Code of Civil Procedure, § 116.620(b)

233

NOTICE OF MOTION

A hearing will be held on this request as follows:

		DATE	DAY	TIME	PLACE
HEARING DATE **FECHA DEL JUICIO**	1.				
	2.				
	3.				
	4.				

COURT ORDER

1. ☐ The judgment debtor shall pay the full amount of the judgment immediately.
2. ☐ The judgment debtor may pay the judgment as follows:
   a. *(If initial lump sum ordered)* Pay $ _____ on *(date):* _____
   b. Pay $ _____ or more on *(specify):* _____ of every *(specify):* _____
   until the judgment is fully paid.
3. *(Missed payments)* On the filing of an affidavit or declaration by the judgment creditor showing that any payment due has not been paid, this order shall be set aside and the clerk may issue a writ of execution immediately, without further order of the court.

Date: _____

_____
(JUDGE OR COMMISSIONER)

WARNING: IF YOU MISS A PAYMENT, THE BALANCE OWING ON THE JUDGMENT WILL BECOME DUE IMMEDIATELY.

CLERK'S CERTIFICATE OF MAILING—NOTICE TO JUDGMENT CREDITOR

I certify that I am not a party to this action. This Notice to Judgment Creditor was mailed first class, postage prepaid, in a sealed envelope to the responding party at the address shown on the reverse. The mailing and this certification occurred
at *(place):* _____, California,
on *(date):* _____

Clerk, by _____, Deputy

CLERK'S CERTIFICATE OF MAILING — NOTICE OF MOTION

I certify that I am not a party to this action. This Notice of Motion was mailed first class, postage prepaid, in a sealed envelope to the responding party at the address shown on the reverse. The mailing and this certification occurred
at *(place):* _____, California,
on *(date):* _____

Clerk, by _____, Deputy

CLERK'S CERTIFICATE OF MAILING — COURT ORDER

I certify that I am not a party to this action. This Court Order was mailed first class, postage prepaid, in a sealed envelope to the responding party at the address shown on the reverse. The mailing and this certification occurred
at *(place):* _____, California,
on *(date):* _____

Clerk, by _____, Deputy

MAIL TO THE JUDGMENT CREDITOR DO NOT FILE WITH THE COURT	SC-133

JUDGMENT CREDITOR (the person or business who won the case) *(name):*

JUDGMENT DEBTOR (the person or business who lost the case and owes money) *(name):*

SMALL CLAIMS CASE NO.:

NOTICE TO JUDGMENT DEBTOR: You *must* (1) pay the judgment or (2) appeal or (3) file a motion to vacate. If you fail to pay or take one of the other two actions, you must complete and mail this form to the judgment creditor. If you do not, you may have to go to court to answer questions and may have penalties imposed on you by the court.	**AVISO AL DEUDOR POR FALLO JUDICIAL:** Usted debe (1) pagar el monto del fallo judicial, o (2) presentar un recurso de apelación o (3) presentar un recurso de nulidad. Si usted no paga el fallo o presenta uno de estos dos recursos, deberá llenar y enviar por correo este formulario a su acreedor por fallo judicial. Si no lo hace, es posible que deba presentarse ante la corte para contestar preguntas y pagar las multas que la corte le pueda imponer.

INSTRUCTIONS

The small claims court has ruled that you owe money to the judgment creditor.

1. You may appeal a judgment against you only on the other party's claim. You may *not* appeal a judgment against you on *your* claim.

   a. If you appeared at the trial and you want to appeal, you must file a *Notice of Appeal* (form SC-140) within 30 days after the date the *Notice of Entry of Judgment* (form SC-130) was mailed or handed to you by the clerk.

   b. If you did not appear at the trial, before you can appeal, you must first file a *Notice of Motion to Vacate Judgment and Declaration (form SC-135)* and pay the required fee within 30 days after the date the *Notice of Entry of Judgment* was mailed or handed to you, and the judgment cannot be collected until the motion is decided. If your motion is denied, you then have 10 days after the date the notice of denial was mailed to file your appeal.

2. Unless you **pay the judgment or appeal or file a motion to vacate, you must fill out this form and mail it to the person who won the case** within **30 days** after the *Notice of Entry of Judgment* was mailed or handed to you by the clerk.

3. If you lose your appeal or motion to vacate, you must pay the judgment, including post-judgment costs and interest, and complete and mail this form to the judgment creditor within **30 days** after the date the clerk mails or delivers to you (a) the denial of your motion to vacate, or (b) the dismissal of your appeal, or (c) the judgment against you on your appeal.

4. As soon as the small claims court denies your motion to vacate and the denial is not appealed, or receives the dismissal of your appeal or judgment from the superior court after appeal, the judgment is no longer suspended and may be immediately enforced against you by the judgment creditor.

If you were sued as an individual, skip this box and begin with item 1 below. Otherwise, check the applicable box, attach the documents indicated, and complete item 15 on the reverse. a. ☐ *(Corporation or partnership)* Attached to this form is a statement describing the nature, value, and exact location of all assets of the corporation or the partners, and a statement showing that the person signing this form is authorized to submit this form on behalf of the corporation or partnership. b. ☐ *(Governmental agency)* Attached to this form is the statement of an authorized representative of the agency stating when the agency will pay the judgment and any reasons for its failure to do so.

JUDGMENT DEBTOR'S STATEMENT OF ASSETS

EMPLOYMENT

1. What are your sources of income and occupation? *(Provide job title and name of division or office in which you work.)*

2. a. Name and address of your business or employer *(include address of your payroll or human resources department, if different):*

   b. If not employed, names and addresses of all sources of income *(specify):*

3. How often are you paid?
   ☐ daily ☐ every two weeks ☐ monthly
   ☐ weekly ☐ twice a month ☐ other *(explain):*

4. What is your gross pay each pay period? $

5. What is your take-home pay each pay period? $

6. If your spouse earns any income, give the name of your spouse, the name and address of the business or employer, job title, and division or office *(specify):*

(Continued on reverse)

Form Approved by the
Judicial Council of California
SC-133 [Rev. January 1, 1998]

JUDGMENT DEBTOR'S STATEMENT OF ASSETS
(Small Claims)

Cal. Rules of Court, rule 982.7(a);
Code of Civil Procedure,
§§ 116.620(a), 116.830

CASH, BANK DEPOSITS

7. How much money do you have in cash?... $

8. How much other money do you have in banks, savings and loans, credit unions, and other financial institutions either in your own name or jointly *(list)*:

Name and address of financial institution	Account number	Individual or joint?	Balance
a.			$
b.			$
c.			$

PROPERTY

9. List all automobiles, other vehicles, and boats owned in your name or jointly:

Make and year	Value	Legal owner if different from registered owner	Amount owed
a.	$		$
b.	$		$
c.	$		$
d.	$		$

10. List all real estate owned in your name or jointly:

Address of real estate	Fair market value	Amount owed
a.	$	$
b.	$	$

OTHER PERSONAL PROPERTY (*Do not list household furniture and furnishings, appliances, or clothing.*)

11. List anything of value not listed above owned in your name or jointly *(continue on attached sheet if necessary)*:

Description	Value	Address where property is located
a.	$	
b.	$	
c.	$	

12. Is anyone holding assets for you? ☐ Yes. ☐ No. If yes, describe the assets and give the name and address of the person or entity holding each asset *(specify)*:

13. Have you disposed of or transferred any asset within the last 60 days? ☐ Yes. ☐ No. If yes, give the name and address of each person or entity who received any asset and describe each asset *(specify)*:

14. If you are not able to pay the judgment in one lump sum, you may be able to make payment arrangements with the person or business who won the case (the judgment creditor). State the amount that you can pay each month: $, beginning on *(date)*:   . If you are unable to agree, you may also ask the court for permission to make installment payments by filing a *Request to Pay Judgment in Installments* (form SC-106).

15. I declare under penalty of perjury under the laws of the State of California that the foregoing is true and correct.

Date:

▶

_____
(TYPE OR PRINT NAME)

_____
(SIGNATURE)

Mail or deliver this completed form to the judgment creditor at the address shown on the Notice of Entry of Judgment form.

JUDGMENT DEBTOR'S STATEMENT OF ASSETS
(Small Claims)

Certificate of Facts RE Unsatisfied Judgment

(Do not complete or sign until 30 days after finality of judgment unless the court ordered installment payments.) **After completion of this form, please mail it with your check or money order in the amount of $20 to: Financial Responsibility, P.O. Box 942884, Sacramento, CA 94284-0001. DO NOT TAKE IT TO YOUR LOCAL DEPARTMENT OF MOTOR VEHICLES.**

In the _____   Court of _____

Court Code _____

STATE OF____CALIFORNIA_____

Plaintiff : _____   Defendant : _____

_____ vs. _____

Case No. : _____   Date Filed : _____

The undersigned Clerk/Judge of the Court hereby certifies as follows:

1. The above judgment was based on a tort claim as a result of a motor vehicle accident.
2. The judgment was entered on _____ 19 ___ , and became final _____ 19 ___ ,and remained unsatisfied for thirty days thereafter.
3. Judgment was entered against _____

   a. Bodily injury _____   d. Costs _____
   b. Damage to property _____   e. Loss of use _____
   c. Wrongful death _____   f. Any other ground _____
   TOTAL _____

4. The court (ordered, did not order) the judgment paid in installments.

   If so ordered, a certified copy of such order must be attached as required by Section 16379 of the Vehicle Code.)

Date _____   SIGNED _____

Official Title ____CLERK OF THE COURT____

By _____

Official Title _____

The undersigned creditor/attorney hereby certifies as follows:

5. Date of accident _____
6. Did accident result from the operation of a motor vehicle in California? _____
7. Vehicle involved was owned by _____
8. Vehicle involved was operated by _____
9. Ownership of vehicle resulted in judgment against _____
10. Operation of vehicle resulted in judgment against _____
11. License number of debtor's vehicle involved in the accident _____
12. Identifying information for judgment debtor(s)—enter "unknown", if information not available.
    Full name _____   Former name, or AKA _____
    Current address _____
    Former address _____
    Birthdate or approximate age _____   Calif. Driver License No. _____
    Other information _____

Date _____   Name and address of Judgment Creditor or Attorney

_____

FOR DMV USE ONLY:

_____

_____

_____   Signed _____

Court Report of Judgments (Reference 16373 V.C.)

The clerk of a court, or the judge of a court which has no clerk, shall issue upon the request of a judgment creditor, a certified copy of the judgment or a certified copy of the docket entries in an action resulting in a judgment for damages, and a certificate of facts relative to such judgment on a form provided by the Department, the rendering and nonpayment of which judgment requires the Department to suspend the driver license of the judgment debtor. The document shall be forwarded immediately upon the expiration of thirty days after the judgment has become final and when the judgment has not been stayed or satisfied within the amounts specified in this chapter as shown by the records of the court. Department of Motor Vehicles, P.O. Box 942884, Sacramento, CA 94284-0001.

DL 30 (REV 3/93)

this page intentionally left blank

ATTORNEY OR PARTY WITHOUT ATTORNEY *(Name and Address)*:

TELEPHONE NO.:

FOR RECORDER'S USE ONLY

Recording requested by and return to:

ATTORNEY FOR   JUDGMENT CREDITOR   ASSIGNEE OF RECORD

NAME OF COURT:

STREET ADDRESS:

MAILING ADDRESS:

CITY AND ZIP CODE:

BRANCH NAME:

PLAINTIFF:

DEFENDANT:

WRIT OF

☐ **EXECUTION (Money Judgment)**
☐ **POSSESSION OF**   ☐ **Personal Property**
                     ☐ **Real Property**
☐ **SALE**

CASE NUMBER:

FOR COURT USE ONLY

1. **To the Sheriff or any Marshal or Constable of the County of:**

   You are directed to enforce the judgment described below with daily interest and your costs as provided by law.

2. **To any registered process server:** You are authorized to serve this writ only in accord with CCP 699.080 or CCP 715.040.

3. *(Name)*:

   is the ☐ judgment creditor   ☐ assignee of record
   whose address is shown on this form above the court's name.

4. **Judgment debtor** *(name and last known address)*:

   ☐ additional judgment debtors on reverse

5. **Judgment entered** on *(date)*:

6. ☐ **Judgment renewed** on *(dates)*:

7. **Notice of sale** under this writ
   a. ☐ has not been requested.
   b. ☐ has been requested *(see reverse)*.

8. ☐ Joint debtor information on reverse.

[SEAL]

9. ☐ See reverse for information on real or personal property to be delivered under a writ of possession or sold under a writ of sale.

10. ☐ This writ is issued on a sister-state judgment.

11. Total judgment . . . . $

12. Costs after judgment (per filed order or memo CCP 685.090) . . . . $

13. Subtotal *(add 11 and 12)* . . . . . . $ _____

14. Credits . . . . $ _____

15. Subtotal *(subtract 14 from 13)* . . . . . $ _____

16. Interest after judgment (per filed affidavit CCP 685.050) . . . . $

17. Fee for issuance of writ . . . . $

18. **Total** *(add 15, 16, and 17)* . . . . . $ _____

19. Levying officer:
    (a) Add daily interest from date of writ (at the legal rate on 15) of. . . . . . $
    (b) Pay directly to court costs included in 11 and 17 (GC 6103.5, 68511.3; CCP 699.520(i)) . . . . $

20. ☐ The amounts called for in items 11-19 are different for each debtor These amounts are stated for each debtor on Attachment 20.

Issued on *(date)*:

Clerk, by _____ , Deputy

— **NOTICE TO PERSON SERVED: SEE REVERSE FOR IMPORTANT INFORMATION.** —

(Continued on reverse)

Form Approved by the
Judicial Council of California
EJ-130 [Rev. January 1, 1997*]

WRIT OF EXECUTION

Code of Civil Procedure, §§ 699.520, 712.010, 715.010

* See note on reverse.

SHORT TITLE: CASE NUMBER:

— Items continued from the first page —

4. ☐ **Additional judgment debtor** (name and last known address):

7. ☐ **Notice of sale** has been requested by (name and address):

8. ☐ **Joint debtor** was declared bound by the judgment (CCP 989-994)
   a. on (date):   a. on (date):
   b. name and address of joint debtor: b. name and address of joint debtor:

   c. ☐ additional costs against certain joint debtors (itemize):

9. ☐ (Writ of Possession or Writ of Sale) **Judgment** was entered for the following:
   a. ☐ Possession of real property: The complaint was filed on (date):   **(Check (1) or (2)):**
       (1) ☐ The Prejudgment Claim of Right to Possession was served in compliance with CCP 415.46.
             The judgment includes all tenants, subtenants, named claimants, and other occupants of the premises.
       (2) ☐ The Prejudgment Claim of Right to Possession was NOT served in compliance with CCP 415.46.
             (a) $ was the daily rental value on the date the complaint was filed.
             (b) The court will hear objections to enforcement of the judgment under CCP 1174.3 on the following
                 dates (specify):
   b. ☐ Possession of personal property
       ☐ If delivery cannot be had, then for the value (itemize in 9e) specified in the judgment or supplemental order.
   c. ☐ Sale of personal property
   d. ☐ Sale of real property
   e. Description of property:

— NOTICE TO PERSON SERVED —

WRIT OF EXECUTION OR SALE. Your rights and duties are indicated on the accompanying Notice of Levy.
WRIT OF POSSESSION OF PERSONAL PROPERTY. If the levying officer is not able to take custody of the property, the levying officer will make a demand upon you for the property. If custody is not obtained following demand, the judgment may be enforced as a money judgment for the value of the property specified in the judgment or in a supplemental order.
WRIT OF POSSESSION OF REAL PROPERTY. If the premises are not vacated within five days after the date of service on the occupant or, if service is by posting, within five days after service on you, the levying officer will remove the occupants from the real property and place the judgment creditor in possession of the property. Except for a mobile home, personal property remaining on the premises will be sold or otherwise disposed of in accordance with CCP 1174 unless you or the owner of the property pays the judgment creditor the reasonable cost of storage and takes possession of the personal property not later than 15 days after the time the judgment creditor takes possession of the premises.
▶ A Claim of Right to Possession form accompanies this writ (unless the Summons was served in compliance with CCP 415.46).

---

* NOTE: Continued use of form EJ-130 (Rev. July 1, 1996) is authorized through December 31, 1997.
EJ-130 [Rev. January 1, 1997*]   **WRIT OF EXECUTION**   Page two

[NOT FOR WAGE GARNISHMENT]
[RETURN TO LEVYING OFFICER. DO NOT FILE WITH COURT]

ATTORNEY OR PARTY WITHOUT ATTORNEY (Name and Address):	TELEPHONE NO.:	LEVYING OFFICER (Name and Address):
ATTORNEY FOR (Name):		

NAME OF COURT, JUDICIAL DISTRICT OR BRANCH COURT, IF ANY:

PLAINTIFF:

DEFENDANT:

CLAIM OF EXEMPTION (Enforcement of Judgment)	LEVYING OFFICER FILE NO.:	COURT CASE NO.:

Copy all the information required above (except the top left space) from the Notice of Levy. The top left space is for your name or your attorney's name and address. The original and one copy of this form must be filed with the levying officer. DO NOT FILE WITH THE COURT.

1. My name is *(specify)*:

2. Papers should be sent to
   ☐ me.
   ☐ my attorney (I have filed with the court and served on the judgment creditor a request that papers be sent to my attorney and my attorney has consented in writing on the request to receive these papers.)

   at the address ☐ shown above ☐ following *(specify)*:

3. ☐ I am not the judgment debtor named in the notice of levy. The name and last known address of the judgment debtor is *(specify)*:

4. The property I claim to be exempt is *(describe)*:

5. The property is claimed to be exempt under the following code and section *(specify)*:

6. The facts which support this claim are *(describe)*:

7. ☐ The claim is made pursuant to a provision exempting property to the extent necessary for the support of the judgment debtor and the spouse and dependents of the judgment debtor. **A Financial Statement form is attached to this claim.**

8. ☐ The property claimed to be exempt is
   a. ☐ a motor vehicle, the proceeds of an execution sale of a motor vehicle, or the proceeds of insurance or other indemnification for the loss, damage, or destruction of a motor vehicle.
   b. ☐ tools, implements, materials, uniforms, furnishings, books, equipment, a commercial motor vehicle, a vessel, or other personal property used in the trade, business or profession of the judgment debtor or spouse.
   c. all other property of the same type owned by the judgment debtor, either alone or in combination with others, is *(describe)*:

9. ☐ The property claimed to be exempt consists of the loan value of unmatured life insurance policies (including endowment and annuity policies) or benefits from matured life insurance policies (including endowment and annuity policies). All other property of the same type owned by the judgment debtor or the spouse of the judgment debtor, either alone or in combination with others, is *(describe)*:

I declare under penalty of perjury under the laws of the State of California that the foregoing is true and correct.

Date:

▶

_____
(TYPE OR PRINT NAME)

_____
(SIGNATURE OF CLAIMANT)

Form Approved by the Judicial Council of California EJ-160 [New July 1, 1983]	**CLAIM OF EXEMPTION** (Enforcement of Judgment)	CCP 703.520

241

this page intentionally left blank

ATTORNEY OR PARTY WITHOUT ATTORNEY *(Name and Address)*:	TELEPHONE NO.:	LEVYING OFFICER *(Name and Address)*:

ATTORNEY FOR *(Name)*:

NAME OF COURT, JUDICIAL DISTRICT OR BRANCH COURT, IF ANY:

PLAINTIFF
:
DEFENDANT:

CLAIM OF EXEMPTION (Wage Garnishment)	LEVYING OFFICER FILE NO.:	COURT CASE NO.:

—READ THE EMPLOYEE INSTRUCTIONS BEFORE COMPLETING THIS FORM—

for your name or your attorney's name and address. The original and one copy of this form with the Financial Statement attached must be filed with the levying officer. DO NOT FILE WITH THE COURT.

1. I need the following earnings to support myself or my family *(check a or b)*:
   a. ☐ All earnings.
   b. ☐ $ _____ each pay period.

2. Please send all papers to
   ☐ me
   ☐ my attorney
   at the address ☐ shown above ☐ following *(specify)*:

3. I am willing for the following amount to be withheld from my earnings **each pay period** during the withholding period. **I understand that the judgment creditor can accept this offer by not opposing the Claim of Exemption, which will result in the following sum being withheld each pay period** *(check a or b)*:
   a. ☐ None
   b. ☐ Withhold $ _____ each pay period.

4. I am paid
   ☐ daily   ☐ every two weeks   ☐ monthly
   ☐ weekly   ☐ twice a month   ☐ other *(specify)*:

NOTE: *You must attach a properly completed Financial Statement form to this Claim of Exemption.*
The Financial Statement form is available without charge from the levying officer.

I declare under penalty of perjury under the laws of the State of California that the foregoing is true and correct.
Date:

....
(TYPE OR PRINT NAME)

▶ _____
(SIGNATURE OF DECLARANT)

Form Adopted by the
Judicial Council of California
982.5(5) [Rev. July 1, 1983]

CLAIM OF EXEMPTION
(Wage Garnishment)

CCP 706.124

243

this page intentionally left blank

ATTORNEY OR PARTY WITHOUT ATTORNEY *(Name and Address)*:	TELEPHONE NO.:	*FOR COURT USE ONLY*

ATTORNEY FOR *(Name)*:

NAME OF COURT, JUDICIAL DISTRICT OR BRANCH COURT, IF ANY:

PLAINTIFF:

DEFENDANT:

NOTICE OF HEARING ON CLAIM OF EXEMPTION (Wage Garnishment—Enforcement of Judgment)	LEVYING OFFICER FILE NO.:	COURT CASE NO.:

1. TO:

    Name and address of levying officer   Name and address of judgment debtor

☐ Claimant, if other than judgment debtor *(name and address)*:   ☐ Judgment debtor's attorney *(name and address)*:

2. **A hearing to determine the claim of exemption of**
   ☐ judgment debtor
   ☐ other claimant
   will be held as follows:

   a. date: time: ☐ dept.:   ☐ div.:   ☐ rm.:

   b. address of court:

3. ☐ **The judgment creditor will not appear at the hearing and submits the issue on the papers filed with the court.**

Date:

. . . .   ▶
(TYPE OR PRINT NAME)   *(SIGNATURE OF JUDGMENT CREDITOR OR ATTORNEY)*

If you do not attend the hearing, the court may determine your claim based on the Claim of Exemption, Financial Statement (when one is required), Notice of Opposition to Claim of Exemption, and other evidence that may be presented.

(Proof of service on reverse)

Form Adopted by the Judicial Council of California 982.5(8), EJ-175 [Rev. July 1, 1983]	**NOTICE OF HEARING ON CLAIM OF EXEMPTION** (Wage Garnishment—Enforcement of Judgment)	CCP 703.550, 706.105

245

SHORT TITLE:	LEVYING OFFICER FILE NO.:	COURT CASE NO.:

PROOF OF SERVICE BY MAIL

I am over the age of 18 and not a party to this cause. I am a resident of or employed in the county where the mailing occurred. My residence or business address is *(specify)*:

I served the attached Notice of Hearing on Claim of Exemption and the attached Notice of Opposition to Claim of Exemption by enclosing true copies in a sealed envelope addressed to each person whose name and address is given below and depositing the envelope in the United States mail with the postage fully prepaid.

(1) Date of deposit: (2) Place of deposit *(city and state)*:

NAME AND ADDRESS OF EACH PERSON TO WHOM NOTICE WAS MAILED

I declare under penalty of perjury under the laws of the State of California that the foregoing is true and correct.

Date:

....   ▶ _____
(TYPE OR PRINT NAME)   *(SIGNATURE OF DECLARANT)*

PROOF OF SERVICE—PERSONAL DELIVERY

I am over the age of 18 and not a party to this cause. My residence or business address is *(specify)*:

I served the attached Notice of Hearing on Claim of Exemption and the attached Notice of Opposition to Claim of Exemption by personally delivering copies to the person served as shown below.

PERSONS SERVED

Name

Delivery At
Date: Time: Address:

I declare under penalty of perjury under the laws of the State of California that the foregoing is true and correct.

Date:

....   ▶ _____
(TYPE OR PRINT NAME)   *(SIGNATURE OF DECLARANT)*

NOTICE OF HEARING ON CLAIM OF EXEMPTION
(Wage Garnishment—Enforcement of Judgment)

982.5(8), EJ-175 [Rev. July 1, 1983]   Page two

form 31

ATTORNEY OR PARTY WITHOUT ATTORNEY *(Name and Address)*:	TELEPHONE NO.:	**FOR COURT USE ONLY**

ATTORNEY FOR *(Name)*:

NAME OF COURT:
STREET ADDRESS:
MAILING ADDRESS:
CITY AND ZIP CODE:
BRANCH NAME:

PLAINTIFF:

DEFENDANT:

	LEVYING OFFICER FILE NO.:	COURT CASE NO.:

NOTICE OF OPPOSITION TO CLAIM OF EXEMPTION
(Enforcement of Judgment)

— DO NOT USE THIS FORM FOR WAGE GARNISHMENTS —

The original of this form and a Notice of Hearing on Claim of Exemption must be filed with the court.

A copy of this Notice of Opposition and the Notice of Hearing *must* be filed with the levying officer.

A copy of this Notice of Opposition and the Notice of Hearing must be served on the judgment debtor and other claimant at least 10 days *before* the hearing.

TO THE LEVYING OFFICER:

1. Name and address of judgment creditor

2. Name and address of judgment debtor

Social Security Number *(if known)*:

3. ☐ Name and address of claimant *(if other than judgment debtor)*

4. The notice of filing claim of exemption states it was mailed on *(date)*:

5. The item or items claimed as exempt are
   a. ☐ not exempt under the statutes relied upon in the Claim of Exemption.
   b. ☐ not exempt because the judgment debtor's equity is greater than the amount provided in the exemption.
   c. ☐ other *(specify)*:

6. The facts necessary to support item 5 are
   ☐ continued on the attachment labeled Attachment 6.
   ☐ as follows:

I declare under penalty of perjury under the laws of the State of California that the foregoing is true and correct.

Date:

....
(TYPE OR PRINT NAME)

▶

_____
(SIGNATURE OF DECLARANT)

Form Approved by the
Judicial Council of California
EJ-170 [New July 1, 1983]

NOTICE OF OPPOSITION TO CLAIM OF EXEMPTION
(Enforcement of Judgment)

CCP 703.550

247

this page intentionally left blank

ATTORNEY OR PARTY WITHOUT ATTORNEY *(Name and Address)*:	TELEPHONE NO.:	FOR COURT USE ONLY

ATTORNEY FOR *(Name)*:

NAME OF COURT, JUDICIAL DISTRICT OR BRANCH COURT, IF ANY:

PLAINTIFF:

DEFENDANT:

NOTICE OF OPPOSITION TO CLAIM OF EXEMPTION (Wage Garnishment)	LEVYING OFFICER FILE NO.:	COURT CASE NO.:

TO THE LEVYING OFFICER:

1. Name and address of judgment creditor

2. Name and address of employee

Social Security Number *(if known)*:

3. The Notice of Filing Claim of Exemption states it was mailed on
   (date):

4. The earnings claimed as exempt are
   a. ☐ not exempt.
   b. ☐ partially exempt. The amount *not* exempt per month is
        $

5. The judgment creditor opposes the claim of exemption because
   a. ☐ the judgment was for the following common necessaries of life *(specify)*:

   b. ☐ the following expenses of the debtor are *not* necessary for the support of the debtor or the debtor's family *(specify)*:

   c. ☐ other *(specify)*:

6. ☐ The judgment creditor will accept $ per pay period for payment on account of this debt.

I declare under penalty of perjury under the laws of the State of California that the foregoing is true and correct.

Date:

▶

_____
(TYPE OR PRINT NAME)

_____
(SIGNATURE OF DECLARANT)

F 0328-245 (6/83)

Form Adopted by the
Judicial Council of California
982.5(7) (Rev. July 1, 1983)

NOTICE OF OPPOSITION TO CLAIM OF EXEMPTION
(Wage Garnishment)

CCP 706.128

this page intentionally left blank

ATTORNEY OR PARTY WITHOUT ATTORNEY *(Name and Address)*:	TELEPHONE NO.:	*FOR COURT USE ONLY*
ATTORNEY FOR *(Name)*:		
PLAINTIFF:		
DEFENDANT:		

ORDER DETERMINING CLAIM OF EXEMPTION (Wage Garnishment—Enforcement of Judgment)	LEVYING OFFICER FILE NO.:	COURT CASE NO.:

1. The application of *(name)*:

   for an order determining the Claim of Exemption of *(name)*:

   was heard on *(date)*:
   (Check boxes to indicate personal presence)
   ☐ Judgment Creditor *(name)*:   ☐ Attorney *(name)*:

   ☐ Judgment Debtor *(name)*:   ☐ Attorney *(name)*:

2. The court considered the evidence in support of and in opposition to the Claim of Exemption.

3. IT IS ORDERED

   a. ☐ The judgment debtor's Claim of Exemption is denied.

   b. ☐ The judgment debtor's Claim of Exemption is granted.

   c. ☐ The levying officer is directed to release any earnings held to the **judgment debtor.**

   d. ☐ The levying officer is directed to release any earnings held to the **judgment creditor** for payment on the **judgment.**

   e. ☐ Other orders *(specify)*:

   f. The clerk shall transmit a certified copy of this order to the levying officer. The levying officer shall notify the employer of any change in the Earnings Withholding Order and release any retained sums as provided in this order.

Date: ▶ _____
                                   (SIGNATURE OF JUDGE)

[SEAL]

CLERK'S CERTIFICATION

I certify that the foregoing is a true and correct copy of the original on file in my office.

Date: Clerk, by _____ , Deputy

Form Adopted by the
Judicial Council of California
982.5(9) [Rev. July 1, 1983]

ORDER DETERMINING CLAIM OF EXEMPTION
(Wage Garnishment—Enforcement of Judgment)

CCP 706.106

this page intentionally left blank

ATTORNEY OR PARTY WITHOUT ATTORNEY (Name and Address):	TELEPHONE NO.:	FOR RECORDER'S OR SECRETARY OF STATE'S USE ONLY

ATTORNEY FOR (Name):

NAME OF COURT:
STREET ADDRESS:
MAILING ADDRESS:
CITY AND ZIP CODE:
BRANCH NAME:

PLAINTIFF:

DEFENDANT:

CASE NUMBER:

ACKNOWLEDGMENT OF SATISFACTION OF JUDGMENT
☐ FULL   ☐ PARTIAL   ☐ MATURED INSTALLMENT

FOR COURT USE ONLY

1. Satisfaction of the judgment is acknowledged as follows (see footnote* before completing):
   a. ☐ Full satisfaction
      (1) ☐ Judgment is satisfied in full.
      (2) ☐ The judgment creditor has accepted payment or performance other than that specified in the judgment in full satisfaction of the judgment.
   b. ☐ Partial satisfaction
      The amount received in partial satisfaction of the judgment is
      $
   c. ☐ Matured installment
      All matured installments under the installment judgment have been satisfied as of (date):

2. Full name and address of judgment creditor:

3. Full name and address of assignee of record, if any:

4. Full name and address of judgment debtor being fully or partially released:

5. a. Judgment entered on (date):
   ☐ (1) in judgment book volume no.:   (2) page no.:
   b. ☐ Renewal entered on (date):
   ☐ (1) in judgment book volume no.:   (2) page no.:

6. ☐ An ☐ abstract of judgment ☐ certified copy of the judgment has been recorded as follows (complete all information for each county where recorded):

COUNTY	DATE OF RECORDING	BOOK NUMBER	PAGE NUMBER

7. ☐ A notice of judgment lien has been filed in the office of the Secretary of State as file number (specify):

NOTICE TO JUDGMENT DEBTOR: If this is an acknowledgment of full satisfaction of judgment, it will have to be recorded in each county shown in item 6 above, if any, in order to release the judgment lien, and will have to be filed in the office of the Secretary of State to terminate any judgment lien on personal property.

Date:

▶ _____
(SIGNATURE OF JUDGMENT CREDITOR OR ASSIGNEE OF CREDITOR OR ATTORNEY)

*The names of the judgment creditor and judgment debtor must be stated as shown in any Abstract of Judgment which was recorded and is being released by this satisfaction. **A separate notary acknowledgment must be attached for each signature.**

Form Approved by the
Judicial Council of California
EJ-100 [Rev. July 1, 1983] (Cor. 7/84)

ACKNOWLEDGMENT OF SATISFACTION OF JUDGMENT

CCP 724.060, 724.120, 724.250

this page intentionally left blank

Name and Address of Court:

SMALL CLAIMS CASE NO.:

ATTORNEY-CLIENT FEE DISPUTE (ATTACHMENT TO PLAINTIFF'S CLAIM)
(Attach to Plaintiff's Claim)

1. **Parties.** At the arbitration hearing, plaintiff was ☐ attorney ☐ client.

2. **Arbitration award.** The award made after the arbitration hearing
   a. ☐ requires the ☐ attorney ☐ client   to pay the other party this amount: $
   b. ☐ requires neither the attorney nor the client to pay the other anything.

3. **Amount in dispute.** The amount of fees and costs in dispute is *(may not exceed $5,000):* $

4. ☐ **Binding award.** The award made after the arbitration hearing was binding because *(check at least one box):*
   a. ☐ the attorney and client agreed in writing to have binding arbitration. *(Attach a copy.)*
   b. ☐ the award document was mailed on *(date):*   , and more than 30 days have passed since then.

5. ☐ **Nonbinding award.** The award made after the arbitration hearing was NOT binding because
   a. the attorney and client did NOT agree in writing *after* the dispute arose to have binding arbitration; and
   b. thirty days have NOT passed since the award document was mailed on *(date):*

6. **Plaintiff's request.**
   a. ☐ *(Trial after arbitration)* I reject the arbitration award and request a TRIAL ("hearing de novo") in small claims court to resolve the dispute. *(NOTE: Do NOT check a box unless you also checked item 5, "Nonbinding award," above.)*
      (1) ☐ I appeared at the arbitration hearing.
      (2) ☐ I did not appear at the arbitration hearing, but the award does not contain a finding that my failure to appear was willful.
      (3) A court action (case) involving this attorney-client fee dispute
          (i) ☐ is not pending.
          (ii) ☐ is pending. *(Your request for a trial must be filed in that court using the same case number.)*

   (NOTE: Do not check boxes b, c, or d, unless you also checked item 4, "Binding award," above.)
   b. ☐ *(Correct award)* I request that the court correct the award as follows:
      (1) Reason award should be corrected *(specify in this box a letter from item 3 on page three):* ☐
      (2) Change requested *(specify):*

   c. ☐ *(Vacate award)* I request that the award be vacated ("canceled") as follows:
      (1) Reason award should be vacated *(specify in this box a letter from item 4 on page three):* ☐
      (2) Explain the circumstances *(specify):*

      (3) I ☐ do not ☐ do   request a new arbitration hearing.
   d. ☐ *(Confirm award)* I request that the award be confirmed.

7. **Copy of award.** A copy of the arbitration award is attached. *(Attach a copy and check this box:* ☐ *)*

▶

. . . .
(TYPE OR PRINT NAME)   (SIGNATURE OF PLAINTIFF)

| — The county provides small claims advisor services free of charge. Read the information on the reverse. — |

(Continued on page two)   **Page one of three**

Form Adopted for Mandatory Use
Judicial Council of California
SC-101 [Rev. July 1, 2001]

**ATTORNEY-CLIENT FEE DISPUTE
(ATTACHMENT TO PLAINTIFF'S CLAIM)**
(Small Claims)

Cal. Rules of Court, rule 982.7
Code of Civil Procedure, §§ 116.220(a)(4), 1280 et seq.
Business & Professions Code, § 6200 et seq.

255

INFORMATION
ATTORNEY-CLIENT FEE DISPUTE CASES IN SMALL CLAIMS COURT

1. Rights After Nonbinding Arbitration

A. What are my rights if the arbitration award is nonbinding?

If the arbitration award is nonbinding, you may have a right to a trial in court. If you did not appear at your fee arbitration hearing, however, you will have to prove to the court that you had a good reason for not being there. If a court determines that your failure to appear was willful, you may not be entitled to a trial after arbitration.

If you are not satisfied with the award, you should follow the instructions below to protect your rights.

B. How long do I have to act?

If you want a trial in court, you must act within 30 days after the date the arbitration award was mailed to you. The date the arbitration award was mailed is written at the end of the notice you received with the award.

C. What must I do to get a trial in court?

You must file papers in the proper court within the 30-day limit.

D. What papers must I file? In what court must I file them?

That depends. Has a lawsuit about the fees already been filed?

(1) *YES—lawsuit already filed*

If a lawsuit about the fees has already been filed, then you must file in that same court. You may need a lawyer's help to file your complaint if it is not a small claims court.

(2) *NO—lawsuit not yet filed*

If no lawsuit about the fees has been filed, then you must file your own lawsuit in the proper court. The small claims court is not the proper court if the amount in dispute is more than $5,000. Also consult the Venue Table on the back of the Plaintiff's Claim *(form SC-100).*

E. What if I am satisfied with the award?

If you are satisfied with the award, do nothing. The award will become binding if the other party does not file papers for a trial in court within the 30-day limit.

F. What are my rights if the award becomes binding? *(Read item 2 below.)*

2. Rights After Binding Arbitration

A. What are my rights if the arbitration award is binding?

If the arbitration award is binding, you must abide by it. There is no appeal from a binding award. Even so, a binding award can be corrected or "vacated" (overturned) by a court, but only in rare cases.

Please read on to learn more about your rights after a binding arbitration.

B. What if I am dissatisfied with the award?

A court has the power to "vacate" (overturn) an arbitration award, but only on very narrow grounds. *(See item 4 on page three.)* A court can also correct obvious mistakes in the award, like an arithmetic mistake. *(See item 3 on page three.)*

If you think you are entitled to correct or vacate the arbitration award, please follow the instructions below to protect your rights.

(1) *What must I do to vacate or correct the arbitration award?*

You must file a petition in the proper court within the 100-day limit.

(2) *How long do I have to act?*

(a) If you want to correct or vacate the award, you must act within 100 days after the date the arbitration award was mailed to you. The date the award was mailed is at the end of the notice mailed with the award.

(b) If, however, you receive notice from a court that the other side has filed a petition to confirm the award, you no longer have 100 days to file your petition. You must then respond by filing your petition to vacate or correct the award within the time stated on the notice from the court.

(3) *What is a petition?*

A petition is a technical legal document that tells the court what you want and why you are entitled to it.

(4) *In what court do I file my petition?*

That depends. Has a lawsuit about the fees already been filed?

(a) *YES—lawsuit already filed*

If a lawsuit about the fees has already been filed, you will file your petition to vacate or correct with that same court.

(b) *NO—lawsuit not yet filed*

If no lawsuit about the fees has been filed, then you will file your petition with the court that has jurisdiction over the amount of the arbitration award. The small claims court is not the proper court if the amount of the arbitration award exceeds $5,000. For awards over $5,000, the superior court is the proper court.

(Continued on page three)

SC-101 [Rev. July 1, 2001]

ATTORNEY-CLIENT FEE DISPUTE
(ATTACHMENT TO PLAINTIFF'S CLAIM)
(Small Claims)

C. What if I am satisfied with the arbitration award?

If the arbitration award says that you are owed money, you should write the other party a letter and demand payment. If you are not paid, and you are the client and your arbitration request was filed on or after January 1, 1994, you have the right to ask the State Bar to assist you. If you want the State Bar to assist you and

(1) 100 days have passed from service of the award and the award is binding, or

(2) the award has become a final judgment after a trial following arbitration or after a petition to vacate, correct, or confirm the award, you can reach the State Bar at

> **Mandatory Fee Arbitration**
> **180 Howard Street, 6th Floor**
> **San Francisco, CA 94105-1639**
> **(415) 538-2020**

D. How do I confirm the arbitration award?

Any party who is owed money has the right to request court orders allowing that party to take property or money from the other party's paycheck and/or bank accounts. To get those court orders, you must first confirm the arbitration award.

(1) *How do I confirm the arbitration award?*

   To confirm the arbitration award, you must petition for confirmation with the proper court.

   (a) What is a petition for confirmation?

   A petition for confirmation is a legal document that tells the court what you want and why you are entitled to it. In small claims court, request confirmation by checking box 6d on page one.

   (b) What is the proper court?

   That depends on the amount owed. If it is $5,000 or less, you may choose to file in small claims court. Or you may choose to file the petition as a limited case in superior court if the amount is $25,000 or less. If the amount you are owed is more than $25,000, you would file an unlimited case in superior court.

(2) *How long do I have to file my petition for confirmation?*

   You must file your petition for confirmation within four years after the date the arbitration award is mailed to you. That date appears at the end of the notice mailed with the award.

(3) *What are my rights after the arbitration award is confirmed?*

   When the arbitration award is confirmed, it becomes a judgment of the court. Once you have a judgment, you have a right to enforce the judgment. That means you can get court orders allowing you to collect your money. Enforcing judgments can be very technical and very complicated. The court has forms to use for this procedure.

E. What if the arbitration award says I owe money?

If you owe money, pay it. If you do not, the other party has a right to get court orders allowing him or her to collect the debt by taking and selling your property and by taking money from your paycheck and your bank account.

---

3. Reasons to Correct the Award *(See item 6b(1) on page one)*

A. The numbers were not calculated correctly or a person, thing, or property was not described correctly.

B. The arbitrators exceeded their authority.

C. The award is imperfect as a matter of form.

---

4. Reasons to "Vacate" (Cancel) the Award *(See item 6c(1) on page one)*

A. The award was obtained by corruption, fraud, or other unfair means.

B. One or more of the arbitrators was corrupt.

C. The misconduct of a neutral arbitrator substantially prejudiced my rights.

D. The arbitrators exceeded their authority and the award cannot be fairly corrected.

E. The arbitrators unfairly refused to postpone the hearing or to hear evidence useful to settle the dispute.

F. An arbitrator should have disqualified himself or herself after I made a demand to do so.

SC-101 [Rev. July 1, 2001]

ATTORNEY-CLIENT FEE DISPUTE
(ATTACHMENT TO PLAINTIFF'S CLAIM)
(Small Claims)

257

this page intentionally left blank

Name and Address of Court:

SMALL CLAIMS CASE NO.:

ATTORNEY-CLIENT FEE DISPUTE (ATTACHMENT TO NOTICE OF ENTRY OF JUDGMENT)
(Attach to Notice of Entry of Judgment)

1. ☐ **Trial after arbitration**. A trial after arbitration of an attorney-client fee dispute
    a. ☐ is denied because
        (1) ☐ the arbitration award is binding.
        (2) ☐ plaintiff willfully failed to appear at the arbitration hearing.

    b. ☐ is granted, and a trial
        (1) ☐ was held on *(date)*:
        (2) ☐ will be held on *(date)*:

2. ☐ **Correction of award**. The arbitration award is
    a. corrected as follows *(specify)*:

    b. ☐ and in all other respects the award is confirmed as indicated below in item 4b.

3. ☐ **Vacation of award**. The arbitration award is vacated ("canceled").
    a. ☐ A new arbitration hearing is ordered before
        (1) ☐ new arbitrators. *(See Code of Civil Procedure section 1287.)*
        (2) ☐ the original arbitrators. *(See Code of Civil Procedure section 1287.)*
        The attorney and client are both ordered to appear at the new arbitration hearing.

    b. ☐ No new arbitration hearing is ordered.

4. ☐ **Confirmation of award**. The arbitration award is
    a. ☐ not confirmed.
        (1) ☐ The award is vacated under item 3 above.
        (2) ☐ The case is dismissed. *(See Code of Civil Procedure section 1287.2.)*

    b. ☐ confirmed
        (1) ☐ as made by the arbitrators. *(A copy of the award is attached.)*
        (2) ☐ as corrected in item 2 above. *(A copy of the award is attached.)*

5. **Payment**.
    a. ☐ The ☐ plaintiff ☐ defendant shall pay to ☐ plaintiff ☐ defendant
        (i) ☐ disputed fees and costs of: $
        (ii) ☐ costs of this proceeding of: $

    b. ☐ Neither the plaintiff nor the defendant shall pay the other anything.

— The county provides small claims advisor services free of charge. —

Form Adopted by the
Judicial Council of California
SC-132 [New January 1, 1997]

**ATTORNEY-CLIENT FEE DISPUTE
(ATTACHMENT TO NOTICE OF ENTRY OF JUDGMENT)
(Small Claims)**

Cal. Rules of Court, rule 982.7
Code of Civil Procedure, §§ 116.220(a)(4),
1280 et seq.
Business & Professions Code, § 6200 et seq.

INFORMATION
ATTORNEY-CLIENT FEE DISPUTE CASES IN SMALL CLAIMS COURT
—*Continued*—

C. What if I am satisfied with the arbitration award?

If the arbitration award says that you are owed money, you should write the other party a letter and demand payment. If you are not paid, and you are the client and your arbitration request was filed on or after January 1, 1994, you have the right to ask the State Bar to assist you. If you want the State Bar to assist you and

(1) 100 days have passed from service of the award and the award is binding, or

(2) the award has become a final judgment after a trial following arbitration or after a petition to vacate, correct, or confirm the award, you can reach the State Bar at

> **Mandatory Fee Arbitration**
> **100 Van Ness Avenue, 28th Floor**
> **San Francisco, CA 94102**
> **(415) 241-2020**

D. How do I confirm the arbitration award?

Any party who is owed money has the right to request court orders allowing that party to take property or money from the other party's paycheck and/or bank accounts. To get those court orders, you must first confirm the arbitration award.

(1) *How do I confirm the arbitration award?*

To confirm the arbitration award, you must petition for confirmation with the proper court.

    (a) What is a petition for confirmation?

    A petition for confirmation is a legal document that tells the court what you want and why you are entitled to it. In small claims court, request confirmation by checking box 6d on page one.

    (b) What is the proper court?

    That depends on the amount you are owed. If it is $5,000 or less, you may choose to file in small claims court or municipal court. If it is $25,000 or less, the municipal court is the proper court. File in superior court if you are owed more than $25,000.

(2) *How long do I have to file my petition for confirmation?*

You must file your petition for confirmation within four years of the date the arbitration award is mailed to you. That date appears at the end of the notice mailed with the award.

(3) *What are my rights after the arbitration award is confirmed?*

When the arbitration award is confirmed, it becomes a judgment of the court. Once you have a judgment, you have a right to enforce the judgment. That means you can get court orders allowing you to collect your money. Enforcing judgments can be very technical and very complicated. The court has forms to use for this procedure.

E. What if the arbitration award says I owe money?

If you owe money, pay it. If you do not, the other party has a right to get court orders allowing him or her to collect the debt by taking and selling your property and by taking money from your paycheck and your bank account.

---

3. Reasons to Correct the Award *(See item 6b(1) on page one)*

    A. The numbers were not calculated correctly or a person, thing, or property was not described correctly.

    B. The arbitrators exceeded their authority.

    C. The award is imperfect as a matter of form.

---

4. Reasons to "Vacate" (Cancel) the Award *(See item 6c(1) on page one)*

    A. The award was obtained by corruption, fraud, or other unfair means.

    B. One or more of the arbitrators was corrupt.

    C. The misconduct of a neutral arbitrator substantially prejudiced my rights.

    D. The arbitrators exceeded their authority and the award cannot be fairly corrected.

    E. The arbitrators unfairly refused to postpone the hearing or to hear evidence useful to settle the dispute.

    F. An arbitrator should have disqualified himself or herself after I made a demand to do so.

982(a)(18.1)

ATTORNEY OR PARTY WITHOUT ATTORNEY *(Name, state bar number, and address)*:	FOR COURT USE ONLY
TELEPHONE NO.: FAX NO.:	
ATTORNEY FOR *(Name)*:	

INSERT NAME OF COURT AND NAME OF JUDICIAL DISTRICT AND BRANCH COURT, IF ANY:

PLAINTIFF/PETITIONER:

DEFENDANT/RESPONDENT:

ORDER ON APPLICATION FOR WAIVER OF <u>ADDITIONAL</u> COURT FEES AND COSTS (Cal. Rules of Court, rule 985(j))	CASE NUMBER:

1. The application was filed on *(date)*: ☐ A previous order was issued on *(date)*:
2. The application was filed by *(name)*:
3. ☐ IT IS ORDERED that the application is **granted** ☐ in whole ☐ in part *(see Cal. Rules of Court, rule 985)*.
   a. ☐ **No payments**. Payment of all the fees and costs listed in California Rules of Court, rule 985(j), **is waived**.
   b. ☐ **Applicant shall pay** all the fees and costs listed in California Rules of Court, rule 985(j), EXCEPT the following:
      (1) ☐ Jury fees and expenses.   (5) ☐ Court-appointed experts.
      (2) ☐ Court-appointed interpreter for witnesses. (6) ☐ Other fees and costs *(specify)*:
      (3) ☐ Witness fees of peace officers.
      (4) ☐ Reporter's fees *(beyond 60 days)*.
   c. **Method of payment**. Applicant shall pay all the fees and costs when charged, EXCEPT as follows:
      (1) ☐ Pay *(specify)*:   percent.
      (2) ☐ Pay: $ per month or more until the balance is paid.
   d. The clerk of the court, county financial officer, or appropriate county officer is authorized to require the litigant to appear before and be examined by the court no sooner than four months from the date of this order, and not more than once in any four-month period.

      ☐ The applicant is ordered to appear for the court's review of the applicant's financial status as follows:

Date:	Time:	Dept.:	oonı.

   e. ☐ *(must be completed if application is granted in part)* Reasons for denial of a requested waiver *(specify)*:

   f. ☐ The clerk is directed to mail a copy of this order to the applicant's attorney or to the applicant if unrepresented.
   g. **All unpaid fees and costs shall be deemed to be taxable costs if applicant is entitled to costs and shall be a lien on any judgment recovered by the applicant and shall be paid directly to the clerk by the judgment debtor upon such recovery.**
4. ☐ IT IS ORDERED that the application **is denied** for the following reasons *(specify)*:

   a. The applicant shall pay any fees and costs due in this action within 10 days from the date of service of this order or any paper filed by the applicant with the clerk will be of no effect.
   b. The clerk is directed to mail a copy of this order to all parties who have appeared in this action.
5. ☐ IT IS ORDERED that **a hearing** be held.
   a. The substantial evidentiary conflict to be resolved by the hearing is *(specify)*:

   b. **Applicant should be present** at the hearing to be held as follows:

Date:	Time:	Dept.:	Room:

   c. The address of the court is *(specify)*:

   d. The clerk is directed to mail a copy of this order to the applicant only.

Date: _____   _____
                                                      JUDICIAL OFFICER

                        (Continued on reverse)

Form Adopted by Rule 982
Judicial Council of California
982(a)(18.1) [Rev. January 1, 1999]

**ORDER ON APPLICATION FOR WAIVER OF
<u>ADDITIONAL</u> COURT FEES AND COSTS
(In Forma Pauperis)**

Government Code, § 68511.3;
Cal. Rules of Court, rule 985

PLAINTIFF/PETITIONER (Name):	CASE NUMBER:
DEFENDANT/RESPONDENT (Name):	

CLERK'S CERTIFICATE OF MAILING

I certify that I am not a party to this cause and that a true copy of the foregoing was mailed first class, postage prepaid, in a sealed envelope addressed as shown below, and that the mailing of the foregoing and execution of this certificate occurred at (place): , California, on (date):

Clerk, by _____ , Deputy

(SEAL)

CLERK'S CERTIFICATE

I certify that the foregoing is a true and correct copy of the original on file in my office.

Date: Clerk, by _____ , Deputy

**ORDER ON APPLICATION FOR WAIVER OF
ADDITIONAL COURT FEES AND COSTS
(In Forma Pauperis)**

APPENDIX J
LIST OF LOCAL FORMS

Contra Costa Consolidated

Motion For Relief From Filing Late Small Claims Appeal
Notice Of Motion Small Claim Appeal [Cc-2]
Plaintiffs Statement

Fresno

Plaintiffs Claim [Fsc 344.1

Kern Consolidated

Small Claims Case Management Rules

Los Angeles Unified

Addendum Information After Judgment
Declaration And Order Re Lost Writ [Civ M 590]
Declaration Of Non Military Service, Request For Dismissal
Instructions To Sheriff's Summons, Orap, Misc
Memorandum Of Costs, Acknowledgment Of Credits and Declaration of Accrued Interest [Ci 66]
Motion And Order For Time Payment Of Judgment [Sc-12]
Plaintiffs Claim To Clerk Fictitious Business Name Declaration [Sc 2 Jc]

Marin Consolidated

Stipulation and Order to Dismiss Action and Submit Causes of Action to Small Claims Jurisdiction

Mariposa Unified

Application For Transfer (Ccp 116.390)
Order Transferring Action
Order Transferring Action (Ccp 116.390]
Request For Postponement [Scm-268]

Monterey Consolidated

Plaintiff's Statement Worksheet (MCS-111)

Napa Consolidated

Corporate Representative Declaration
Minor Offense Small Claims

Orange Unified

Small Claims Appeal Request For Dismissal [543]
Small Claims Authorization To Appear [1069]
Small Claims Certified Mail Statement [1091]
Small Claims Declararion Of Lost Document [1088]
Small Claims Declaration And Order Of Satisfaction Of Judgment [1070]
Small Claims Declaration Of Default Non Compliance And Order [1152]
Small Claims Defendants Statement [1092]
Small Claims Mediation Settlement Stipulation For Entry Of Judgment [1151]
Small Claims Plaintiffs Statement [1090]
Small Claims Request For Postponement [1093]

Riverside Consolidated

Request for Postponement Order

San Diego Unified

Application And Order To Produce Statement Of Assets And To Appear For Examination [SC-134]
Declaration In Support Of Appearance By Representative-Employee [SC-21]
Declaration Of Military Status-Request For Dismissal [SC-20]

Judgment Debtors Statement Of Assets [SC-133]
Request For Reset Or Continuance Of Small Claims Trial [SC-34]
Request To Enter Satisfaction Of Judgment [SC-19]
Small Claims Filing Packet [SC-22]
Small Claims Information Sheet 1 How To Name The Parties [SC-23]
Small Claims Information Sheet 2 Serving The Parties [SC-24]
Small Claims Information Sheet 3 Notice Of Courts Motion To Dismiss [SC-25]Small
Claims Work Sheet [SC-26]

San Luis Obispo

Declaration Of Default In Payments And Request For Court Hearing
Declaration Re Default In Payments [2510-423]
Declaration To Correct Name [2510-311]
Request For Postponement [2510-418]

San Mateo Superior

Plaintiffs Statement to the Clerk (SC-14)

Santa Barbara Unified

Declaration Designating Company-Corporation Representative [SC-7002]
Instruction Sheet For Small Claims Forms [SC-7000]
Motion To Vacate Mediated Stipulated Judgment And Motion For Rehearing [SC-7010]
Notice Of Appeal Parking [SC-7012]
Plaintiffs Statement [SC7001]
Proof Of Service Notice Of Appeal Parking [SC-7013]
Request For Dismissal Satisfaction Of Judgment [SC-7008]
Request For Small Claims Continuance [SC-7006]
Request To Correct Or Amend A Small Claims Judgment [SC-7007]
Small Claims Declaration Re Default In Payments [SC-7009]

Santa Cruz

Authorization To Appear Pursuant To CCP 116.540 (e)(f)(g)
Declaration Of The Party [SUPSC-024]
Cost Bill After Judgment And Accrued Interest [SUPSC-009]
Declaration And Order For Examination Of Garnishee [SUPSC-011]
Declaration Of Judgment Debtor And Request To File Satisfaction Of Judgment

[SUPSC-013]

Declaration Re Default In Payments [SUPSC-022]

Declaration To Appear Pursuant To CCP 116.540 (b)(c)(d)(h) [SUPSC-025]

Instructions For Filling Out Small Claims Forms And Declaration Of Non Military Service [SUPSC-001]

Notice Of Hearing And Time To Appear[SUPOP-002]

Order To Amend Name After Judgment [SUPSC-028]

Petition And Order For Appointment Of Guardian Ad Litem [SUPOP-118]

Petition And Order For Hearing On Third Party Claim [SUPSC-006]

Request To Amend Name After Judgment [SUPSC-027]

Solano Consolidated

Amendment Of Claim Prior To Judgment [7090]

Application For Postponement Of Trial Date [7015]

Declaration Re Default In Payments And Order Setting Aside Order Providing Payment Of Judgment In Installments [7060]

Judgment After Trial By Court Unlawful Detainer [7040]

Judgment Debtors Statement Re Request To Enter Satisfaction Of Judgment [7000]

Notice Re Appearance [7002]

Plaintiffs Statement To Clerk [7020]

Request For Dismissal [7023]

Resolution Appointing A Corporation Representative [7070]

Sonoma Unified

Resolution Small Claims Appointing A Corporation Representative [SC-02]

Warrant of Atttachment [SC-06]

Yolo Unified

Business Plaintiff Statement To The Clerk [SC-111]

Ex Parte Request For Entry Of Judgment [YOCV 0138]

Individual Plaintiff Statement To The Clerk [SC-111]

Order For Entry Of Judgment [YOCV 0173]

Order Upon Failure To Appear For Examination Of Judgment Debtor [YOCV 0180]

Proof Of Service By Mail [YOCV 0190]

Yuba Unified

Request For Postponement of Small Claims Hearing [SC-106]

INDEX

personal injury, 2, 3, 8, 55, 56, 98
pet deposit, 58
piercing the corporate veil, 28
plaintiff, 4, 5, 29, 31, 34, 64, 66, 68, 75, 76, 90
plaintiff's claim and order to defendant, 34, 63, 75, 183
preponderance of evidence, 86
probate, 19
process servers, 36
product, 2, 13, 54
    as is, 13
products liability, 54-55
profit, 20
promissory note, 68
proof, 14-18, 86
proof of service, 38, 199
property, 2, 3, 12, 28, 32, 36, 38, 39, 50, 57, 58, 59, 67, 93, 95, 96
    exempt, 96
    management, 2
    personal, 96
    real, 15, 29, 50, 69, 96
    rental, 28, 32, 36, 57
public entities, 2
public policy, 44
punitive damages, 8

R

real estate. *See property*
reformation, 4
release, 73
rent, 12, 60
reorganization, 73
request for dismissal, 215
request for postponement, 33, 203
request to correct or vacate judgment, 92, 227
request to pay judgment in installments, 77, 233
request to pay judgment to court, 77, 231
rescission, 4, 41-61
residence, 15
restaurants, 3, 72
restitution, 4
rules of procedure, 1, 5

S

sales, 13, 32
school districts, 2
security deposit, 2, 32, 58
services, 33, 35-38, 53, 71
    personal, 35
    substitute, 36
settlement, 16, 70, 74
small claims advisor, 7, 22

small claims subpoena, 79, 82
small claims subpoena for personal appearance and production of documents, 211
sole proprietorship, 26
special damages, 59
specific performance, 4
spouse, 16, 26
statement of assets, 94
statute of frauds, 69
statute of limitations, 17, 41
stipulation to stay entry of judgment, 74
stop payment, 42-43
store owner, 3
subpoena, 23, 83, 88
summons, 63-64

T

tenant, 19, 60
testimony, 80, 83-86
    telephone, 84
third party, 76
torts, 32
trial, 11, 87-92, 101

U

unemployment, 15
Uniform Commercial Code (UCC), 73
uninhabitable rental unit, 59
Unruh Civil Rights Act, 60
usury, 71

V

venue, 31

W

wages, 8, 94
waiver, 33, 72
warranty, 41, 45-47, 54
    breach, 45
    express, 45, 46
    implied, 45, 46
warranty of merchantability, 45, 46-47
warranty of fitness, 45, 47
warranty of title, 45, 46
witnesses, 5, 8, 82, 87
    expert, 84
writ of execution, 95, 96, 239

Y

Youth Authority, 29

SPHINX® PUBLISHING ORDER FORM

BILL TO: **SHIP TO:**

| Phone # | Terms | F.O.B. | Chicago, IL | Ship Date |

Charge my: ☐ VISA   ☐ MasterCard   ☐ American Express

☐ **Money Order or Personal Check**

Credit Card Number   Expiration Date

Qty	ISBN	Title	Retail	Ext.
		SPHINX PUBLISHING NATIONAL TITLES		
	1-57248-148-X	Cómo Hacer su Propio Testamento	$16.95	
	1-57248-147-1	Cómo Solicitar su Propio Divorcio	$24.95	
	1-57248-166-8	The Complete Book of Corporate Forms	$24.95	
	1-57248-163-3	Crime Victim's Guide to Justice (2E)	$21.95	
	1-57248-159-5	Essential Guide to Real Estate Contracts	$18.95	
	1-57248-160-9	Essential Guide to Real Estate Leases	$18.95	
	1-57248-139-0	Grandparents' Rights (3E)	$24.95	
	1-57248-188-9	Guía de Inmigración a Estados Unidos (3E)	$24.95	
	1-57248-187-0	Guía de Justicia para Víctimas del Crimen	$21.95	
	1-57248-103-X	Help Your Lawyer Win Your Case (2E)	$14.95	
	1-57248-164-1	How to Buy a Condominium or Townhome (2E)	$19.95	
	1-57248-191-9	How to File Your Own Bankruptcy (5E)	$21.95	
	1-57248-132-3	How to File Your Own Divorce (4E)	$24.95	
	1-57248-100-5	How to Form a DE Corporation from Any State	$24.95	
	1-57248-083-1	How to Form a Limited Liability Company	$22.95	
	1-57248-099-8	How to Form a Nonprofit Corporation	$24.95	
	1-57248-133-1	How to Form Your Own Corporation (3E)	$24.95	
	1-57248-224-9	How to Form Your Own Partnership (2E)	$24.95	
	1-57248-119-6	How to Make Your Own Will (2E)	$16.95	
	1-57248-200-1	How to Register Your Own Copyright (4E)	$24.95	
	1-57248-104-8	How to Register Your Own Trademark (3E)	$21.95	
	1-57071-349-9	How to Win Your Unemployment Compensation Claim	$21.95	
	1-57248-118-8	How to Write Your Own Living Will (2E)	$16.95	
	1-57248-156-0	How to Write Your Own Premarital Agreement (3E)	$24.95	
	1-57248-158-7	Incorporate in Nevada from Any State	$24.95	
	1-57071-333-2	Jurors' Rights (2E)	$12.95	
	1-57071-400-2	Legal Research Made Easy (2E)	$16.95	
	1-57248-165-X	Living Trusts and Other Ways to Avoid Probate (3E)	$24.95	

Qty	ISBN	Title	Retail	Ext.
	1-57248-186-2	Manual de Beneficios para el Seguro Social	$18.95	
	1-57248-220-6	Mastering the MBE	$16.95	
	1-57248-167-6	Most Valuable Bus. Legal Forms You'll Ever Need (3E)	$21.95	
	1-57248-130-7	Most Valuable Personal Legal Forms You'll Ever Need	$24.95	
	1-57248-098-X	The Nanny and Domestic Help Legal Kit	$22.95	
	1-57248-089-0	Neighbor v. Neighbor (2E)	$16.95	
	1-57248-169-2	The Power of Attorney Handbook (4E)	$19.95	
	1-57248-149-8	Repair Your Own Credit and Deal with Debt	$18.95	
	1-57248-168-4	The Social Security Benefits Handbook (3E)	$18.95	
	1-57071-399-5	Unmarried Parents' Rights	$19.95	
	1-57071-354-5	U.S.A. Immigration Guide (3E)	$19.95	
	1-57248-192-7	The Visitation Handbook	$18.95	
	1-57248-138-2	Winning Your Personal Injury Claim (2E)	$24.95	
	1-57248-162-5	Your Right to Child Custody, Visitation and Support (2E)	$24.95	
	1-57248-157-9	Your Rights When You Owe Too Much	$16.95	
		CALIFORNIA TITLES		
	1-57248-150-1	CA Power of Attorney Handbook (2E)	$18.95	
	1-57248-151-X	How to File for Divorce in CA (3E)	$26.95	
	1-57071-356-1	How to Make a CA Will	$16.95	
	1-57248-145-5	How to Probate and Settle an Estate in California	$26.95	
	1-57248-146-3	How to Start a Business in CA	$18.95	
	1-57248-194-3	How to Win in Small Claims Court in CA (2E)	$18.95	
	1-57248-196-X	The Landlord's Legal Guide in CA	$24.95	
		FLORIDA TITLES		
	1-57071-363-4	Florida Power of Attorney Handbook (2E)	$16.95	
	1-57248-176-5	How to File for Divorce in FL (7E)	$26.95	
	1-57248-177-3	How to Form a Corporation in FL (5E)	$24.95	
	1-57248-203-6	How to Form a Limited Liability Co. in FL (2E)	$24.95	
	1-57071-401-0	How to Form a Partnership in FL	$22.95	

Form Continued on Following Page   **SUBTOTAL**

To order, call Sourcebooks at 1-800-432-7444 or FAX (630) 961-2168 (Bookstores, libraries, wholesalers—please call for discount)
Prices are subject to change without notice.
Find more legal information at: www.SphinxLegal.com

SPHINX® PUBLISHING ORDER FORM

Qty	ISBN	Title	Retail	Ext.
	1-57248-113-7	How to Make a FL Will (6E)	$16.95	
	1-57248-088-2	How to Modify Your FL Divorce Judgment (4E)	$24.95	
	1-57248-144-7	How to Probate and Settle an Estate in FL (4E)	$26.95	
	1-57248-081-5	How to Start a Business in FL (5E)	$16.95	
	1-57071-362-6	How to Win in Small Claims Court in FL (6E)	$16.95	
	1-57248-202-8	Land Trusts in Florida (6E)	$29.95	
	1-57248-123-4	Landlords' Rights and Duties in FL (8E)	$21.95	
		GEORGIA TITLES		
	1-57248-137-4	How to File for Divorce in GA (4E)	$21.95	
	1-57248-180-3	How to Make a GA Will (4E)	$21.95	
	1-57248-140-4	How to Start a Business in Georgia (2E)	$16.95	
		ILLINOIS TITLES		
	1-57071-405-3	How to File for Divorce in IL (2E)	$21.95	
	1-57248-170-6	How to Make an IL Will (3E)	$16.95	
	1-57071-416-9	How to Start a Business in IL (2E)	$18.95	
	1-57248-078-5	Landlords' Rights & Duties in IL	$21.95	
		MASSACHUSETTS TITLES		
	1-57248-128-5	How to File for Divorce in MA (3E)	$24.95	
	1-57248-115-3	How to Form a Corporation in MA	$24.95	
	1-57248-108-0	How to Make a MA Will (2E)	$16.95	
	1-57248-106-4	How to Start a Business in MA (2E)	$18.95	
	1-57248-209-5	The Landlord's Legal Guide in MA	$24.95	
		MICHIGAN TITLES		
	1-57071-409-6	How to File for Divorce in MI (2E)	$21.95	
	1-57248-182-X	How to Make a MI Will (3E)	$16.95	
	1-57248-183-8	How to Start a Business in MI (3E)	$18.95	
		MINNESOTA TITLES		
	1-57248-142-0	How to File for Divorce in MN	$21.95	
	1-57248-179-X	How to Form a Corporation in MN	$24.95	
	1-57248-178-1	How to Make a MN Will (2E)	$16.95	
		NEW YORK TITLES		
	1-57248-193-5	Child Custody, Visitation and Support in NY	$26.95	
	1-57248-141-2	How to File for Divorce in NY (2E)	$26.95	
	1-57248-105-6	How to Form a Corporation in NY	$24.95	
	1-57248-095-5	How to Make a NY Will (2E)	$16.95	
	1-57071-185-2	How to Start a Business in NY	$18.95	

Qty	ISBN	Title	Retail	Ext.
	1-57248-198-6	How to Win in Small Claims Court in NY (2E)	$18.95	
	1-57071-186-0	Landlords' Rights and Duties in NY	$21.95	
	1-57071-188-7	New York Power of Attorney Handbook	$19.95	
	1-57248-122-6	Tenants' Rights in NY	$21.95	
		NORTH CAROLINA TITLES		
	1-57248-185-4	How to File for Divorce in NC (3E)	$22.95	
	1-57248-129-3	How to Make a NC Will (3E)	$16.95	
	1-57248-184-6	How to Start a Business in NC (3E)	$18.95	
	1-57248-091-2	Landlords' Rights & Duties in NC	$21.95	
		OHIO TITLES		
	1-57248-190-0	How to File for Divorce in OH (2E)	$24.95	
	1-57248-174-9	How to Form a Corporation in OH	$24.95	
	1-57248-173-0	How to Make an OH Will	$16.95	
		PENNSYLVANIA TITLES		
	1-57248-211-7	How to File for Divorce in PA (3E)	$26.95	
	1-57248-094-7	How to Make a PA Will (2E)	$16.95	
	1-57248-112-9	How to Start a Business in PA (2E)	$18.95	
	1-57071-179-8	Landlords' Rights and Duties in PA	$19.95	
		TEXAS TITLES		
	1-57248-171-4	Child Custody, Visitation, and Support in TX	$22.95	
	1-57248-172-2	How to File for Divorce in TX (3E)	$24.95	
	1-57248-114-5	How to Form a Corporation in TX (2E)	$24.95	
	1-57071-417-7	How to Make a TX Will (2E)	$16.95	
	1-57248-214-1	How to Probate and Settle an Estate in TX (3E)	$26.95	
	1-57248-228-1	How to Start a Business in TX (3E)	$18.95	
	1-57248-111-0	How to Win in Small Claims Court in TX (2E)	$16.95	
	1-57248-110-2	Landlords' Rights and Duties in TX (2E)	$21.95	

SUBTOTAL THIS PAGE _____

SUBTOTAL PREVIOUS PAGE _____

Shipping— $5.00 for 1st book, $1.00 each additional _____

Illinois residents add 6.75% sales tax _____

Connecticut residents add 6.00% sales tax _____

TOTAL _____

To order, call Sourcebooks at 1-800-432-7444 or FAX (630) 961-2168 (Bookstores, libraries, wholesalers—please call for discount)
Prices are subject to change without notice.
Find more legal information at: www.SphinxLegal.com